NEW DIRECTIONS
IN AFRICAN EDUCATION:

CHALLENGES AND POSSIBILITIES

NEW DIRECTIONS
IN AFRICAN EDUCATION:

CHALLENGES AND POSSIBILITIES

Edited by S. Nombuso Dlamini

UNIVERSITY OF
CALGARY
PRESS

University of Calgary Press
2500 University Drive NW
Calgary, Alberta
Canada T2N 1N4
www.uofcpress.com

LIBRARY AND ARCHIVES CANADA CATALOGUING IN PUBLICATION

New directions in African education : challenges and possibilities /
edited by S. Nombuso Dlamini.

(Africa, missing voices series, 1703-1826 ; 4)
Includes bibliographical references and index.
ISBN 978-1-55238-212-7

1. Education—Africa. I. Dlamini, S. Nombuso, 1962- II. Series.

LA1501.N49 2007   370.96'09045   C2007-904002-0

The University of Calgary Press acknowledges the support of the Alberta Foundation for
the Arts for our publications. We acknowledge the financial support of the Government
of Canada through the Book Publishing Industry Development Program (BPIDP) for our
publishing activities. We acknowledge the financial support of the Canada Council for the
Arts for our publishing program.

This book has been published with the help of a grant from the Canadian Federation for the
Humanities and Social Sciences, through the Aid to Scholarly Publications Programme,
using funds provided by the Social Sciences and Humanities Research Council of Canada.

Cover design, page design and typesetting by Melina Cusano

TABLE OF CONTENTS

ABOUT THE CONTRIBUTORS

S. Nombuso Dlamini is Associate Professor in the Faculty of Education and holds the position of Research Leadership Chair, University of Windsor. She has a PhD from the OISE/University of Toronto. Born in South Africa, Nombuso received her undergraduate degree from the University of Swaziland, worked in Community Development, and taught at high school and university in South Africa before migrating to Canada. Her teaching and research are in the areas of socio-cultural studies in education, literacy and critical sociolinguistics, migration and diaspora studies, and gender and youth matters. She has conducted several research projects funded by various agencies such as the Social Sciences and Humanities Research Council, Canadian Council on Learning, and Canadian Race Relations Foundation and has published in several international journals. Nombuso Dlamini is the author of *Youth and Identity Politics in South Africa 1990–1994* (University of Toronto Press, 2005).

Eva Aboagye was born, bred, and educated in Ghana, West Africa. Currently she is working as Manager of Strategic Institutional Planning and Performance at Centennial College, Toronto. She believes strongly in the transforming power of higher education both for the individual and for society and that access to that transforming power is not just based on one's academic potential; rather, it is often restricted by lack of access to the financial resources needed to succeed in higher education. Her research interests include looking at ways of making higher education financing more equitable.

Uzo Anucha is Assistant Professor in the Atkinson School of Social Work, York University, Toronto. Her educational background includes a master's degree in Psychology from the University of Benin, Nigeria, and a doctorate in Social Work from the University of Toronto, Canada. Uzo Anucha's interest in international social work has focussed on building the capacity of social work in Nigeria to promote gender equity. She is also engaged in several research projects that examine social issues such as homelessness among diverse and low social economic populations in Ontario, She is the principal investigator of Social Work in Nigeria, a 1 million dollar AUCC/CIDA collaborative project between the University of Benin and the University of Windsor. She serves as a member of the Board of Accreditation, Canadian Association of Schools of Social Work.

Grace Bunyi is a Senior Lecturer in Curriculum Studies at Kenyatta University, Kenya. She has published journal articles and chapters in edited volumes on language in education policy and practices in Kenya. Her research interests are sociolinguistic practices in schools and gender education. She has published several journal articles on gender inequalities in higher education in Kenya and other parts of Africa.

George J. Sefa Dei is Professor and Chair, Department of Sociology and Equity Studies, OISE/University of Toronto. Between 1996 and 2000, he served as the first Director of the Centre for Integrative Anti-Racism Studies at OISE/UT. His teaching and research interests are in the areas of Anti-Racism, Minority Schooling, International Development, and Anti-Colonial Thought. His published books include: *Anti-Racism Education: Theory and Practice* (1996); *Hardships and Survival in Rural West Africa* (published in both English and French, 1992); *Schooling and Education in Africa: The Case of Ghana* (2004); and *Critical Issues in Anti-Racist Research Methodologies* (co-edited with Gurpreet Singh Johal, 2005). George Dei is the recipient of the Race, Gender, and Class Project Academic Award (2002). He also received the African-Canadian Outstanding Achievement in Education Award from *Pride Magazine* in Toronto (2003), and the City of Toronto's William P. Hubbard Award for Race Relations (2003). In 2005 he received the ANKH Ann Ramsey Award for Intellectual

Initiative and Academic Action at the Annual International Conference of the Association of Nubian Kemetic Heritage, Philadelphia.

Wanja Gitari is Assistant Professor cross-appointed between the Transitional Year Programme and the Department of Curriculum, Teaching and Learning at OISE/ University of Toronto. She undertook her undergraduate studies at Kenyatta University, Kenya, and, before pursuing graduate studies, taught high school science. Her scholarship is in science education with research interests in the ways in which knowledge in everyday life can be used to meet science education goals.

Zephania Matanga holds a doctorate in Human Development and Applied Psychology from the OISE/University of Toronto. He has experience in teaching in elementary, secondary, and university settings, a sound knowledge base in special education, and advanced understanding of educational technology and its application in special education. Currently he works as an instructor of special education at the University of Manitoba, and he is the Executive Director of the African Canadian Disability Community Association.

Selina Mushi is Associate Professor of Teacher Education at Northeastern Illinois University. She holds a PhD from the OISE/University of Toronto. She conducted her undergraduate studies at the University of Dar es Salaam, Tanzania, where she also taught for three years before migrating to North America. Her focus is on the preparation of high-quality, interculturally competent teacher candidates. She has published over fifteen journal articles and book chapters; some of these are reports in the areas of evaluation of classroom assessment practices, technology in teaching, multicultural competencies, and multiple languages and learning.

Jacinta Muteshi is the Chairperson of the National Commission on Gender and Development, Kenya. In 2006 she was appointed to the Committee of Eminent Persons to undertake an evaluation of the Kenya constitutional review process to provide a road map for the conclusion of the process. As a consultant she works on issues related to legislating women's rights, gender equity in the workplace, gender mainstreaming for institutional change, women's health, FGC/FGM, violence against women, and human rights. Until 2005, she was on the Board of Directors of the Kenya Human Rights Commission. She holds a PhD from the OISE/University of Toronto, an MA in Education from McGill University, and a Bachelor of Science from the State University of New York.

Grace Khwaya Puja is a Senior Lecturer and Head of the Department of Educational Foundations at the Faculty of Education, University of Dar es Salaam, Tanzania. She is a citizen of Tanzania. Her research interests are in the areas of gender issues in higher education and the effect of language of instruction in Africa. She is engaged in a variety of research projects examining the economic strategies used by women in rural Tanzania. She is also consultant to a number of overseas internationally funded research projects.

INTRODUCTION

S. Nombuso Dlamini

The purpose of this volume is to reconceptualize and reinvent education in order to suit and serve pressing socioeconomic needs in the African continent. The chapters in this book are written by continental African scholars who, prior to pursuing graduate studies in North America, did the majority of their schooling in educational institutions in Africa. Each respected scholars in their respective disciplinary areas, contributors in this volume present perspectives that provide a current view of the conditions for and of education in Africa and put forward measures that need to be taken to address what has been referred to as an educational crisis on the continent.

Now academics, with experiences of teaching in African and/or North American classrooms, the contributors are well aware of the needs and levels of understanding of their students and colleagues about the African continent. Their chapters reflect their intimate and informed knowledge and experiences, and each chapter is enlivened with thick description (Geertz, 1973) emerging from a blending of empirical studies and theoretical writings about Africa and the Americas, and offer readers thoughtful analyses of the complex intricacies inherent in the educational concepts, curricula, and sociocultural issues that the authors address in their texts.

In examining the state of education in Africa, chapters in this volume have a common narrative thread that borrows from Mbembe's notion of the "postcolony," which concerns itself "specifically [with] a given historical trajectory – that of societies recently emerging from the experience of colonisation and the violence which the colonial relationship involves. … the postcolony is chaotically pluralistic; it has nonetheless an internal coherence" (2001, p. 102). From this vantage point, in the postcolony, state power is understood as creating:

> … through administrative and bureaucratic practices, its own world of meanings – a master code that, while becoming the society's central code, ends by governing, perhaps paradoxically, the logics that underlie all other meanings within that society; (2) attempts to institutionalise this world view of meanings as a "socio-historical world" and to make the world real, turning it into people's "common sense" not only by instilling it in the minds of the *cibles* or "target population," but also by integrating it into the period's consciousness. (2001, p. 103 – emphasis in the original)

In looking at the colonial roots of the current educational crisis in Africa, the authors have moved forward to examine the complex relationship that postcolonial African leaders have had with the colonial past, their efforts in drawing from indigenous knowledge and ways of being while simultaneously working to create a common sense that suits their personal and often corrupt economic interest, thereby suppressing political consciousnesses that might result in exposing their corruption and hegemonic tendencies. In other words, in their examination of relations of power in the postcolony, these authors have moved away from using simple oppositional binaries in which the Colonial Era is characterized by social, cultural, economic, and political violence and political independence is presented as the beginning of freedom marking emerging civil liberties and social and cultural reconstruction.

The chapters in this volume perceptively illustrate some of the many ways in which the past, imbued as it is with violent practices, is intertwined with the present, and how, to borrow from Mikhail Bakhtin, within "non-official" cultures, especially those that have been created in the postcolonial era, systems and structures of domination and subordination are found. Differently stated, the education crisis in Africa is said to be also rooted in the practices of African leaders who, since independence, have done little to change the malfunctioning policies and practices inherited from colonial regimes. As authors in this volume demonstrate, post-independence leaders have not embarked on meaningful activities towards transforming education in Africa, and, where such actions have been taken, they have been devastatingly shaped by commercial and capitalist interests. These authors are products of this crisis- and conflict-laden education system that, while aiming to offer intellectual tools with which to "write back" to the empire, in many ways, failed to offer them lenses for understanding and appreciating indigenous knowledge. The education received by these authors was presented in Western terms; for instance, the meanings of "power," "peace," and "freedom" were presented as Western phenomena, and, when mentioned, the African continent was presented only in the context of the "white man's" involvement with it. Textbooks used in schools only testified to the power of whites as great thinkers and great inventors: Galileo unlocked the workings of the heavens, Gutenberg discovered printing, and Newton solved the mysteries of gravity in physics. In this regard, the chapters in this book call for a need for African education to rid itself of this Eurocentric legacy of white supremacy.

What, then, are the educational areas of focus that should be examined and reconfigured in order to make new directions in the education of African children? There are three crosscutting themes that emerge in the way educational issues are discussed in this volume. First are discussions about gendered relations in the postcolony and how gendered inequities impact the practice of educating and women's chances of enjoying human rights. Another theme is that of language, which is intricately examined as an important resource affecting the delivery of curriculum content as well as influencing chances of economic development and success. The third theme woven throughout this volume attends to social and cultural issues, including the social welfare of citizens, especially of those with physical disabilities. Implicit throughout this volume are the authors' articulations and explorations of new initiatives as well as new directions towards a politically informed action-oriented education in Africa.

Actions that would improve the social role and economic livelihood of women have always been part of discourses in both the colony and the postcolony (Dlamini, 2001); yet to date, women in Africa are still disadvantaged by restrictive application of human rights policies, limited opportunities, and economic inequalities. Related to the lack of rights and economic inequalities, women face a system of sexist oppression, which pervades every aspect of life – that is, women face the rule of patriarchy and erroneous patriarchal relations of power, of gender inequity, that others have argued, run deeper than class exploitation and racial discrimination (see, for example, Millett, 1990). Examining the relationship between class and gender in Burkina Faso, Sankara (1988) argues that there is a close parallel between class exploitation and women's inferior status and that women's subjugation has survived and has been consolidated, both in the activities of everyday life and in intellectual and moral repression. Thus, in the postcolony, to facilitate patriarchal relations of power, traditions are rediscovered, and in some instances created, and practices that have long been contested are restored and given a central defining role, and signs regulating gender relations become bound up with notions of cultural reconstruction and authenticity.

In the chapters "Reproductive Health in Kenya" and "Gender, Post-Secondary Education, and Employment Opportunities for Women in Tanzania," Jacinta Muteshi and Grace Puja, respectively, take a detailed look at the various discourses that, when enacted, ensure women's subjugation and gender inequality in Africa. Although many advances and contributions to the status of women in Africa have been made, these authors argue that there is a pressing need for African governments to seriously put women, as a social category, at the forefront of national agendas. In colonial Africa, struggles for women's emancipation did not go hand in hand with national resistance movements; consequently, the "women's issue" failed to become part of the nationalist agenda. Currently, the problem of continued marginalization of women in Africa is compounded by what Kristeva (1986) argues is the globalization of problems of women in different milieux, ages, civilizations, and varying psychic structures. In this regard, Jacinta Muteshi's chapter "Reproductive Health in Kenya" argues that issues facing Kenyan women require local solutions. Further, she points out the limitations of comparing the struggles of women in Kenya to the struggles experienced in other countries, suggesting as an alternative the need and utility of contextualizing the social position of Kenyan women within the context of Kenyan Nationalist discourses. Writing on the role education can play in redressing the sexual and reproduction health rights of women in Kenya, Muteshi demonstrates how a comparative lens, if used to understand reproductive health issues in Kenya, can do more damage than it can offer solutions for girls. Muteshi demonstrates this danger in discussing, for example, access to sexual reproductive health services, in which she states that, while studies indicate that "it is common for young people in Kenya to start having sex in their early teens ... what is not so well known is that, unlike in western nations, where sexually active adolescents are unmarried, in developing countries most are married and therefore face different challenges from their single counterparts." Conversely, Muteshi argues that, since access to health services and to education is a human right yet to be realized by many Kenyans, strategies to combat this social issue need to be formulated within the context from which they emerge rather than through borrowing a global approach to gender inequities. According to Muteshi, another related concern is that the language used to write policy documents about this human right should be illustrative of government commitment and should include stipulated measures of accountability.

Following a view that, in the west, has come to be associated with Millett, Puja argues that the social organization of families, whereby girls are expected to perform certain house chores that boys are not, affects girls' success in schools and further conditions boys for roles of power and domination from a very early age. The concern about the right of women to education is also part of Puja's basis for arguing that the government of Tanzania must rethink its policies regarding women's access to post-secondary education, which ultimately contour women's employment opportunities in the labour market. Furthermore, Puja analyzes the ways in which in the post-colony, Eurocentric capitalist ideologies have combined with African patriarchal cultures to establish Tanzania's current education system. The result of this combination is women's under-representation in higher and technical education and their subsequent limited employment opportunity. Puja stresses the need for research that looks for alternatives to current educational policies so that education better promotes equity and improves women's employment opportunities.

LANGUAGE USE, PEDAGOGY, AND DEVELOPMENT

Language has always been a central and often perilous theme in education debates in the postcolony. In many African countries, formal education was introduced by missionaries with the aims of colonizing and training converts to proselytize and spread Christianity as taught in the mission schools. This meant that the Bible was translated into many indigenous languages for teaching purposes. However, not all subjects (geography, history, mathematics, and so on) received the same level of translation. Consequently, as others have argued, this, together with the use of non-indigenous languages as the medium of instruction in schools, may very well account for the failure of modern science and technology to take root and flourish over the past century. Additionally, African education systems of the past and present do not acknowledge the incompatibility of the language of the home and immediate community and that of the school. In many African countries, indigenous communities are multi-ethnic, and children learn their mother language first, then, through early social relations, they acquire other languages that are spoken by the children from one or more other ethnic groups. This means that in cases where, for example, English is used as a medium of instruction, it may not be the students' second language (as in the popular, now globally understood "English as a second language" conceptualization), even after many years of schooling. Furthermore, in many schools, students do not typically speak English to one another or with their teachers outside the classroom (Dlamini, 2005).

In her chapter "Some Issues of Science Education in Africa," Wanja Gitari discusses the fragmentation and disconnection between school knowledge (e.g., in science) and the knowledge students make in their everyday interactions within the local community and family. Several resolutions have been suggested to address this disconnect resulting from the use of languages with colonial origins in education in the postcolony. Some have advocated the use of European languages, arguing that using/writing in African languages causes the learner/ writer to lose both other African readers and Western audiences (e.g., Ojaide, 2005); others have advocated the use of indigenous languages in schools in teaching all courses, including science and technology (Dlodlo, 1999; Bunyi, this volume).

The active force of language in society, its use by individuals and groups to control others, or to defend themselves against being controlled, to change society or to prevent others from changing it (Burke, 1988) has been widely discussed in critical theory and sociolinguistic studies (see, for example, Foucault, 1989, on labelling; Bourdieu, 1982, on symbolic domination; Heller, 1995, on language choice and social institutions; and, Dlamini, 2001, on linguistic discourses). This means that any discussion of the languages of education in the postcolony cannot be divorced from questions of power and cannot be understood without reference to the society in which they are spoken. As part of ideology (used here in the Althusserian sense in which ideology is a system of representations with material existence that works to structure the relationships of individuals to their real conditions of existence; that is, it acts as a guide to social reality), languages have been a central force used in the postcolony to convince others about their role in accessing valued resources, both symbolic and material. This is the heart of Grace Bunyi's examination of the current state of language use in Kenyan schools in her chapter "The Place of African Indigenous Knowledge and Languages in Education for Development: The Case of Kenya." Significantly, she examines practices of language use in schools in Kenya and how they are intertwined with societal attitudes, the myth of development, and social, cultural, and economic progress.

In Kenya, Kiswahili, a traditional *lingua franca* encouraged by the British colonizing forces because it facilitated local administration, was given a new function during the independence movement since it was seen as a means of facilitating unity between different ethnic groups in a common political project, of giving them a common consciousness. Ironically, English, the language of former rulers, was also given the same role. Post-independence Kenya, however, witnessed a devaluing of African indigenous languages, including Kiswahili, and a rise in the value of English. By looking at elementary schools in Kenya, some in which English is used as a medium of instruction from the first grade, and others in which Kiswahili is used as a medium of instruction for the first five years of schooling, Bunyi examines the processes through which African indigenous languages have been delegitimized and denigrated in education. She argues that a meaningful solution to the problem of language in education lies in creating policies that place high value on the role that indigenous languages play in the lives of African children. In this vein, Bunyi's chapter provides a case for why indigenous African languages should be given more of a central role in education.

The question of how teachers teach and what is taught in schools remains the focus of educational debates in both the developed and developing worlds. A well-known way of describing the forms of teacher practice in education is offered by the Brazilian educator Paulo Freire (1970), who distinguishes between what he calls a "banking system of education" and a "problem-posing" approach to knowledge production. A banking system of education is one that ignores students' knowledge and in which knowledge is transmitted to students with the aim of having them accept the status quo. In this system, students are considered empty vessels to be filled by the knowledgeable teacher and the historicity of individuals in the learning process is ignored. Conversely, within the framework of a problem-posing education, which places emphasis on dialogue and local knowledge, the students' historicity is taken as the starting point, and the students' knowledge claims are valued.

In the chapter "Some Issues of Science Education in Africa," Wanja Gitari argues that a problem-posing approach to science education in Africa would address the disjointedness of classroom-based information and its applicability to students' everyday lives. Gitari eloquently expresses the uselessness of being well-informed, of having accumulated endless inert knowledge, if one cannot engage with that knowledge. She goes on to discuss education with production, constructivist teaching, science, technology, society, and the environment, anti-racist science teaching, and co-operative learning as equally relevant models of teaching science education. The reason for proposing these models is threefold: first, to elevate the achievement and representation of girls and women in science; second, to examine the soundness of the content knowledge learned in school; and third, to ensure that science graduates are able to readily transfer the science knowledge they gained at school to everyday problem-solving situations. For Gitari, all these models would provide hands-on experience in learning, facilitate students' self-esteem, lead towards deconstruction and radicalizing the milieu of science discourses and facilitate the overall learning of science. Moreover, Gitari argues that, since these learning approaches appeal to women's ways of knowing, they will enable girls to place science within the context of everyday life.

Access to education, especially to higher education, while a taken-for-granted right in the West, is still a challenge for young people in the postcolony. Moreover, as Eva Aboagye's chapter "Financing Students in Higher Education: Examining Trends and Funding Options in Africa and Canada" indicates, post-secondary education in Africa is under the command of international funding institutions such as the International Monetary Fund, whose interests are more corporate than educational. In her Canada-Ghana comparative study of financing higher education, Aboagye argues that, even though these two areas are different economically, socially, and politically, the issues of cost recovery facing students and governments in these countries are the same. Consequently, in Ghana, preoccupation with cost recovery leads to minute resources being directed towards education; the result is a poor quality of education with declining standards.

In the chapter "Possibilities in African Schooling and Education," George Dei contends that, in order to imagine new possibilities, African peoples must deconstruct the myth of "development" using local, traditional, and indigenous cultural knowledge. He argues that a significant challenge is to unravel how dominant thinking shapes what constitutes development. Today, local peoples continue to struggle for new cultural, economic, and political imaginings and imaginaries. There is a need for new visions and counter-theoretical perspectives of education and development to disentangle "development" and "education" from the grip of dominant paradigms. By working with critical and alternative ideas, educators can think creatively about "education and development" in ways that avoid an easy slippage into the form, logic, and implicit assumptions and postulations of what exactly is being contested. In other words, education for development is not just about an increase in physical and human capital. Education for development requires changes both in ways of thinking and in the social, political, cultural, and economic institutions of society. Local peoples have not been passive recipients of "development" knowledge. Local cultural knowledge and subjectivities have, and can, become important sites of power and resistance to dominant discursive practices. It is incumbent upon critical scholarship to employ an anti-colonial prism to examine some key issues of African schooling and development, specifically the role of culture: indigenous/local cultural resource knowledge and education in the search for genuine development and educational options for the continent (see Dei, 2004). The reference to anti-colonial thought is relevant in stressing local understandings of the nature and contexts of colonized relations and practices, as well as the recourse to power and subjective agency for resistance, and the promotion of genuine "development" (Dei & Asgharzadeh, 2000).

In calling for localized solutions to the African education problem, writers in this volume realize that a call to the local should not mean a return to purity. Instead, the position taken follows that articulated by Stuart Hall (1997), in which the global and the local constitute two aspects of the same phenomenon. Hall sees a return to the local as a response to the seeming homogenization and globalization of culture, which can only work for social change if it is not rooted in "exclusive and defensive enclaves" (p. 36). Arguing against the portrayal of the "local" as inherently wholesome and better than the "global," Hall writes:

> The homeland is not waiting back there for the new ethnics to rediscover it. There is a past to be learned about, but the past is now seen, and it has to be grasped as a history, as something that has to be told. It is narrated. It is grasped through desire. It is grasped through reconstruction. It is not just a fact that has been waiting to ground our identities. (1997, p. 38)

ENGAGING NEW INITIATIVES IN AFRICAN EDUCATION

The creation of the new homeland – through the use of history, the present as well as futuristic desires – is now being shaped by access to new technologies. Information Technology (IT) has challenged old and simplistic concepts of the neat north-south divide, which are now replaced by new geographies of power and access that have re-configured the world. As such, education in Africa needs to recognize the urgency of responding to a new communication order. Research in the area of IT advances in Africa indicates that several institutions of higher learning have adapted to the changes in communication methods and that, to some degree, IT has become central in the teaching and learning of Information Science/Service because of the great influence of these technologies on the profession (Minish-Mananja, 2004). Such changes in the use of IT come from the realization of a need to produce, for efficiency and effectiveness, graduates equipped with competencies for working in the current information environment, which, though still traditional, is increasingly becoming dependent on IT. Many studies, however, indicate that there is an important need for schools to increase the use of IT in teaching and learning as well as in school administration so as to foster effectiveness and full participation of students in the social, economic, and political realms of life (Burbules and Callister, 2000). Moreover, others point to the need to increase access in order to overcome an already existing digital divide (Mushi, this volume), the need to tap into the unique possibilities offered by IT, and the need to engage in sustained research that examines how IT interfaces with other transformative processes happening simultaneously (Czerniewicz, 2004).

In her chapter "Information Technology and the Curriculum Process," Selina Mushi addresses this pervasiveness of Information Technology around the world and its implications for the education process. She argues that the use of IT in teaching and learning changes the traditional role of the teacher; yet, this use and access to IT is not evenly experienced across countries because IT trends seem to follow those of the print media. A few centuries ago when the printing press began to emerge in societies, books began to be mass-produced. It was at this juncture that people (mostly the rich) began to immerse themselves in the readily available literature of the time. Many poor and disadvantaged people could not afford books. As a result, those who could afford books emerged as the most literate in societies, leaving the poor and disadvantaged behind. Mushi documents a similar situation with computers and the Internet, which is causing disparities and inequality within communities and nations. Drawing on her experiences as a new graduate student in Toronto, Mushi documents the challenges she faced, which resulted from underexposure to IT in her undergraduate work in Africa. Mushi argues that exposure to IT allowed her to participate more in the learning process, which consequently led her to examine how teachers respond to students' engagement with technology. Her chapter, then, is an analysis of teachers' responses to students' exposure to IT and concludes that, since students use technology to inform themselves, and are often more knowledgeable than the teacher, teachers' responses to students' knowledge are often not empowering and do not encourage independent learning.

In "Envisioning African Social Work Education," Uzo Anucha critically examines current social work models in Africa and argues that there is a need for new context-based models in the profession. According to Anucha, social work models in Africa have been exported from the West; yet, there is plenty of evidence that the West has failed to come up with answers to many of its own problems, including homelessness, neglect and abuse of children, alcohol and drug abuse, crime, and so on. For this reason, Anucha critiques the transfer of these botched models to other contexts and calls for an African social work education based within an indigenous framework – one that addresses African challenges. She discusses some particular areas of social welfare and development in Africa that would benefit most from an indigenized social work education.

Zephania Matanga's thought-provoking chapter demonstrates how countries all over the world need to critically examine how they treat their citizens who have disabilities. Having conducted a Zimbabwe-Canada comparative study, Matanga contends that challenges faced by people with disabilities all over the world are similar; that they are not community-based but, rather, percolate through national and cultural boundaries. He also challenges the notion that discriminatory practices perpetuated against people with disabilities are either self-inflicted by the disability itself or else merely isolated incidences and localized problems, which are especially prevalent and mostly confined in third world countries. For Matanga, these discriminatory practices persist because of the public's silence, which he considers tantamount to gross neglect and mistreatment.

In conclusion, *New Directions in African Education* conveys the pressing need to rethink how education addresses gender parity, reconfigures the meaning of and engagement in socio-cultural and economic development activities, moves towards new ways of conducting education subjects in and through indigenous languages, engages in the creation of citizens who will be involved in both the production and consumption of new information technologies, addresses issues of financing education in schools and especially in post-secondary institutions, and moves towards forms of pedagogy that draw from the African experience, resources, knowledge, and local communities. Each chapter begins with an introductory account and a list of ideas or concepts pertinent to the topic; this is followed by a discussion of the content, as well as the theoretical framework or the controversial interpretations that have dominated the ideas conveyed, and a succinct examination of the author's position, which is tied to suggestions about new directions that exist or should be taken in order to fully envelop the theme discussed. A relatively full reference list, which has informed the author's position and may be consulted to get a fuller understanding of the topic and fulfill further scholarly interests, concludes each chapter. It is hoped that by reading these pages many will begin to see how, in the words of Walter Rodney (1972), Europe underdeveloped Africa and how Africa is beginning to deal with the trauma of colonialism and underdevelopment.

REFERENCES

Bourdieu, P. (1982). Lecture on the lecture. In *In other words* (pp. 177–198). Cambridge: Polity Press.

Burbules, N., & Callister, C. (2000). *Watch IT: The risk and promise of information technologies for education.* Boulder, CO: Westview Press.

Burke, P., & Porter, R. (1988). *The social history of language.* Cambridge: Cambridge University Press.

Czerniewicz, L. (2004). Cape of storms or Cape of Good Hope? Educational technology in a changing environment. *British Journal of Educational Technology, 35*(2), 145–58.

Dei, G.J.S. (2004). *Schooling and education in Africa: The case of Ghana.* Trenton, NJ: Africa World Press/Red Rose.

Dei, G.J.S., & Asgharzadeh, A. (2000). The power of social theory: Towards an anti-colonial discursive framework. *Journal of Educational Thought, 35*(3), 297–323.

Dlodlo, T. S. (1999). Science nomenclature in Africa: Physics in Nguni. *Journal of Research in Science Teaching, 36*(3), 321–31.

Dlamini, S. N. (2001). Literacy, womanism and struggle: Reflections on the practices of an African woman. *Journal of International Women's Studies, 2*(3), 78–93.

Dlamini, S. N. (2005). *Youth and identity politics in South Africa: 1990–1994.* Toronto: University of Toronto Press.

Foucault, M. (1989). *The birth of the clinic. An archaeology of medical perception.* London and New York: Routledge.

Freire, P. (1970). *Pedagogy of the Oppressed.* New York: Continuum.

Geertz, C. (1973). *The interpretation of cultures.* New York: Basic Books.

Hall, S. (1997). The local and the global: Globalisation and ethnicity. In A. D. King (Ed.), *Culture, globalisation and the world-system: Contemporary conditions for the representation of identity* (pp. 19–40). Minneapolis: University of Minesota Press.

Heller, M. (1995). Language choice, social institutions, and symbolic domination. *Language and Society, 24*(3) 373–405.

Kristeva, J. (1986). Women's time. In M. Toril (Ed.), *The Kristeva reader* (pp. 160–86). New York: Columbia University Press.

Mbembe, A. (2001). *On the postcolony.* Berkeley: University of California Press.

Millett, K. (1990). *Sexual politics.* New York: Simon and Schuster.

Minish-Mananja, M. (2004). Information and communication technologies in library and information science education in South Africa. *Mousaion, 22*(2), 150–71.

Ojaide, T. (2005). Literature in Africa and the Caribbean. In M. Azevedo (Ed.), *Africana Studies: A survey of Africa and the African Diaspora*, 3rd ed. (pp. 325–78). Durham, NC: Academic Press.

Rodney, W. (1972). *How Europe underdeveloped Africa.* London: Bogle-L'Ouverture.

Sankara, T. (1988). *Thomas Sankara speaks: The Burkina Faso revolution, 1983–87.* New York: Pathfinder.

1

THE PLACE OF AFRICAN INDIGENOUS KNOWLEDGE AND LANGUAGES IN EDUCATION FOR DEVELOPMENT: THE CASE OF KENYA

Grace W. Bunyi

ABSTRACT

Nearly five decades after political independence in some countries, education has had little demonstrable impact on the problems that confront the people as development has continued to elude Africa. In this chapter, the author explores how education is the tool to empower the African people to seek and find solutions of the problems that confront them; specifically the author argues that African indigenous knowledge and languages must play greater roles in an education that will lead to greater development of African countries. The author begins by extricating the ties between language, education, and development and underscores the central role of African indigenous knowledge and languages in Africa's development. She focuses on Kenya as she discusses the socio-political and economic processes that have led to the marginalization of African indigenous knowledge and languages in education before critically analyzing the reasons often given for the non-use of indigenous languages as languages of instruction. The chapter ends with a discussion of the major challenges to the use of indigenous languages as languages of instruction and concludes with suggestions to ensure the empowering use of these languages, which she argues will consequently lead to greater socio-economic independence.

INTRODUCTION

The problems that confront African nations at the beginning of the twenty-first century are enormous and permeate all areas of human life. An enumeration of problems that the human race faces reveals Africa taking the lead in nearly all areas. The people of Africa struggle daily with basic problems of hunger, war, and civil strife, and with new and old diseases. Diseases such as HIV/AIDS and malaria continue to wreak havoc on their lives, reducing life expectancy rates to below forty years in some countries and impoverishing survivors. Poverty levels in Africa are appalling, with more than half of the populations in many countries having been declared officially poor on account of living on less than one U.S. dollar a day. These everyday problems of the African people are usually characterized as problems of development or the lack of it.

It must be pointed out that this characterization of African countries' problems as problems of development is not entirely new in Africa. Indeed, on the attainment of independence by various countries starting late in the 1950s, African leaders preached the gospel of development. In Kenya, for example, the first president Mzee Jomo Kenyatta's rallying call was that all should unite to bring *maendeleo* (the Kiswahili word for development) through tackling three enemies: ignorance, disease, and poverty. Indeed, as is the case today, within the development discourse of the time, education was seen as key to the solution of the other development problems and African governments set about expanding their educational systems with some success. At the time of independence in Kenya in 1963, there were 6,058 primary and 151 secondary schools with enrolments of 891,553 and 30,121 pupils, respectively. In 2004, there were 17,804 public primary and 3,621 public secondary schools with respective enrolments of 7,122,407 and 923,134 pupils (Government of Kenya, 1998; Ministry of Education, Science, and Technology, 2005). However, rather than rethink and transform the European education models transplanted into Africa courtesy of European missionaries and colonial administrators, African governments adopted these models with slight curriculum changes such as introducing the geography and history of Africa. African indigenous knowledge and culture, which had been disparagingly characterized as primitive and pagan therefore continued to be considered unfit as educational resources and to be excluded from education. Further, African indigenous languages, the symbols of and media through which African knowledge and culture is transmitted, suffered devaluation in colonial society due to their contact with the languages of the political, social, and economic power wielding European colonials in spite of being given some roles in education by some imperial powers such as the British.

Nearly five decades after political independence in some countries, education has had little demonstrable impact on the problems that confront the people as development has continued to elude Africa. In this chapter, I argue that, if education is to empower the African people to seek and find solutions of the problems that confront them and thus contribute to their own and their countries' development, there is need for African indigenous knowledge and languages to play a greater role in education. I start by extricating the ties between language, education, and development and underscoring the central role of African indigenous knowledge and languages in Africa's development. I then focus on Kenya and discuss the socio-political and economic processes that have led to the marginalization of African indigenous knowledge and languages in education before critically analyzing the reasons often given for the non-use of indigenous languages as languages of instruction. The chapter ends with a discussion of the major challenges to the use of indigenous languages as languages of instruction.

LANGUAGE, EDUCATION, AND DEVELOPMENT

Economic theories, with their emphasis on economic growth, have traditionally dominated development scholarship. However, development models based solely on economic considerations have been found to be inadequate. Critics of such models have argued that economic growth manifested in improved GNPs or GDPs does not necessarily translate into improved living conditions for the people, and calls have been made for a more expanded view of development (Mohochi, 2005). Supporting an expanded view of development, Bartoli argues that, when viewed widely, development encompasses the general improvement of a people's material well being, with areas of concern including food, health, education, and life expectancy (cited in Mohochi, 2005). This view is in line with the United Nations Development Programme's approach to development, where the concern is with human development, which it holds refers to development of the people, by the people, and for the people (Bartoli, cited in Mohochi, 2005). Participatory development has become the rallying call of this approach to development, which puts the ordinary people at the centre of the development process as active participants in their individual and societal development and transformation. Participatory development is by implication interactive. Since grass root African people interact in their indigenous languages, these languages are key tools in the development process. Further, when there is a disconnect between the language of the leaders and the experts who have been educated in European languages and the language of the people who are proficient only in their indigenous languages, no development can occur, as the two cannot communicate.

A different formulation of the expanded view of development posits that development is a multi-dimensional concept encompassing the socio-cultural, political, and economic spheres of human life. According to Bodomo (n.d.), a comprehensive view of development calls for a complete transformation of the socio-political and economic belief systems of a particular society to suit its present needs. This view places the cultural capital of any society at the centre of its development. Bodomo further argues that, since language is a repository and a tool for the expression and communication of these very socio-cultural, political, and economic belief systems, successful conceptualization and implementation of this societal transformation can only be achieved through the use of the languages that are indigenous to the society. The implication here is that African indigenous languages have a key role to play in the continent's development. Clearly, whichever way you look at development, language is a key tool and African indigenous languages should be an integral component of the conceptualization and implementation of development efforts.

On the other hand, few would argue with the proposition that education or knowledge is a key development tool. In both Western and African educational thought, cultural transmission has been identified as one of the most fundamental functions of education (Dewey, 1916; Kenyatta, 1953). In this view, a people's culture or indigenous knowledge constitutes the content of education. For centuries before the advent of European education and education systems in Africa, African indigenous knowledge sustained African societies for generations. African indigenous knowledge spans all areas of human life – economic, culture, politics, science, and technology. Using African indigenous knowledge in areas such as agriculture, politics, and medicine, African societies were able to address problems of food security, peaceful co-existence, and health. Though excluded from formal education in the colonial and postcolonial eras, to date, African indigenous knowledge is part of the lived experience of African people, especially the rural poor, and it is stored and communicated in songs, dances, beliefs, proverbs, and folklore. It is also to be found in the social institutions, traditions, and practices of the people.

Development literature acknowledges that indigenous knowledge continues to be an integral part of the culture and history of African local communities and that it continues to be used at the local community level as the basis for decisions pertaining to food security, human and animal health, education, natural resource management, and other vital activities (Gorjestani, n.d.). Indeed, some express the opinion that the gradual erosion of indigenous knowledge and accompanying destruction of natural wealth – plants, animals, insects, soils, clean air, and water – and human cultural wealth such as songs, proverbs, folklore, and social-cooperation is the greatest threat to economic stability of the African continent (Burford et al., n.d.). A good indication that African indigenous knowledge continues to be an important resource is the fact that the informal economic sector, which in some countries represents as much as 50 per cent of the total economic growth, draws from the accumulated skills and expertise and indigenous knowledge systems (Emeagwali, 2003). Emphasizing the importance of indigenous knowledge in development, Abdalla (cited in Mohochi, 2005) states, "third world countries must see development as being first of all based on the assertion of their cultural identity" (p. 3). African indigenous languages are part of indigenous knowledge and culture, which are so crucial to Africa's development.

Many scholars have shown that language is not only part of culture but that it is the repository of culture and therefore embodies culture. Many have emphasized the intricate ties that exist between a language and the culture it symbolizes (Fanon, 1967; Goke-Pariola, 1993; Spencer, 1985). For example, Fanon (1967) states, "To speak [a language] … means above all to assume a culture, to support the weight of a civilization.… A man who has a language consequently possesses the world expressed and implied by that language" (pp. 17–18). This statement underscores the fact that a language symbolizes its native speakers' culture and that any language is also constitutive of the culture of those who speak it natively.

Language plays a key role in education and cultural transmission, whether within the indigenous education model, which was and continues to be informal, or the Western model, which is formal. Indeed, few would dispute the contention that language is the tool for education. In the informal education processes, constituted of the interactive activities of children, their parents and/or other caregivers, teaching and learning take place through oral/aural language. Within formal education, it is mainly through verbal interactions between the teacher and the learners and among the learners themselves and through learners interacting with written language by reading and writing that knowledge is constructed and acquired in the teaching-learning process. Indeed, language learning itself is seen by many as an important part of what becoming educated is all about. As Obanya (1999) has observed, "In promoting the development of every child, the primary focus is on language development" (p. 18). Indeed, many of a child's early years in school are spent on developing linguistic skills or what some language and learning scholars have described as learning to use language as a tool for thought (Wells, 1989). In this regard, scholars have argued that, in a multilingual environment, the use and development of the child's indigenous language in his/her early years of education is best suited for his/her cognitive and emotional development (Cummins, 1981).

European languages that have dominated education in Africa have not been of much help in the African people's development endeavours. Education scholars focused on language issues have argued that only education that is anchored in African indigenous knowledge and languages can serve the goal of national development in Africa. Prah (cited in Brock-Utne, 2005) has, for example, observed thus, "it is the empowerment of Africans with their native languages, which would make the difference between whether Africa develops, or not" (p. 178). On the other hand, Spencer's (1985) observation is worth noting: "No developed or affluent nations, though many of these have minority languages, utilize a language for education and other national purposes which is of external origin and the mother tongue of none, or at most few of its people" (p. 390).

In the foregoing paragraphs, I have tried to explicate the relationship between language, education, and development and to show why it is that any effort aimed at transforming the lives of African people (and through them the countries) must take account of African indigenous knowledge and languages. However, this has not been the case. European languages introduced to Africa through colonialism continue to be the key languages of education in Africa today. In the next section, I focus on Kenya as a case study of the colonial, post-colonial, socio-economic, and political processes that have led to the entrenchment of English in education and the marginalization of indigenous languages and the indigenous cultures that they embody before discussing the impacts that this has had on education.

THE KENYA CASE: SOCIOLINGUISTIC CONTEXT

There are four language categories in Kenya: African indigenous languages, of which there are over 40 (Abdulazizz, 1982); non-Kenyan languages, including Indo-Asiatic languages and European languages other than English; Kiswahili, Kenya's national language; and, English, the official language. Whereas nearly everybody in Kenya speaks an indigenous Kenyan language, it is estimated that 75 per cent of the population have varying levels of competence in Kiswahili and that only 15 per cent of the population know English well enough to use it effectively in all areas of life (Abdulaziz, 1982). Although spoken by a small minority, English continues to play the dominant role in education at the expense of indigenous languages.

COLONIAL ROOTS OF THE MARGINALIZATION OF INDIGENOUS LANGUAGES IN EDUCATION

The marginalization of Kenyan indigenous languages during British colonial rule had to do with shifts in the reasons why these languages were used in education.[1] The missionaries introduced Western-type education to Kenya in 1844 when Johann Kraph established a mission station at Rabai near the coast. The colonial government only started taking an interest in education in 1909. In this period, the missionaries taught and used the indigenous languages as languages of instruction for ideological reasons. They saw these languages as the most effective in reaching the souls of the Africans and thereby achieving their conversion to Christianity. The missionary interests in proselytization were well served by indigenous languages. Education in the indigenous languages meant that graduates of missionary schools could read the scriptures for themselves and for others.

The teaching of and through African indigenous languages was encouraged in British colonies (Bamgbose, 1991; Spencer, 1974). This was because, unlike the French and the Portuguese colonial powers that sought to assimilate a few Africans into French and Portuguese culture and therefore did not teach indigenous African languages, British colonialism pursued separatist policies. The other colonials with a presence in Kenya were the white farmers, known as white settlers, who were perfectly happy with this racist practice. They supported indigenous language education for Africans, whom they saw as "people destined to till the land" (Crampton, 1986) and therefore not fit to learn English, the language of colonial power. Consequently, in the early part of British colonial rule in Kenya, the practice was to teach indigenous languages and to switch to Kiswahili in Standard 3 and to continue teaching in Kiswahili in junior secondary.

In the latter part of British colonialism in Kenya, indigenous languages were marginalized through the expansion of the teaching of English in African schools. Following the two Beecher Reports of 1942 and 1949, which recommended that English replace Kiswahili as the *lingua franca*, colonial education started to lay more emphasis on the teaching of English. The colonial government's Education Department Annual Report of 1951 called for the teaching of English in the lower classes of primary school, and English as the language of instruction right from Standard 1 was introduced in 1962 (Mbaabu, 1996). According to wa Thiong'o (1981), the colonial government realized that its days were numbered and therefore found it necessary to ensure that in its absence its interests would be served by those Africans who took over power. The colonial government therefore expanded the teaching of English as a way of passing on British values and standards to the incoming African elite.

Consequently, by the end of colonial rule in 1963, the indigenous languages were losing even the small traditionally uncontested roles that they had as the languages of instruction in the first years of school. In addition, there was a tendency among teachers to neglect the teaching of these languages entirely (Gachukia, 1970).

It must be pointed out that the Africans themselves were opposed to teaching of and in the indigenous languages. This is because English had become the language of political power and elevated socio-economic status in Kenya. It was the language spoken by the politically and economically powerful white people and the African functionaries in the colonial civil service. Writing about the situation in Nigeria, in particular, and in British colonial Africa, in general, Goke-Pariola (1993) states that, for the Africans, "To speak that language in itself was power … the local person who understood the White man's language increased his own power dramatically: he became a man before whom others stood in awe" (p. 223). At the same time, insofar as they gained employment in junior positions of the colonial administration, those Africans who acquired English language skills gained inclusion into colonial power. According to wa Thiong'o (1986), in Kenya, "English was the official vehicle and formula to colonial elitedom" (p. 115). Consequently, African parents demanded that their children be taught English. They saw indigenous language education as third-rate education meant to deny them English and hence the economic and political power controlled by those who spoke it.

POSTCOLONIAL EDUCATION AND THE INDIGENOUS LANGUAGES

Indigenous languages were dealt an almost fatal blow by the first post-independence education commission in Kenya, popularly known as the Ominde Commission; the blow came through its recommendation that English be the medium of instruction from Standard 1 and characterization of indigenous languages as "essential languages of verbal communication." The commission observed, "We see no cause for assigning to [the indigenous languages] a role for which they are ill adapted, namely, the role of educational medium in the critical early years of schooling" (Republic of Kenya, 1964, p. 60).

The second post-independence education commission, the Gachathi Commission of 1976, subsequently reversed this policy (Republic of Kenya, 1976). However, the attitudes towards indigenous languages expressed in the Ominde Commission Report continue to influence the position of these languages in education. Current language in education policy as regards indigenous languages is that they are to be taught and used as languages of instruction for the first three years of school in linguistically homogeneous areas.[2] According to this policy, indigenous languages have only a bridging role between the language of the home and English, the language of education in Kenya. They do not have a place in the education of Kenyan children beyond Standard 3, and they have no role in the education of all those Kenyan children in linguistically heterogeneous areas. Further, in practice, for various reasons, including the mistaken belief that the earlier English is used as the medium of instruction the more quickly the children will learn it and learn in it and the lack of teaching-learning resources such as textbooks in the indigenous languages, many teachers rush into using English as the language of instruction right from Standard 1.

Currently, the discourse in support of the strengthening of the teaching of English centres on science, technology, and globalization. It is argued that English is the language of science and technology and that school curricula should emphasize computer-based technology and English as the language of such technologies. Further, one hears more and more about the need for Kenya's education system to produce graduates for the global labour market and therefore the need to emphasize English, the global language.

In addition, there are those who express concern about the falling standards of English and argue for emphasis on the language. For the last three decades or so, Kenyan newspapers have carried articles that decry the poor English skills of primary and even secondary and college students. "The Big English Problem," "Language Experts Concern...," "Declining Standards of English Language...," "English Standards are Falling" are all fairly common features of newspaper article titles. Such articles offer opinions about the causes of the falling standards and suggestions concerning how the teaching and learning of English can be strengthened. In the emerging discourse, indigenous languages are seen as hindrances to the effective learning of English and as languages of little value – languages that cannot take one anywhere.

As already indicated, right from independence in 1963, Kenya has looked to education for the necessary knowledge, skills, and attitudes to enable Kenyans to attain development. However, development is not in sight for Kenyans as good numbers of them continue to suffer from the lack of fulfilment of even the most basic needs. Each year, communities living in arid and semi-arid areas are confronted by food shortage problems. In the worst years, several million people are reduced to depending on famine food relief which causes the government to declare the famine a national disaster. Clearly, the Eurocentric, English-language-dominated education has not been of much use to the majority of Kenyans who live in linguistically homogenous communities in the rural areas and draw on their indigenous knowledge for survival.

At the same time, the education system has enormous problems of its own as it struggles towards the United Nation's Education for All (EFA) goals of access, quality, and equity. Educational problems are multidimensional and are often caused by a variety of factors. In the case of education in Africa, language of instruction has been identified as key to the problems (Obanya, cited in Brock-Utne, 2005). In what follows, I discuss some of the problems that are associated with the use of English – a second or even third language for the majority of the learners – as the language of instruction in the primary school in Kenya.

PROBLEMS ASSOCIATED WITH THE USE OF ENGLISH AS THE MEDIUM OF INSTRUCTION

Access

While enrolment figures showed a dramatic rise in 2003 when free primary education[3] was introduced in the country, reports indicate that over 1.7 million primary school age children are still out of school. The children who took advantage of the free primary education policy and re-entered school and the majority of those out of school are children of the poor and marginalized inhabitants of the rural areas and urban slum communities. One would have thought that the very marginalized pastoralist, nomadic, and largely Islamic communities in the North Eastern province, for example, would have taken advantage of the free primary education policy and enrolled their children in school in large numbers. However, extremely low enrolment rates are still common. The province attained a net enrolment ratio of only 19.6 per cent (and a gross enrolment ratio of 26.9 per cent) in 2004. I believe there is a linguistic and cultural explanation that plays into the equation. These low enrolment communities are the same communities that are culturally far removed from the Eurocentric culture of the Kenyan elite and English. The latter are considered the legitimate social capital resources in education in Kenya. These communities, which invest in a different form of social capital, therefore, do not see the need of enrolling their children in school.

The introduction of free primary education as part of the renewed efforts towards universal primary education is an important step in opening up access to the masses of Kenyan children. However, for all Kenyan children to access and benefit from education, their indigenous languages need to play the crucial role of languages of instruction for much of primary education.

Repetition and dropout

It has also been observed that once children enrol in school, many fail to make progress. For example, the Ministry of Education's statistics show that the grade repetition phenomenon is considerable and that the highest repetition rate of 17.2 per cent is at Standard 1 (Ministry of Education, Science, and Technology, 2003). The report indicates that most of these children repeat because they fail to acquire literacy. The fact that children at this level do not learn how to read and write in Kenyan primary schools is understandable since the official curriculum expects them to acquire literacy in two or three languages – English, Kiswahili, and the indigenous languages – simultaneously. It would make better sense for the curriculum to be designed so as to allow children to acquire initial literacy skills first in their indigenous languages, which they already know and which they would therefore learn to read in more easily. They could then transfer the skills to acquiring literacy in Kiswahili and then English (Cummins, 1981).

Furthermore, school dropout rates in Kenya are high. Less than half of the children who enrol in Standard 1 complete the eight years of primary education. Many reasons contribute to children dropping out of school. One of these must surely be their experience of schooling. Owing to the use of English as the medium of instruction, many children do not have empowering school experiences. Obanya (cited in Brock-Utne, 2005) has pointed out:

> It has always been felt by African educators that the African child's major learning problem is a linguistic problem. Instruction is given in a language that is not normally used in his immediate environment, a language which neither the learner nor the teacher understands and uses well enough. (p. 173)

In agreeing with Obanya, Brock-Utne (2005) asserts that the major learning problem for the African child is linguistic; if the children lack the language of the school they are "stamped as dumb." I would argue that such experiences cause many children to drop out of school.

Educational outcomes

Educational outcomes, even when narrowly measured by students' achievement in national examinations and other types of assessment tests, are low in Kenya. For example, there are indications that Kenyan primary school learners are not attaining literacy skills necessary for successful learning. The 1998 SACMEQ criterion-referenced English reading test administered to a representative national sample indicated that 77 per cent of Kenyan Standard 6 pupils had not attained the English reading mastery level deemed desirable for successful learning in Standard 7 (UNESCO IIEP, 2001).

On the other hand, in a report accompanying the 2005 issue of the Kenya Certificate of Primary Education (KCPE) examination results, the Kenya National Examinations Council reported that some of the candidates should not have gone beyond Standard 1 as they had not learned anything by the time they sat for the examination in Standard 8. According to the report, in the English composition paper, some candidates spent their examination time copying the lead sentence over and over again instead of constructing a piece of narrative in line with the sentence.

The above learning achievement reports suggest that many Kenyan children are leaving school before they acquire basic literacy – perhaps the least of the skills that are controlled by the school. This is not helping Kenya's fight against illiteracy. Reports indicate that there are over 4 million illiterate Kenyans – a figure that comprises those adults and out-of-school youth who have never enrolled in school and those who enrolled but got little in the way of literacy skills out of the experience.

Curriculum and pedagogy

The quality of education in Kenyan primary schools is poor. Classroom ethnographers who have sought to document classroom processes reveal that the use of English as the language of instruction is associated with intellectually unchallenging curriculum and pedagogy. I will use data from my study of language use in a rural Standard 1 class to demonstrate this.

From my discussions with the teachers in this school, I found that because of their lack of English on arrival in school, the children in this school were being characterized as having learning problems. The headmaster of the school told me, "Language is another problem we have especially in lower primary. Because the children come without any knowledge of English, they take a long time before they can understand and communicate in English."

The teachers in the school also constantly told me that the children did not learn easily and that they did not understand easily. The Standard 1 teacher explained that her solution to the "learning problems" of these students was to keep repeating the same thing over and over again. She said, "You have to keep repeating so that they understand and you keep repeating what you have already done so that they don't forget."

The following excerpts from a reading lesson in Standard 1 illustrate what the teacher was saying. The lesson started with the reading of the new words in the text as follows. In the excerpts, *T* stands for teacher, *SS* for students and *T* and *SS* for teacher and students:

T:	So let us first of all read the new words. The new words are on page 17. Okay. The first word here is ride. Say riding.
SS:	Riding.
T:	Riding.
SS:	Riding.
T:	Again.
SS:	Riding.
T:	Once again.
SS:	Riding.

The other two new words in the reading text, "reading," and "beanbag" were treated in the same manner. The reading activity then moved into reading of sentences and proceeded as follows:

T:	Tom has a book and Mary has a book too.
T and *SS:*	Tom has a book and Mary has a book too.
T:	Tom has a book and Mary has a book too.
T and *SS:*	Tom has a book and Mary has a book too.
T:	Tom has a book and Mary has a book too.
T and *SS:*	Tom has a book and Mary has a book too.
T:	Again.
T and *SS:*	Tom has a book and Mary has a book too.

The teacher then asked different groups of children to read the sentence and then individuals. The sentences "Tom is reading his book and Mary is reading her book" and "Tom's book is green and Mary's book is green too" were read in the same manner. This is how these Standard 1 children were introduced to reading. They spent most of their reading time repeating pieces of the reading text after the teacher over and over again. Some of the children did not have the reading textbooks while others did not even bother to look at what was being read but they "read" nevertheless. Clearly, for many of these children, reading translated into memorizing bits of the reading text. In content area subjects lessons, these learners spent much of their learning time participating in oral/aural drills during which they mindlessly repeated bits and pieces of supposedly important information – usually that which was likely to appear in examinations and other school-based assessments. Writing activities in their turn engaged the learners in copying from the blackboard or textbooks and doing endless fill-in-the-blanks exercises. These repetitive, boring, and intellectually unchallenging learning activities constituted the experienced curriculum for these Standard 1 children.

These lessons fall within what Freire (1970) has referred to as the "banking model" of education. Freire argues that the banking model of education treats learners as empty vessels to be filled by the teacher, rather than as active participants in the production and acquisition of knowledge. According to Freire, this model of education does not empower the learner to take charge of his or her own life and transform it. In Africa, education that is non-transformatory is insufficient; given the role that education is expected to play in the development and transformation of African societies.

Equity

The discussion on the colonial roots of the marginalization of indigenous languages revealed that the introduction of Western education in Kenya in the colonial era led to social stratification based on English-language skills and education. The privileged few Africans who gained some education and English-language skills constituted the new elites. Through the use of English as the language of education, the new elite has been reproduced and strengthened. School ethnography studies have documented these social reproduction processes. In my study, for example, I documented classroom interactional processes in two primary schools and demonstrated that children from elite backgrounds and those from poor backgrounds received unequal educational treatments (Bunyi, 2001). While the class with elite background children was exposed to a fairly challenging and interesting curriculum, the reverse was the case in the class with poor background children. I argue that such differential treatment leads to educational success and social mobility for the elite children and to educational failure and social stagnation for the non-elite children.

The foregoing discussion has highlighted some educational problems that are associated with the use of English as the medium of instruction in primary schools in Kenya. In spite of these problems, several reasons for not using indigenous languages as languages of instruction in Kenya and elsewhere in Africa have been advanced. Obanya (1999) refers to these reasons as popular fallacies. I will now critically discuss some of these popular fallacies.

POPULAR FALLACIES ABOUT INDIGENOUS AFRICAN LANGUAGES AS LANGUAGES OF INSTRUCTION

There are too many languages

It is often argued that, because of the multiplicity of indigenous languages, it is difficult to choose one as the language of instruction as this would be seen as favouring the community that speaks the language natively. This argument does not hold for Kenya since we have the national language Kiswahili, which could be used as the language of instruction in the primary school as in Tanzania without much ethnic resistance. Furthermore, research has shown that rural and urban poor Kenyan children are more comfortable speaking Kiswahili and find it easier to learn than English (Muthwii, 2002).

In her critique of the too many languages argument, Brock-Utne (2005) has written about what she calls the myth of the many languages of Africa and argued, "The demographics of language and linguistic diversity in Africa are not really different from what obtains in other parts of the world" (p. 176). Brock-Utne blames the missionaries for the fragmentation of African languages in their work of identifying linguistic communities and developing orthographies. She singles out the Summer Institute of Linguistics (SIL) for criticism for continuing to fragment African languages in its work.[4] Brock-Utne argues that the fragmentation of African indigenous languages serves the economic interests of the strong publishing industry in the West, while working against the use of these languages as languages of instruction.

Costs of the production of materials and teacher training

The cost of producing teaching-learning materials and training teachers in all the indigenous languages is often said to be prohibitive.

However, language in education scholars have been quick to point out that the African children's educational failure as manifested in high school dropout and repetition rates, poor learning achievement, and poor educational outcomes such as low literacy rates are all due to the use of European languages and carry an even higher cost (Bamgbose, 1991; Brock-Utne, 2005; Obura, 1986).

At the same time, there are examples of cost-effective ways of producing indigenous language teaching-learning materials in Africa. These include the Rivers Readers Project, which began in 1970 in Nigeria with the aim of producing literacy materials in twenty minority languages. The project showed that, by making use of uniform formats and illustrations and by using cheaper materials, it is possible to reduce the production costs of teaching-learning materials considerably (Williamson, 1976). With advancement in technology and the advent of desktop publishing, the costs of producing materials can be brought down even lower.

Indigenous languages are underdeveloped

The argument here is that African indigenous languages lack terms to express scientific and technological concepts, which constitute a big portion of school subjects, while many are yet to acquire orthographies. Fortunately, no one denies that African indigenous languages like other languages have the potential to develop to meet the communicative needs of their users. It is in fact because the need to use the languages in education has not arisen that they continue to lack the necessary linguistic resources (Phillipson & Skutnabb-Kangas, 1994). Once the need is created, African indigenous languages have risen to the occasion, as was the case in Tanzania when Kiswahili became the language of instruction for the entire primary level.

On the other hand, developing orthographies for indigenous African languages is not an impossible task. What is required is commitment and determination. Nineteenth-century European missionaries with less training and resources than are available in Africa today developed orthographies for some of the languages. Though criticized for fragmenting indigenous languages, the fact that SIL is cost-effectively developing orthographies for many minority languages in Africa is proof that it can be done.

Use of indigenous languages threatens national unity

It has been argued that current boundaries in Africa were *concocted* by European colonial powers at conference tables in Berlin in 1885, rather than being *natural*, and that therefore African countries are made up of peoples of varied ethno-linguistic backgrounds (Laitin, 1992). Consequently, an emphasis on indigenous languages in education might lead to divisiveness and ethnic tensions. However, linguistic homogeneity has not always engendered peace in Africa, as ethnic wars in Somalia where Somali is the sole language and in Rwanda with Kinyaruanda is the sole language have shown. Further, as Pattanayak (1988) has observed, "'languages' do not quarrel. When representatives of languages do, the reasons are mostly extra-linguistic" (p. 380). More often than not, the reasons for the ethnic tensions have to do with the sharing of power and resources among the various linguistic groups in the country. Furthermore, it can also be argued that, whereas indigenous languages may divide people along ethnic lines, English divides people along class lines. Divisions along ethnic lines are more visible and therefore quicker to detect than divisions along class lines, which are hegemonic and therefore less obvious and thus difficult to detect and resolve.

In the above discussion, I have tried to demonstrate that critical analyses of the reasons that are often given to justify the non-use of African indigenous languages in education do not hold much water. These reasons leave the question: "Why have African indigenous languages not been given their rightful role (i.e., that of languages of instruction) in the education of African children?" without a satisfactory answer. In the next section, to conclude this chapter, I offer what I consider to be the real explanation, which I refer to as major challenges.

MAJOR CHALLENGES TO INDIGENOUS LANGUAGES AS LANGUAGES OF INSTRUCTION

The major challenges that confront the use of indigenous languages as languages of instruction can be appreciated by looking inwardly at the postcolonial community itself and outwardly at how the community is positioned in relation to the globally powerful First World nations (Stroud, 2000). Within the community, language attitudes of both the elite and the non-elite denigrate indigenous languages and legitimize European languages. This is so because, for the elite, European languages constitute a valued resource that they have access to and control over – a resource that they can use to benefit not only locally but also in the global labour marketplace (Mazrui, 1997, cited in Stroud, 2000). The non-elite, on the other hand, see their lack of the European language as the reason for their marginalization, and therefore in their misguided view that more means better, they want their children taught in European languages as early as possible. Consequently, education policies and practices around language promote the use of European languages for instruction as early as possible; thus excluding indigenous languages from education gets the support of all in the community.

The above formulation mirrors the situation in Kenya where, even when poor primary school students, their parents, and teachers admit that the students have difficulties understanding lessons taught in English, they still say that they prefer English as the language of instruction (Muthwii, 2002). The elite in their turn have no doubt that English should remain the language of instruction. They argue that education should prepare one to work anywhere in the world and that since English is the global language it should receive emphasis in the school.

At a global level, African countries' economic dependence on the developed world countries leaves them little room for cultural, political, and even educational self-determination. Stroud (2000) has argued that the problems faced by African indigenous languages are not about inadequate resources or even about education; "they are fundamentally about who is to exercise the power of deciding what social and symbolic capital should accrue to different languages" (p. 4). In summing up this theoretical formulation, Stroud (2000) says that the problems that indigenous languages face are basically "problems of deprivation, marginality, and poverty of the speakers of the languages" (p. 3). In their encounter with the languages of the economically and politically powerful nations, as in the colonial era, African indigenous languages have a poor start as languages of the socio-economically and politically powerless.

Further, education in African countries is heavily dependent on foreign donor support. Such support, especially from former colonial powers, comes with economic interests of the publishing companies back home, which are better served through education in European languages (Brock-Utne, 2005). To push their cultural and linguistic agenda, donor countries such as Britain place strong cultural institutions such as the British Council in their former colonies. The imperialistic mandate of the British Council is to promote and transform the English language into a world language (Ogunjimi, 1995).

From the foregoing discussion, it is clear that the problems African indigenous languages face are both those that are from the local discourses and those that are global in making. Since the problems emanate from dependence, Africa will have to come up with development models that look into the strengths within Africa so as to be empowered enough to take charge of its own development.

All the same, African children cannot wait until the problem of Africa's dependence on others is solved to receive a meaningful education. Implementation of transformatory language in education policies and practices must be part of the process of overcoming dependence. Tanzania is often cited as one of the few African countries that transformed education by making Kiswahili, a language spoken fluently by more than 95 per cent of the population, the language of instruction throughout primary education through its Swhilization policy of 1967. English is introduced as a subject in Standard 3, taking over as the language of instruction in the secondary school (Rubanza, 1998).[5] Tanzania has therefore chosen to have only two languages (Kiswahili and English) in education and has not provided any educational role for its more than 120 indigenous languages (Rubanza, 1998).

I would not recommend the two-language Tanzanian model for Kenya. For one, unlike in Tanzania, although Kiswahili serves as the *lingua franca* in Kenya, a variety of other indigenous languages are the only languages spoken fluently by a large majority of Kenyans, especially those living in the rural areas. Secondly, adopting the two-language model in education in Kenya would signal the beginning of the death of the currently vibrant indigenous languages. Thus, even in the context of globalization, I believe that education should lead the way in the revaluing of indigenous Kenyan languages and through them the indigenous knowledge they symbolize and carry.

However, a policy that could be interpreted as denying children English would be undesirable and not acceptable to the elite and the poor alike. Consequently, I believe that Kenya would do well to seriously implement the three-language model (indigenous Kenyan languages, Kiswahili, and English) already implied in current policy with some modifications.

My proposal is that *all* Kenyan children learn an indigenous language from Standard 1 to 8 and that they be examined in the language in which they learn. This will ensure that *all* children are taught the languages equally. Currently, when indigenous languages are taught, they are taught only in the rural area, which causes them to be negatively regarded. Kiswahili and English should be introduced in Standard 1 but only the oral/aural forms so as to allow students to attain literacy in the indigenous languages – the languages they already know – first. As regards the language of instruction, I would propose that indigenous languages be used from Standard 1 to 5 instead of up to Standard 3 as current policy stipulates. This is so as to allow children to acquire meaningful English competence levels to enable it to be used as a medium for learning other subjects. I would propose a gradual switch so that some subjects such as social studies and literature in the form of oral literature can continue to be taught in the indigenous languages right up to the end of the primary school level.

All the same, owing to the complex socio-linguistic context in Kenya, a uniform language of instruction policy may not be workable. For example, there should be provisions for children who speak Kiswahili or even English in their homes and community – and who therefore have higher linguistic competencies in these languages than in indigenous languages – to use them as languages of instruction from Standard 1, with those using Kiswahili switching to English in Standard 5 just like those using the indigenous languages. I believe that what all parents want is that their children experience school success and receive a good education in order to improve their quality of life. The implication here is that the quality of education in schools using indigenous languages and Kiswahili as language of instruction should be as good as, if not better than, the quality of education provided in the schools using English as the language of instruction in Standards 1 to 5. This has implications for teacher training and retraining, as well as for teaching-learning materials production and availability.

REFERENCES

Abdulazizz, M. H. (1982). Patterns of language acquisition and use in Kenya: Rural-urban differences. *International Journal of the Sociology of Language, 34*, 95–120.

Bamgbose, A. (1991). *Language and the nation: The language question in Sub-Sahara Africa.* Edinburgh: Edinburgh University Press.

Bodomo, A. B. (n.d.). *On language and development in Africa: The case of Ghana.* Retrieved January 3, 2006, from http://www.ghanaweb.com/GhanaHomePage/features/artikel.php?ID=19656.

Brock-Utne, B. (2005). Language in education policies and practices in Africa with a special focus on Tanzania and South Africa – insights from research in progress. In A.M.Y. Lin & P. M. Martin (Eds.), *Decolonisation, globalisation. Language-in-education policy and practice* (pp. 153–73). Clevedon: Multilingual Matters.

Bunyi, G. W. (2001). Language and education inequalities in Kenya. In M. Martin-Jones and M. Heller (Eds.), *Voices of authority: Education and linguistic difference* (pp. 77–100). London: Ablex.

Burford, G., Ngila, L., & Rafiki, Y. (n.d.). *Education, indigenous knowledge and globalisation.* Retrieved January 3, 2006, from http://www.scienceinafrica.co.za/2003/march/ik.htm.

Crampton, D. (1986). Language policy in Kenya. *Rassegna Italiana di Linguistica Applicata, 18*(3), 109–22.

Cummins, J. (1981). The role of primary language development in promoting educational success for language minority students. In *Schooling and Minority Students: A Theoretical Framework* (pp. 3–49). Los Angeles: Evaluation Dissemination and Assessment Center.

Dewey, J. (1916). *Democracy and education.* Toronto: The Free Press.

Emeagwali, G. (2003). African indigenous knowledge systems (AIK). Implications for the curriculum [Electronic version]. In T. Falola (Ed.), *Ghana in Africa and the world: Essays in honour of Adu Boahen* (pp. n.p.). New Jersey: Africa World Press. Retrieved April 23, 2005 from http://www.africahistory.net/AIK.htm

Fanon, F. (1967). *Black skins, white masks.* New York: Grove Press.

Freire, P. (1970). *Pedagogy of the oppressed.* New York: Continuum.

Gachukia, E. (1970). The teaching of vernacular languages in Kenyan primary schools. In T. P. Gorman (Ed.), *Language in education in Eastern Africa* (pp. 18–29). Nairobi: Oxford University Press.

Goke-Pariola, A. (1993). Language and symbolic power: Bourdieu and the legacy of Euro-American colonialism in an African society. *Language and Communication 13*(3), 219–34.

Gorjestani, N. (n.d.). *Indigenous knowledge for development: Opportunities and challenges.* Retrieved January 3, 2006, from http://www.worldbank.org/afr/ik/ikpaper_0102.pdf.

Government of Kenya. (1998). *Master plan on education and training 1997–2010.* Nairobi: Jomo Kenyatta Foundation.

Kenyatta, J. (1953). *Facing Mount Kenya: The tribal life of the Gĩkũyũ.* London: Secker and Warburg.

Laitin, D. (1992). *Language, repertoires, and state construction in Africa*. New York: Cambridge University Press.

Mbaabu, I. (1996). *Language policy in East Africa*. Nairobi: Educational Research and Publication.

Ministry of Education, Science, and Technology. (2003). *Report of the Sector Review and Development*. Nairobi: MOEST.

Ministry of Education, Science and Technology. (2005). Education Statistical Booklet (Draft). Nairobi: MOEST.

Mohochi, S. (2005). *Turning to indigenous languages for increased citizen participation in the African development process*. Retrieved January 3, 2006, from http://www.codesria.org/Links/conferences/general_assembly11/papers/mohochi.pdf.

Muthwii, M. (2002). *Language policy and practices in education in Kenya and Uganda*. Nairobi: Phoenix.

Obanya, P. (1999). Education, equity, and transformation from the perspective of language education. In L. Limage (Ed.), *Comparative perspectives on language and literacy. Selected papers from the work of the language and literacy commission of the 10th World Congress of Comparative Education Societies* (pp. 17–30). Dakar: UNESCO-BREDA.

Ogunjimi, B. (1995). Currents on language debates in Africa [Electronic version]. *Languages of Africa, 2*(3), 1–6; http://www.ccsu.edu/afstudy/upd2-3.html#Z3.

Obura, A. (1986). Research issues and perspectives in language in education in Africa: An agenda for the next decade. In University of Edinburgh (Ed.), *Proceedings of a seminar held in the Centre of African Studies* (pp. 415–44). Edinburgh: University of Edinburgh.

Pattanayak, D. P. (1988). Monolingual myopia and petals of the Indian lotus. In T. Skutnabb-Kangas & J. Cummins (Eds.), *Minority education: From shame to struggle* (pp. 279–389). Clevedon: Multilingual Matters.

Phillipson, R., & Skutnabb-Kangas, T. (1994). Language rights in postcolonial Africa. In T. Skutnabb-Kangas & R. Phillipson (Eds.), *Linguistic human rights: Overcoming linguistic discrimination* (pp. 335–45). New York: Mouton de Gruyter.

Republic of Kenya. (1964). *Kenya education commission report*. Nairobi: Government Printers.

Republic of Kenya. (1976). *Report of the national committee on educational objectives and policies*. Nairobi: Government Printers.

Rubanza, Y. I. (1998). In search of a meaningful language policy in Tanzania. *Southern African Review of Education 4*, 29–41.

Spencer, J. (1974). Colonial language policies and their legacies in Sub-Saharan Africa. In J. Fishman (Ed.), *Advances in language planning* (pp. 164–75). New York: Mouton.

Spencer, J. (1985). Language and development in Africa: The unequal equation. In N. Wolfson & J. Manes (Eds.), *Language of inequality* (pp. 123–43). New York: Mouton.

Stroud, C. (2000). *Developing alternative agendas for multilingual education*. Stockholm University Centre for Research on Bilingualism. Retrieved January 3, 2006, from http://www.biling.su.se.

Summer Institue of Linguistics. (1997). *Summer Institute of Linguistics Africa Area annual literacy report 1996*. Nairobi: Summer Institute of Linguistics – Africa Area.

UNESCO IIEP. (2001). *The Quality of education: Some policy suggestions based on a survey of schools, Kenya*. Paris: UNESCO IIEP.

wa Thiong'o, N. (1981). *Writers in politics. Essays*. London: Heinemann.

wa Thiong'o, N. (1986). *Decolonising the mind. The politics of language in African literature*. Nairobi: Heinemann.

Wells, G. (1989). Language in the classroom: Literacy and collaborative talk. *Language and Education, 3*(4), 251–73.

Williamson, K. (1976). The Rivers Readers Project in Nigeria. In A. Bamgbose (Ed.), *Mother tongue education: The West African experience* (pp. 135–53). Paris: UNESCO Press.

Notes

1 Colonial education was based on racial segregation with separate schools and curricula for the whites, the Asians, and the Africans.

2 English is taught from Standard 1 and is the medium of instruction in all schools from Standard 3 onwards. Kiswahili is taught as a compulsory and examinable subject from Standard 1 to Form 4 – the end of the secondary level.

3 Under this program, no direct fees or levies are charged and children are supplied with teaching-learning materials such as text books.

4 SIL has a significant presence in Africa, where it works in more than two hundred languages in over twenty countries (Summer Institute of Linguistics, 1997). In Kenya, SIL works under the auspices of a local NGO – Bible Translation and Literacy – whose objective is to develop minority languages.

5 Initially, the plans were that Kiswahili would eventually be used as the language of instruction at all levels of education including tertiary.

2

SOME ISSUES OF SCIENCE EDUCATION IN AFRICA

Wanja Gitari

ABSTRACT

This chapter explores issues that dominate science education debate in Africa today. Two key focal points of the chapter are gender inequity, which results in an under-representation of girls and women in science, and the efficacy of content learned in schools, which is highlighted by the inability of science graduates to readily transfer the knowledge they gained in school to everyday problem-solving situations. The chapter illustrates that these problems may be moderated through the adaptation of various teaching approaches. Five approaches are targeted as beneficial in addressing gender inequalities and knowledge adaptation: (1) Education with Production, (2) constructivist teaching, (3) Science, Technology, Society and the Environment, (4) anti-racist science teaching, and (5) co-operative learning. The chapter highlights the need for policy-makers, educational institutions, and teachers to recognize that they must work together to make transformative education a reality in

African nations. It concludes by affirming the need for transformative education for students by teachers who are prepared with sufficient resources to engage their pupils.

INTRODUCTION

Until the 1980s, the primary concerns of science educators and policy-makers had been the availability of textbooks, the use of more realistic, practical, and experimental work, and the use of more appropriate teaching methods. Clearly, educators were grappling with ways to improve how students acquire scientific knowledge, which included increasing the number of textbooks and making certain that experiments were part of science learning. Emphasis was, therefore, laid on the experimental method as a means for teaching scientific inquiry with the hope that students would think like scientists. Yet, the science-centred orientation did not enable science education to achieve its goal of applying science knowledge to everyday situations, and educators continued to question its effectiveness.

There are two key pedagogical issues currently dominating the science education debate in Africa: (1) the underachievement and under-representation of girls and women in science; (2) the efficacy of the content knowledge learned in school, that is, the inability of the majority of science graduates to transfer the science knowledge they gained in school to everyday problem-solving situations. Educators suggest that some of these problems might be minimized through the adaptation of various teaching approaches. This chapter offers insight into the science pedagogy debate in Africa, through a discussion of the two issues. The chapter then highlights five teaching approaches as possible and desirable learning models: (1) Education with Production (EwP), (2) constructivist teaching, (3) Science, Technology, Society and the Environment (STSE), (4) anti-racist science teaching, and (5) co-operative learning.

These approaches are discussed in the context of three pedagogical orientations to science curricula: science-centred, learner-centred, and society-centred. All three orientations may find expression in a single curriculum, although in most cases curricula tend to lean towards one of them. These orientations are important to understand because many of their elements have been adopted by the five teaching approaches itemized above.

In the science-centred orientation, emphasis is on content knowledge, structure of science, or scientific inquiry. Curricula are geared towards the acquisition of scientific facts, procedures, and processes. Textbooks, laboratory, and laboratory materials are very important learning tools and most of the teaching proceeds through didactic methods of instruction.

In the learner-centred orientation, focus is on learning activities that enhance the development of the student's affective, normative, and psychomotor domains, and an attempt is made to integrate science learning with the child's environment. For example, in a lesson on plants a child learns about different plants and their functions by visiting surroundings where plants are found. There is a belief in the ability of the child to construct knowledge from experience. Examples of teaching approaches that are adopted for learner-centred orientation are discovery learning and the constructivist method of learning.

In a society-centred orientation, the curriculum is planned so as to enable school science to benefit society in more defined ways. For instance, the likelihood that the study of science will result in a scientifically literate society is considered when planning curriculum activities. The relevance of scientific knowledge for the development of industry and technology and environmental solutions is also considered. Also, there is a tendency to plan science curriculum along lines that follow science careers presently available for science graduates. Resulting from its focus on the needs of society, this approach tends to link education with production and to be concerned with knowledge discontinuity and elements of gender and contextualized knowledge. Two teaching approaches that incorporate the society-centred orientation are Education with Production (EwP) and Science, Technology, Society and the Environment (STSE).

In the late 1960s, the feminist movement laid the foundations for problematizing women's status in science and technology (Rose, 1994). Researchers have since grappled with different aspects of this issue. For example, sociological, feminist, and psychological paradigms have enabled researchers to gain knowledge into social and psychological factors that contribute to the underachievement and under-representation of women in science and technology. Gilligan (1982) reported that many women tend to avoid both science- and technology-related professions that take too much time away from important family roles and relationships. A consideration of personal effect, together with the development of interpersonal relations, is therefore central to the way in which women appropriate knowledge (Hodson, 2003).

Globally, there is a persistent concern for girls' and women's underachievement and under-representation in science (UNESCO-CAMSTE, 2001; Jenkins, 2003; Sjøberg, 1998; UNESCO, 2004). The causes are broad and varied, often embedded in the socio-historical, economic, and political facets of society. Feminist scholarship has contributed insightful theories and frameworks in the study of women's participation (or lack thereof) in the sciences, in European and North American contexts. Although the implications of this body of literature in an African context are not clear, in general, research has pinpointed problematic areas in science education globally. Factors such as sex-stereotyping in textbooks, teaching methods, teacher's attitudes, inequality in the breadth of subject matter (Kinyanjui, 1985; 1993), and bias in teaching and structure of science curricula are considered as possible impediments to women's participation (Woodhouse & Ndongko, 1993; Harding & Apea, 1990). Some of these impediments can be narrowed down to particular aspects of the science curricula. Women's participation, for instance, is restricted through the use of gender stereotyping in the curricula, gender streaming by subject, and limited recruiting of girls into scientific and technical education (Kinyanjui, 1985).

Another factor that has been identified as key to gender inequity is the school structure. In Cameroon, for instance, Woodhouse and Ndongko (1993) found that covert and systematic forms of discrimination are hard to identify, therefore, more difficult to overcome. According to these authors, on average, educators are able to identify overt factors that determine achievement in science, for example, the preferential questioning and encouragement of boys by teachers. Covert factors such as the organization of the school system in a way that enables boys to learn science better (in a well-equipped-all-boys' school) than girls (in a poorly equipped girls' school) are not easily identifiable. Arguably, covert factors are largely responsible for the current status of girls and women in science.

A 1991 UNICEF study reported that, despite quantitative expansion, which resulted in massive enrolment of girls at all levels of schooling in Africa in the 1980s and 1990s, less than 20 per cent of girls chose science as a career (UNICEF, 1991). Kinyanjui (1985) argued that it is not only questions of how many enrol in science but also what kind of science is offered. Others have argued that science learning that over-emphasizes the acquisition of scientific knowledge as facts and "truth" may not appeal to girls. Baker and Leary (1995) identified an aspect of school science that may work against girls as the lack of a genuine connection with the socio-cultural and environmental contexts in which people live. They observed that, when girls are presented with a science that is more socially and environmentally centred, they tend to participate more.

Within the African context, a genuine connection that enhances a personal identification with science requires an appreciation and use of the "fundamental scientific and technological principles, theories, and concepts of the indigenous practices within African society" (Jegede 1994, p. 126). Science education in Africa has neglected this aspect of science teaching – even as the goals of teaching science in Africa have shifted throughout the years to ensure that science serves people better (Ogunniyi, 2005).

CONTEXTUALIZED SCIENTIFIC KNOWLEDGE

Traditionally, the teaching of science emphasized concepts, ideas, and theories that were of interest and importance to scientists but not to the learner (Hodson, 1988). This tradition can be traced to a hypothetico-deductive model of doing science where the natural world is believed to have an objective existence. According to this belief it is possible to know reality as it exists in the natural world through orderly and repeatable procedures like planned experiments. By employing objective methods, like experimental procedures, scientists acquire facts about natural phenomena.[1] The knowledge so acquired is said to be unbiased and universal, and separate from the background (social, political, economic) of the scientist. The extent to which the questions asked or the methods used are culturally determined is not an issue. The philosophy behind this view of science is commonly referred to as "natural humanism" or "positivism."

Natural humanism is transmitted to students when scientific knowledge is depicted as facts, and when observation in experimental procedure is depicted as an accurate means of fact acquisition. The message the learner receives is that what one requires in order to discover the laws of the universe are experimental procedures and careful observations. Given this approach to science, the role of the learner is a passive one because all the necessary tools, namely experimental procedures and rules of observation, are provided.

To counter this view of science and to engage students in an active learning of science, educators are advocating a "constructivist" way of teaching that is based on Kuhn's (1970) concept of "consensus building" and reconceptualist ideologies (Eisner, 1992). The constructivist view argues that the nature of science is constituted of symbols, is socially negotiated, has an empirical basis, and does not rely solely on observable and verifiable facts. Accordingly, constructivists argue that to view scientific knowledge as culturally neutral, value-free, absolute, and unproblematic is to promote a particular bias and a particular set of values (Hodson, 2003).

In following the constructivist view of science, for the purposes of science education in Africa, one would want to know to what extent the science taught in schools is culturally determined and what teaching approaches would be appropriate in exposing the distortions and inaccuracies promoted by conventional science curricula (Nyamnjoh, 2004). Within Western science studies, the History, Philosophy, and Sociology (HPS) of science is a branch of science studies that addresses the questions of how, why, and in what contexts scientific knowledge is constructed. In school curriculum, HPS is taught through Science, Technology, Society, and the Environment (STSE) courses. Other teaching approaches that are used to expose the distortions and inaccuracies of science promoted by conventional science curricula are anti-racist and anti-sexist science teaching (Atwater, 1996; Keller, 1989; Vance, 1987). The application of these teaching approaches in Africa remains questionable, since, according to Nyamnjoh (2004) their efficacy in the attainment of science education goals in Africa in the context of specific learner characteristics, teacher preparedness, curricula structures, general education policies, and the social economic context of learning in the African region has not been systematically studied. Moreover, most African countries are currently focusing on resolving major educational issues in funding, policy, and curricula restructuring and do not have the resources to invest in systematic studies on pedagogy. Issues of learner characteristics and teacher preparedness that are so central to effective teaching and learning may have to wait until the major problems of education have been resolved. The current situation on pedagogy is captured in part by an observation by Ogunniyi (2005): "The conventionally trained science teachers at our higher educational institutions have been so schooled in the scientific mode of inquiry that they can hardly perceive the enormous difficulties that learners from indigenous cultures encounter in their classrooms" (p. 3).

The essence of a science curriculum should never be taken for granted. Fensham (1988) argues that, since definitions of science evolve within the context of developed countries, their usefulness to science discourses in developing countries should be questioned. Also, imported courses make unrealistic assumptions about the general milieu of the school, which includes prevailing world views, learner characteristics, school equipment, teacher training, and out-of-school environments (Sjøberg, 1998). Such importation also inhibits more appropriate local development of ideas and innovations (Reiss, 1993). The historical transferability of curriculum from developed to developing countries was partly based on the belief in the "universal" and absolute aspects of science. However, this belief fell apart as science educators in Africa became aware that curricula adapted from developed countries did not help to achieve most of the science education goals set out by the African ministries of education (see Urevbu, 1984).

In Africa, other concerns for contextualized scientific knowledge that have taken centre stage are the extent to which alternative viewpoints influence the learning and teaching of science (Ogunniyi et al., 1995; Ogunniyi, 2005); the use of aspects of African[2] indigenous science that are of value to science education (Yakubu, 1994); and the inclusion of the scientific achievements of African scientists in school curriculum (Murfin, 1994). It is of paramount importance to rid the curriculum of views of universalism, imperialism, and racism (Rose, 1994) ingrained within the colonizing medium and whose purpose was to "sanitize and civilize" the "primitive" African cultures (Jegede, 1994). The force behind the civilizing mission was the belief that African educational thought was organized around a supernatural mode of thought. Consequently, defining the African world view as one based on the supernatural led to the erroneous belief that Africa did not contribute to modern science. However, new evidence that has traced the growth of modern science to ancient Egypt, then occupied by black Africans, has rendered these earlier claims false and racially motivated (Ogunniyi, 2005; Sertima, 1983). Similar views of women's contributions to science are refuted by current feminist scholarship.

The Western notion that there is a distinction between the supernatural and the natural is a highly contested one in the study of African thought. Horton (1971) argues against the stereotype that the products of a supernatural mode of thought are inevitably magical, irrational, and unscientific. He states that, in African traditional thought, supernatural notions have certain important features which, when critically analyzed, can be said to be objective and, therefore, should not be dismissed as irrational. Certainly, an understanding and a distinction of what constitutes supernatural and natural ways of explaining and understanding natural phenomena is critical in the evolution of appropriate science curricula (Gitari, 2003). This is more so because, within African philosophy, both the natural and supernatural are viewed as interwoven in causal explanation and understanding of natural phenomena. Similarly, writing in the context of health and healing, Gbadegesin (1991) argues that supernatural and natural explanations provide a range of evidence from which people explain and understand natural phenomena.

In another context, Kilbourn (1980) has shown that students' world views do influence their understanding of scientific concepts. Further, in a study to investigate the relationship between African traditional cosmology and students' acquisition of a science process skill, Jegede and Okebukola (1991) concluded that "correct" scientific observations are dependent on students' beliefs. African traditional cosmology[3] was understood to shape how students explained natural phenomena; students used this cosmology as a conceptual framework for constructing personal ideas about natural phenomena.

One way to begin understanding the ideas students have about natural phenomena is to refer to the root metaphors that prevail in their world views. A root metaphor provides the "basic material out of which all the facts of the universe can be generated" (Pepper, 1970, p. 93). When such facts are available, they are organized in a meaningful way in reference to the existing socio-cultural milieu of values, beliefs, and myths (Ogunniyi et al., 1995). The totality of facts that emanate from a root metaphor, and their entire organization within the socio-cultural milieu, constitutes the person's world view. In a broader sense, a community of people with similar socio-cultural and historical backgrounds could be said to have a world view. A people's world view is central to the way they understand and explain natural phenomena. Subsequently, a world view influences the way people construct and validate knowledge, including scientific knowledge. As already stated, the assumption that all scientific knowledge is objective and thereby universal has been strongly challenged. What has resulted from this challenge is a growing interest in the notion of a multicultural, anti-racist, and anti-sexist science. Interest in the latter notions of science also comes from the realization that a large proportion of students are not benefiting from the "universal" science.

Feminist and African studies have produced a large body of literature that is concerned with addressing the question, whose science is considered universal or worthy science? It is important to note that women's studies and African studies have a common heritage in the popular movements of the 1960s and 1970s, which led to a critique of the modernization theory that perceived society as if on a linear path from "traditional" to "modern" environments (Stamp, 1989). The implications of this dichotomy are that "traditional" is viewed as fossilized, belonging to the sphere of women and non-progressive, while "modern" is regarded as progressive, belonging to the West and in the public or male domain (Robertson, 1987). In this respect, indigenous practices are seen as obstacles to progress. Such a view denigrates indigenous practices by rendering them unsuitable for progressive considerations such as modern schooling. Also, it equates modern with Westernization, thereby implying that non-Western societies do not contribute to the "modern." Furthermore, it depicts modern science and technology as solely a Western heritage. Harding (1991) and Warren et al. (1995) argue that, although a Western world view predominates modern science, modern science (especially biology and medicine) has benefited from different world views of various international communities found within institutions of higher learning throughout the world.

Arguments such as those offered by Harding (1991) and Warren et al. (1995) are based on the notion of alternative sources of knowledge production and validation that are outside existing Eurocentric frameworks. Models of teaching science in Africa are historically related to the colonial experience of the early nineteenth to the mid-twentieth centuries. The colonial experience "damaged" indigenous knowledge (local knowledge that is unique to a given culture or society) to the extent that even today it is not legitimized at the high-school level (Gitari, 2003). This is because indigenous knowledge is said not to meet the standards of high-school science. Yet, as postcolonial discourses indicate, standard ways of doing things often reflect hegemonic perspectives of certain powerful groups. As such, it is worthwhile for researchers to interrogate alternative ways of doing things. In the context of schooling, alternative ways of doing things are sought when people are faced with everyday problems whose solutions are not attainable solely with the help of scientific knowledge acquired at school. Indeed, it is becoming increasingly clear that the transfer of school knowledge to out-of-school contexts is not the result of simply being trained in science.

KNOWLEDGE ADAPTATION

It is not fully understood why science graduates rarely find it useful to draw upon knowledge or skills acquired during schooling; yet knowledge and skills acquired informally seem to be used in a variety of everyday problem-solving situations. For instance, it has been noted that in Africa most learners retain indigenous notions of natural phenomena in spite of the content of school science. For example, in a study on the everyday use of scientific knowledge among Sotho

(South Africa) men and women who had previously acquired the scientific notion of heat, Hewson and Hamilyn (1985) found that both genders largely applied the traditional heat metaphor as a conceptual tool in explaining the phenomenon of heat, instead of the notion of heat acquired in their schooling. A study of how Tanzanian teachers linked local technology to school science revealed that few teachers in very few instances used school science language (scientific terms) to describe the traditional fermentation process (Knamiller et al., 1995). The study revealed a clear disconnection between school science and everyday problem-solving. Further, Knamiller posits that "much of the knowledge and certainly the perceptions that African children have of science are wrapped up in their experiences with the happenings that surround them in their local communities" (p. 68).

Examining the transfer of knowledge from school contexts, such as the laboratory, to non-school contexts, such as the workplace, has generated an interesting body of literature. One consistent observation is that

> ... thinking is intricately interwoven with the context of the problem to be solved. The context includes the problem's physical and conceptual structure as well as the purpose of the activity and the social milieu in which it is embedded. One must attend to the content and the context of intellectual activity in order to understand thought processes. This is the case for any situation in which thinking is studied, including the laboratory context, which is not context-free as researchers frequently assume. (Rogoff, 1984, pp. 2–3)

As Rogoff points out, cognitive skills are limited in their generality and a skill developed within a laboratory situation may not serve a useful purpose outside that context. In laboratory settings science experiments are routinely performed and, compared to learning contexts in everyday life, lack emotive events or story-specific episodes that help in knowledge acquisition (Hodson, 1988).[4] The integration of school knowledge into everyday social interactions is what makes school knowledge relevant. This approach is associated with Dewey's 1916 monograph on interest and effort. Dewey's philosophy of education would later address knowledge discontinuity by focusing on individual interests in learning, a learner-centred orientation.

The importance of relevance in education cannot be overstated. The observation that nearly all formal curricula have official goals that aim to enable learners to use knowledge and skills acquired during schooling in everyday life underscores this valued position. However, such official positions are informed by different opinions of what schools should be doing, that is by conservative, liberal, or radical views of schooling (Giroux & Simon, 1989). Therefore, it is not enough to desire knowledge transferability in learners; indeed, the underpinning ideologies that concern such a desire should be explicated and problematized since curriculum goals act as a form of educational accountability, which is a necessary step if relevance is to be achieved.

Making certain that school science is put into practice is another form of educational accountability. Putting science into practice may necessitate the merging of science and technology within the science curriculum, consequently, giving learners a forum for using science skills in everyday life problem-solving. Besides, the separation of science and technology is not by virtue of a distinctive operating procedure or a conceptual framework; rather, this separation exists because of different goals (Cajas, 2001; Layton, 1991; Hodson & Reid, 1988). At the theoretical level the primary goal of science is knowing *that*, whereas the primary goal of technology is knowing *how*, that is, finding practical solutions to everyday problems (Hodson, 2003; Jenkins, 2003). But in practice, the historical development of science and technology reveals an intricate and diffuse relationship consisting of incidences where (1) the invention of technological devices aided in scientific discoveries, (2) scientific discoveries were first made before the invention of technological devices that would later help in explaining and advancing the discoveries, (3) technological innovations and scientific discoveries were independent of each other, and (4) scientific discoveries and technological innovations were mutually dependent on each other (Hodson, 2003).

In addressing the problem of applicability, one may begin by asking why science is not taught along with technology, and whose interests are served when science is taught as distinct from technology (Hodson, 2003). Although answers to these questions are beyond the scope of this chapter, posing them helps one to reflect on other important aspects of the science pedagogy debate. Also, to ponder such basic questions is to initiate discussion of the history of school science and technology in Africa.

The history of school science and technology dates back to the colonization of Africa. The spread of modern science and technology from Europe to Africa by way of colonialism and neo-colonialism was overly successful, perhaps because the vandalism of colonialism was accompanied by industrial and capitalist institutions of modernity into which science and technology were woven. The spread of modern institutions across the world, originally a Western phenomenon, made Western expansion seemingly irresistible (Geddis, 1990). This spread also destroyed the indigenous technological basis of many African societies (see Ocaya-Lakidi & Mazrui, 1975). Urevbu (1991) also argues that "Africa possessed a technological base on which a technological revolution and successful industrial development might have been achieved, but for the historical disaster of slavery" (p. 71).

In Africa, foreign science and technology were more successful in transferring their products and consumption than their essence, therefore becoming a liability (Ocaya-Lakidi & Mazrui, 1975; Blackett, 1969). Unlike most other foreign concepts, for example, the teaching of liberal arts, which were readily Africanized, "science" has remained a foreign form of knowledge, probably because science and technology are forms of knowledge whose development require a context where there is indelible harmony between values and skills (Mazrui, 1978). This observation underscores the need to contextualize scientific knowledge, as discussed earlier. Even as concerns for gender equity, knowledge contextualization, and knowledge adaptation take centre stage in Africa, educators express the need for more appropriate teaching approaches. Traditional teaching approaches (for instance, didactic process and discovery learning) depict scientific knowledge as absolute and unproblematic. They also have not enhanced knowledge transfer for effective socio-economic changes and are therefore inadequate to meet current needs. In view of this, African educators see the need to experiment with more appropriate teaching and learning approaches to overcome gaps and inadequacies.

EDUCATION WITH PRODUCTION (EWP)

Education with Production (EwP) "refers to arrangements whereby socially and economically meaningful components of production have been combined with education or training" (Hoppers & Komba, 1995, p. 9). EwP is different from vocational training in its philosophy and practice. Vocationalization aims to prepare students for work by incorporating work-related skills, for instance, needle work, carpentry, and masonry, into general education, whereas EwP advocates self-reliance through the incorporation of an "educative value of work" in the general curriculum and through adopting a participative role within the community. EwP is linked to the populist traditions that stemmed from dissatisfaction with the outcomes of formal schooling (where students were alienated from their communities) and rapid changes in socio-economic environments. In developing countries, populist traditions were based on the ideas of national leaders such as Mahatma Gandhi of India or Julius Nyerere of Tanzania (Hoppers & Komba, 1995). In North America, populist traditions found expression in the progressive movement of the 1930s and later in colleges that taught work skills created to cater to youth unemployment in the 1970s and 1980s. But, as employment opportunities improved, such programs lost their focus and were incorporated into general curricula as careers and guidance programs.

In Africa, manual labour has long been viewed as undesirable, a view that has a lot to do with the history of formal schooling. During colonial times, Africans were trained for manual labour because Europeans believed that manual labour matched the intellectual capabilities of indigenous Africans. In view of this, the use of EwP in Africa should be twofold: to offer learning experiences that reflect the philosophy of indigenous education where theory and practice go hand in hand, and to incorporate productive work in general schooling as a basis for moving away from current methods, structures, and goals of learning. Other purposes of EwP should be:

- the reduction of incidences of rural-urban migrations by developing in students, teachers, and members of the local community a broad range of practical and problem-solving skills or relevant production skills;

- lowering barriers between school and the local community by directly introducing learners to the realities of work; and
- enhancing character development in learners.

EwP is not without disadvantages. For instance, because children are involved in productive labour, care must be taken not to exploit them for cheap labour. Sometimes EwP has been used to justify tracking in the classroom, that is, categorizing students into those who are ready for academic disciplines and those who are not. The end result is that certain groups of children are trained for elite professions while others are prepared to serve in the lower cadres of the socio-economic structure. In view of its potential misuse, those who advocate EwP stress the need to reconceptualize and problematize the concept over time to reflect changes in political, social, and economic aspects of individuals and their communities (Hoppers & Komba, 1995). Such reconceptualization may enable those involved in the implementation of EwP to avoid tracking and exploitation. When used as a framework with which to provide meaningful education, EwP can enhance the learning process in various ways (Van Rensburg, 2005).

EwP can create direct benefits to science teaching and learning when the content of science is drawn from and linked to local scientific knowledge. This could possibly happen as teachers and students grapple with ways in which to apply theory to practice within the local community in the context of existing productions or in the creation of new productions. For the purposes of instruction, teachers could draw materials, expertise, and practical and theoretical knowledge from the local community. Consequently, students could gain respect for knowledge that emanates from the local community and in so doing be able to build a context from which to draw intellectual inspiration and test problem-solving skills.

Finally, EwP has the potential to alter the gender equation in science. For example, girls working in science-related productions may be encouraged to change their minds about pursuing science as a career. A hands-on experience in repairing a car engine, for instance, may not only link theoretical knowledge to real-life situations, it may also make the unfamiliar familiar. Solutions to real-life situations and familiarity with the theoretical aspects of practice and vice versa are two elements that make science more meaningful to girls (Sjøberg, 2001; Solomon, 1994). Whereas EwP makes scientific concepts commonplace and recognizes indigenous knowledge, it does not address aspects of teaching and learning that deal with how students come to know; therefore, such issues may be addressed through constructivist teaching (Jenkins, 2003).

CONSTRUCTIVIST TEACHING

Underlying the constructivist paradigm is the understanding that learners actively build knowledge based on their interactions with physical events in daily life (Bereiter, 1994; Falk & Adelman, 2003). The nature and quality of students' constructions are taken as a general orientating framework for instructional purposes. Such frameworks embody clear strategies for influencing conceptual change and problem-solving attitudes.

One area in which constructivist teaching could be used to redress science education problems is in promoting a view of science that encourages teachers to take note of students' observations and experiences of natural phenomena. For instance, students bring to science lessons their own observations or experiences that are based on a world view derived from the social environment in which they grew up. To that end, the aim of a planned learning activity should not be to replace prior experiences with scientific facts. Rather, it should be to isolate students' observations or experiences of natural phenomena and to (1) present scientific claims and discussion on how scientific claims are similar or different from students' experiences; (2) discuss which explanations and observations are more plausible and give reasons why; (3) explore the reasons for adopting one way of explaining and rejecting others, or the values of retaining all explanations; and (4) stimulate discussions on the application of different explanations for real-life situations.

This process of knowledge construction is also suitable for importing practical knowledge into the theoretical aspects of any science lesson. Practical knowledge refers to the skills that students use to design, make, or improve artefacts, and the knowledge students' use in their day-to-day life to explain and understand natural phenomena. Such a process of knowledge construction will, therefore, enable the technology component of science to be drawn into discussions, thus facilitating the teaching of technology alongside science. An incorporation of technology into science lessons is attractive to students who value a practical element in learning.

Girls, for instance, are said to value the component of technology in science (Sjøberg, 2001); therefore, they are likely to find a constructivist approach amenable in rebuilding the "intimate association of knowing and doing" (Layton, 1991, p. 44). To that end, constructivist teaching is suitable for redressing this issue of knowledge adaptation as well as adopting science teaching strategies that inhere in women's ways of knowing. Because the process of knowledge construction allows one to move, conceptually, from what one knows to what one does not know, it is a method that enables students to debate and examine other world views, become conversant with their own world views, and appropriate other world views.

One drawback of constructivist teaching is its tendency to focus on the constructions of the individual while not paying equal attention to societal factors. Adhering to a constructivist approach exclusively has the potential of taking note of students' constructions without necessarily helping students understand how these constructions have come about. Societal factors have a direct bearing on the knowledge that students, and anyone else including scientists, construct: therefore, societal factors should be incorporated into science lessons.

Incorporating a discussion of the social, environmental, economic, and political factors that influence the building of knowledge is important. It is particularly important for students to gain insight into how scientific knowledge is constructed. Constructivist teaching is limited in this regard. Other teaching approaches such as Science, Technology, Society and the Environment (STSE) and anti-racism, are better able to bring these factors into a science lesson. STSE teaching incorporates the societal and environmental dimensions in developing science concepts, while anti-racist teaching critiques societal conditions under which knowledge is constructed.

SCIENCE, TECHNOLOGY, SOCIETY, AND THE ENVIRONMENT (STSE)

Teaching science through STSE ensures that meaningful context and evaluative dimensions of technology, society, and the environment are included (Hodson, 2003; Solomon, 1994). Sociological, historical, and philosophical aspects of the epistemology of science and other sub-disciplines, like economics, sociology, and politics inform this approach. The emphasis is on science subject matter and skills, their connection to the student's everyday life and the politicization of science education contexts followed by social action (Hodson, 2003; Solomon & Aikenhead, 1994). Instructional approaches ensure that students make *personal* sense out of science concepts and develop "higher reasoning capabilities associated with creativity and critical thinking" (Aikenhead, 1988, p. 4).

Arguably, STSE has the potential for making epistemological, historical, and cultural arguments of how substantive structures of scientific knowledge are constructed and of how they come to be known to science teachers and students. An understanding of the factors that influence the building and testing of theory, the relationship between theory and observation, the place of models, theories, experiments, and logic in the building of scientific knowledge is likely to happen through the study of the history, philosophy, and sociology of science as offered in STSE courses. By laying out fundamental concepts, principles, and processes on which scientific knowledge is based, STSE sets the stage for an articulation of the scientific world view, while helping students explore their own world views. Such an exploration provides students with the knowledge and skills with which to integrate scientific concepts into other world views, without a sense of alienation and confusion (Aikenhead & Jegede, 1999).

An explication of the fundamental concepts, principles, and processes of science will lead to a better understanding of the nature of science, especially with regard to the role of theory in the building of scientific knowledge. In science text books, for instance, observations of phenomena are not preceded by an explanation of the theory that supports such observations. Overall, there is a tendency to separate theory from observation. What such a distinction does is to encourage students to *observe* or *discover* natural phenomena and scientific concepts without an in-depth understanding of the guiding principles and underlying frames of reference in scientific inquiry (Hodson, 1988).

STSE also enables students to begin to explore current gender inequity in science. An understanding of how women are socialized could enable them to reconsider their career choices and actively challenge the social markers that structure their subjugation. However, overall STSE is limited in fully *questioning* current structural and systemic dimensions of power, economics, and the cultural domination in which science discourses happen, a dimension that is the focus of anti-racist science teaching.

ANTI-RACIST SCIENCE TEACHING

The underlying strategy of anti-racist teaching is to problematize the taken-for-granted, to subvert hegemonic traditions, and to foster an informed interest in science while at the same time challenging racist attitudes and their origins. The discourse levels of an anti-racist approach are instructional, transactional, and interactional (Dei, 1994; Nyamnjoh, 2004). This approach is suitable as a tool for reconstructing the context within which science discourses happen. For instance, based on a study conducted in Britain by Gill, et al. (1987) four key issues should be addressed by an anti-racist perspective in science: "(i) the colonial history which underlies racism in British society; (ii) the devaluation of 'non-Western' cultures; (iii) development and underdevelopment; (iv) racism in contemporary society" (p. 173).

The anti-racist approach could be used to examine curricula materials for sexist views, to encourage students to question traditional ways of viewing women as passive and as having intelligence inferior to men, and for considering science as a preserve for men. Epistemologically, educators could revise all instructional materials to rid them of existing content biases and ideologies of racism, sexism, and classism. Similarly, educators could examine and question where school science comes from and why, and by so doing help foster students' critical skills so that they can make more informed choices in their lives.

The value of anti-racist teaching in redressing issues of knowledge adaptation is founded on its focus on empowerment, which ensures that students' critical and creative skills are directed toward reclaiming their heritage. Students' knowledge of the colonial history of science education in Africa and the damage inflicted on indigenous knowledges by colonial practices help students to see science as a human construction. Most importantly, they see the value in their cultural knowledge and the potential for its further development. Consequently, students come to see the need for creating knowledge and skills that are appropriate for their environment and relevant to everyday problem-solving. Anti-racist teaching is easily carried out when students are in small groups. This ensures that students explore and express their experiences within the curriculum. Small group learning, also referred to as co-operative learning, provides for the creative and constructive exploration of experience.

CO-OPERATIVE LEARNING

Co-operative learning is the use of small groups as a strategy to enhance instruction, problem-solving, classroom management, and instilling social consciousness (Schniedewind, 2004). This approach is based on the notion that knowledge acquisition requires a climate where the creators of knowledge can represent events, negotiate meaning, and agree on acceptable views (Wells et al., 1990). Co-operative learning has a very long history and is widely used – for example, when small groups are used as an instructional strategy or when a team of people are brought together by the need to resolve a problem. These are common occurrences in school and in out-of-school settings all over the world. Noteworthy is that research on co-operative learning has only emerged within the past two decades, necessitated by the realization that co-operative learning may be deployed as an approach for resolving many challenges prevalent in schools today. Some of the many benefits of co-operative learning are that it:

1. enhances self-esteem by promoting mutual support and the exchange of ideas, thereby stimulating students' interest in learning;
2. improves achievement because it enables students to reflect on their study skills, mastery and retention, quality of reasoning strategies, new ideas and solutions (Johnson & Johnson, 1990);
3. enables the teacher to cater to individual interests in relation to the abilities of other students;
4. improves classroom management; and,
5. enhances socialization, especially in ethnically heterogeneous classrooms.

Notably, few studies address science-related disciplines (Okebukola & Ogunniyi, 1984). For the purposes of this discussion, co-operative learning could be used in a science class as a basis for generating indigenous notions of how people explain and understand natural phenomena. In small group settings, students could be encouraged to share their views and develop more acceptable ideas about indigenous science. Students could plan to test some of these ideas through experimentation, leading to revision and further testing of the ideas. In so doing they re-enact processes and procedures that are encountered in the production and validation of school scientific knowledge.

Sherman (1994) observed that co-operative learning can help to "achieve a variety of academic and social goals in the classroom setting" (p. 226). For instance, in the safety of small groups, issues which emanate from the study of the history, philosophy, and sociology of science (e.g., gender issues) would be more likely to stimulate productive discussions than when the entire class is involved. Johnson and Johnson (1990) have observed that individuals in co-operative learning groups use elaborative and metacognitive strategies more frequently than individuals working competitively and individualistically and therefore perform at a higher level.

A drawback of co-operative learning is that it could encourage "free riders" – those who could get away with doing less would do less than others. This could cause more productive group members to work less in order to avoid being taken advantage of. This dynamic of course would have detrimental effects on the entire co-operative process. However, as already stated, there are many benefits – development of skills, stronger and deeper insights, team solidarity, and so on – all of which enhance the learning experience and override the drawbacks (Iwai, 2004). Because of this, co-operative learning could be used to enhance the effects of EwP, constructivist teaching, STSE, and anti-racist science teaching.

As the twenty-first century advances, questions of how to deal with gender, knowledge application, and epistemology remain unanswered. Undoubtedly, some of the current constraints of science education in Africa are rooted in the nature of science content and the context in which science is learned. Regrettably, constraints of science education militate against desirable outcomes, such as the promotion and the acquisition of creative abilities and critical skills, the linkage between scientific knowledge and skills and problem-solving. Nevertheless, there is hope that the appropriate teaching strategies discussed in this chapter can overcome some of these problems. EwP provides a hands-on experience in learning, while co-operative learning enhances self-esteem in students and facilitates the learning of subject matter. Anti-racist teaching enables students and teachers to deconstruct and radicalize the milieu of science discourses, while constructivist teaching and STSE approaches are progressive techniques for learning science concepts. As well, these learning approaches appeal to women's ways of knowing, helping girls and boys to place science within the context of everyday life, and teaching them how to construct knowledge that is applicable in everyday problem-solving.

STRATEGIC INTERVENTIONS AND FUTURE DIRECTIONS: TRANSFORMATIVE AND SUSTAINABLE SCIENCE EDUCATION

This chapter has highlighted two major issues of science education in Africa, namely gender inequality and the apparent lack of knowledge application to everyday life. The chapter has made suggestions of how to redress the two issues through teaching approaches: Education with Production, constructivist teaching, Science, Technology, Society, and Environment instruction, co-operative learning and anti-racist teaching. In the last several decades these two issues of science education significantly informed science education research and policy activities in Africa. Perusing the documents of the Association for the Development of Education in Africa (ADEA), one frequently encounters the issues of gender and knowledge application; however, by far, gender is the most targeted of the two issues.

For instance, a sub-group of ADEA's working group, Working Group for Female Participation (WGFP) convened by Rockefeller and led by the Norwegian Agency for Development Cooperation (NORAD), focuses on women's participation in science, mathematics, and Technology. The WGFP has promoted gender fair science curricula in countries such as Cameroon, Ghana, Tanzania, and Uganda, through the gender, math, and science project known as Female Education in Mathematics and Science in Africa (FEMSA) (Sjøberg, 1998). The Forum for African Women Educationalists (FAWE) is a lead agency in FEMSA's activities. Although FAWE activists do not specifically target science education, their projects and policy activities impact access and achievement of girls in education in general.

In addition to FEMSA's efforts, there are other forums and organizations solely devoted to gender issues in science education. Sjøberg (1998) provides an extensive list of organizations and forums that focus on promoting gender equity in education, all of which are indicative of the important initiatives being made towards addressing issues of gender and science education in various regions of Africa. This list of gender-focused forums include: Girls and Science and Technology (GASAT), in Ghana in 1999, and the International Organization for Science and Technology Education (IOSTE) hosted in Durban, South Africa, in 1999. Other organizations include the African Forum for Children's Literacy in Science and Technology (AFCLST) located in South Africa and Malawi and United Nations Educational, Scientific and Cultural Organization (UNESCO), whose participation in the promotion of women and girls in science is through organizations such as ADEA.

Overall the issue of knowledge application and relevance has significantly inspired policy changes and curriculum restructuring throughout the continent. It is widely recognized that science and technology education will play a key role in the desired socio-economic development of the region (ACTS, 2001; UNESCO, 1999; UNESCO-CAMSTE, 2001). Additionally, the pressing problems of the HIV/AIDS pandemic, abject poverty, and unemployment have reawakened African educators to the notion of relevance and the role that science and technology will play in resolving the problems

(ADEA, 2005). Of course the need for relevant science education in Africa is not new. For instance, the history of curriculum restructuring in East Africa is marked by recurring reference to the application of school science in everyday life (Bogonko, 1992a). Moreover, Kenya's curriculum restructuring in the 1980s was mainly to redress the problem of irrelevance. In particular, science and technology education were targeted as needing special consideration. It was declared that science and technology instruction be geared to the needs of local communities. Unfortunately, the complete and effective implementation of the science curriculum was hindered by an unrealistic time frame, bureaucracy, lack of teacher preparedness, and lack of materials and laboratory equipment, among other obstacles (Bogonko, 1992b). In a similar way, South Africa's learner-centred and society-oriented curriculum implementation has experienced similar setbacks (Howie, 2002).

Problems that hinder complete and effective curricula implementation are widespread across Africa. The World Bank (2002), for instance, discusses the need to critically re-evaluate teacher education/preparedness, teaching methods, pupil assessment, curricula relevance, and learning materials. Stressing the urgent requirement for the re-evaluation of science education in Africa, the World Bank also acknowledges obstacles that will demand concerted effort in policy implementation and generous allocation of funds to the science education sector. Noting that in 1998 in Botswana 56 per cent of science and mathematics teachers were expatriates, the World Bank asserts that "science education has only deteriorated over the last decade in most African countries" (2002, p. 17). This is especially deplorable because of the urgency to contextualize and to utilize the new technologies, namely biotechnology and Information and Communications Technologies (ICTs) to alleviate the enduring socio-economic, health, and environmental problems. In a report prepared by the African Centre for Technological Studies (ACTS), there is a firm call to plan and mobilize resources in time for the anticipated rapid growth of both ICT & biotechnology (ACTS, 2001; UNESCO, 1999).

Indeed, it is a sombre picture for science education in Africa. Nevertheless, it is evident from current literature that teachers in African may be utilizing some of the teaching approaches that were outlined earlier in this chapter (ADEA, 2005). Chepyator and Thomson (2005) reported that primary and secondary teachers in the Keiyo district of Kenya use cultural knowledge among their students to help in the construction of scientific knowledge. Keiyo teachers used community-based learning opportunities to teach science to students. And, although teachers in Africa may not label their pedagogical strategies as anti-racist teaching, STSE instruction, constructivist teaching, or co-operative learning, their efforts are laudable and do resemble some of these methods. Teachers in Africa contextualize science learning and use available resources to help their pupils acquire relevant knowledge. In regard to contextualized science content, Sjøberg (2000) demonstrated that cultural knowledge is a key factor in the way pupils view science content and learning and that the use of cultural knowledge in science learning is therefore likely to impart relevance to the subject matter.

In regard to the identification of the teaching methods that teachers use in their classrooms, Education with Production (EwP) is unlike the other teacher approaches described in this chapter. The use of EwP is easy to identify because of its distinct feature production. EwP also has a long-standing presence in Africa and there is evidence that educators and policy-makers in Botswana, Lesotho, Zambia, Zimbabwe, and South Africa are utilizing EwP to enhance the application of science subject matter to everyday life (Van Rensburg, 2005).

It is indisputable that teachers everywhere in Africa are, in one way or other, doing their best to make science relevant to their students. The question, however, is to what extent are teaching methods such as EwP, constructivist teaching, STSE, anti-racist science teaching, and co-operative learning utilized to enhance gender equity and knowledge application? Although the argument is strong for these teaching approaches as desirable methods to address gender inequality and knowledge application, it is important to systematically study their efficacy in Africa. It is necessary to document what is really going on in science pedagogy in Africa by doing classroom observations or conducting inquiries among teachers. Such studies of pedagogy are rare and are rarely duplicated. A study like the one conducted by Ogunniyi's (2005) is worth duplicating. Ogunniyi's study with secondary teachers in South Africa involved a module designed to find out the extent to which teachers were aware of their pupils' culturally informed learning characteristics. At the end of the study the majority of teachers confessed to having been ignorant of the culturally informed learning characteristics of their learners. Another strategy of gathering data would be a one-time, widespread and systematic study across Africa. The approach used by Sjøberg (2001) in the Relevance Of Science Education (ROSE) project may accomplish the goals of such a systematic regional study. Even more profitable would be to involve teachers in researching their science teaching practices, taking stock and planning changes. Participatory research and action research methodologies may help in accomplishing the goal of training teacher researchers (Hodson, 2003). Informed teachers are equipped to participate in the continued restructuring of the science curricula. Furthermore, they are updated on suitable teaching methods for accomplishing educational goals such as gender equity and knowledge application.

Eventually when science educators, curriculum planners, and policy-makers understand ways in which teachers attempt to eradicate gender inequity and promote knowledge application, they can mobilize resources to give teachers more training and autonomy in the interpretation and implementation of curricula and assessment of pupils. The current standardized national examinations, typically found in most African countries, are not conducive to the kind of teacher creativity implied here. Standardized exams force teachers to rely on textbooks as a sole teaching resource and to gear their teaching toward correct answers to exam questions, inadvertently nurturing a science-centred curriculum and didactic teaching. In a climate of professional autonomy, teachers will be at liberty to experiment and report on the teaching approaches outlined in this chapter, emerging approaches and modules such as the one developed by Ogunniyi (2005), methods of teaching biology like the one authored by Griffiths (2003), or suggestions made by Gitari (2005). Gitari suggested the use of local ways of knowing as conceptual tools for knowledge construction. In her paper she includes questions that teachers can use in planning lesson units.

Finally when teachers are well prepared and there are adequate materials and resources for teachers to effectively engage with science subject matter, it will be worthwhile to reflect on the observation that,

... whatever learning theory is espoused, the central task of the teacher in promoting learning remains that of choosing and deploying the method(s) most likely to help students learn what the teacher wishes them to know, understand or be able to do. In other words, the relative merits of different teaching strategies are to be judged principally by reference to student learning, although other factors are likely to be involved, such as the facilities and level of resources required, and the implications for class management and assessment. In broad terms, students learn most effectively when they are set *clear objectives*, are *actively involved in their own learning*, appreciate the *relevance of their studies* and receive *regular and constructive feedback* about their progress. (Jenkins, 2003, p. 26; emphasis added)

Equitable, relevant, transformative, and sustainable science education will be accomplished in Africa when the four conditions outlined by Griffith are met; it is then that the desirable "science culture" will emerge (UNESCO, 1999). Eventually, learner-centred and society-oriented curricula will be realized throughout the region.

REFERENCES

ACTS (African Centre for Technology Studies). (2001). Report on the 1st Roundtable on Africa, Science and Technology in the Age of Globalization. Organized by the Africa Centre for Technology Studies in collaboration with the African Technology Policy Studies (ATPS), August 7–8, 2001.

ADEA (Association for the Development of Education in Africa). (2005). *1999 prospective, stock review taking of education in Africa.* Retrieved December 20, 2005, from http://adeanet.org/programs/pstr99/en_pstr99.html.

Aikenhead, G. S. (1988). Teaching science through a science-technology-society-environment approach: An instruction guide. Saskatchewan Instructional Development and Research Unit (SIDRU), Report No. 12, July.

Aikenhead, G., & Jegede, O. J. (1999). Cross-cultural science education: A cognitive explanation of a cultural phenomenon. *Journal of Research in Science Teaching, 36*(3), 269–87.

Atwater, M. M. (1996). Social constructivism: Infusion into the multicultural science education research agenda. *Journal of Research in Science Teaching, 33*(8), 821–37.

Baker, D., & Leary, R. (1995). Letting girls speak out about science. *Journal of Research in Science Teaching, 32*(1), 3–27.

Bereiter, C. (1994). Constructivism, socioculturalism, and Popper's world. *Educational Researcher, 23*(7), 21–23.

Blackett, P.M.S. (1969). Reflections on science and technology in developing countries. *Gandhi memorial lecture*, University of Nairobi, Kenya. Nairobi: East African Publishing House.

Bogonko, S. (1992a). *A history of modern education in Kenya (1895–1991)*. Nairobi, Kenya: Evans Brothers.

Bogonko, S. (1992b). *Reflections on education in East Africa*. Nairobi, Kenya: Oxford University Press.

Cajas, F. (2001). The science/technology interaction: Implications for science literacy. *Journal of Research in Science Teaching, 38*(7), 715–29.

Chepyator, J. R., & Thomson, N. (2005). Formalization of informal science knowledge in Kenyan Public schools: Teachers' use of indigenous ideas and examples in science subjects. Paper presented at the National Association for Research in Science Teaching (NARST), Dallas, TX, April 4–7, 2005.

Dei, G.J.S. (1994). The challenges of anti-racist education research in the African context. *Africa Development, 29*(3), 5–25.

Dewey, J. (1916). *Democracy and education*. New York: Macmillan.

Dzobo, N. K. (1975). Values and indigenous African education. In G. N. Brown & M. Hiskett (Eds.), *Conflict and harmony in education in tropical Africa* (pp. 76–90). London: George Allen & Unwin.

Eisner, E. (1992). Curriculum ideologies. In P. W. Jackson (Ed.), *Handbook of research on curriculum: A project of the American educational research association* (pp. 302–26). New York: Macmillan.

Falk, J. H., & Adelman, L. M. (2003). Investigating the impact of prior knowledge and interest on aquarium visitor learning. *Journal of Research in Science Teaching, 40*(2), 163–76.

Fensham, P. J. (1988). Familiar but different: Some dilemmas and new directions in science education. In P. J. Fensham (Ed.), *Development and dilemmas in science education* (pp. 1–26). Lewes: Falmer Press.

Gbadegesin, S. (1991). *African philosophy: Traditional Yoruba philosophy and contemporary African realities*. New York: Peter Lang.

Geddis, A. (1990). *The consequences of modernity*. Stanford: Stanford University Press.

Gill, D., Patel, V., Sethi, A., & Smith, H. (1987). Science curriculum innovation at Holland Park School. In D. Gill & L. Levidow (Eds.), *Anti-racist science teaching* (pp. 147–74). London: Free Association Books.

Gilligan, C. (1982). *In a different voice*. Cambridge, MA: Harvard University Press.

Giroux, H. A., & Simon. R. I. (1989). Schooling, popular culture, and a pedagogy of possibility. In H. A. Giroux & R. I. Simon (Eds.), *Popular culture: Schooling & everyday life* (pp. 219–36). New York: Bergin & Garvey.

Gitari, W. (2003). An inquiry into the integration of indigenous knowledges and skills into the Kenyan secondary science curriculum: A case of human health knowledge. *Canadian Journal of Science, Mathematics and Technology Education, 3*(2), 195–212.

Gitari, W. (2005). Everyday objects of learning about health and healing and implications for science education. *Journal of Research in Science Education, 43*(2), 172–93.

Griffiths, A.J.F. (2003). Community-based biology: UNESCO-IUBS Bioliteracy Series No.1. International Union of Biological Sciences. Retrieved June 20, 2005, from http://www.iubs.org/cbe/Community%20based%20Biology.htm.

Harding, J., & Apea, E. (1990). *Women too in science and technology in Africa: A resource book for counselling girls and young women*. London: Commonwealth Secretariat, Education Programme, Human Resources Group.

Harding, S. (1991). *Whose science? Whose knowledge*. Ithaca, New York: Cornell University Press.

Hewson, M.G.A., & Hamilyn, D. (1985). Cultural metaphors: Some implications for science education. *Anthropology & Education Quarterly, 16*(1), 31–46.

Hodson, D. (1988). Experiments in science and science teaching. *Educational Philosophy and Theory, 20*(2), 53–66.

Hodson, D. (1992). *Teaching and learning about science: Considerations in the philosophy and sociology of science*. Manuscript, Ontario Institute for Studies in Education.

Hodson, D. (2003). Time for action: Science education for alternative future. *International Journal of Science Education, 25*(6), 645–70.

Hodson, D., & Reid, D. J. (1988). Science for all: Motives, meanings and implications. *School Science Review, 69*, 653–61.

Hoppers, W., & Komba, D. (Eds.). (1995). *Productive work in education and training: A state-of-the-art in Eastern Africa*. Kortenaerkade 11, Netherlands: Center for the Study of Education in Developing Countries (CESO).

Horton, R. (1971). African traditional thought and western science. In M.F.D. Young (Ed.), *Knowledge and control* (pp. 208–66). London: Collier-MacMillan.

Howie, S. J. (2002). Renewal of Secondary Education Curriculum and Assessment in South Africa. In the World Bank, *Secondary Education in Africa: Strategies for Renewal. World Bank presentations at the December 2001 UNESCO/BREDA-World Bank Regional Workshop in Mauritius on the Renewal of Secondary Education in Africa. Document #25246* (pp. 41–53). Washington, DC: The World Bank.

Iwai, T. (2004). Learning language in cooperatively structured groups in a first-year level university classroom: A case study of Japanese as a foreign language. Thesis, Ontario Institute of Studies in Education, University of Toronto.

Jegede, O. (1994). African cultural perspectives and the teaching of science. In J. Solomon & G. Aikenhead (Eds.), *STS education: International perspectives on reform* (pp. 120–30). New York: Teachers College Press.

Jegede, O. J., & Okebukola, P. A. (1991). The relationship between African traditional cosmology and students' acquisition of a science process skill. *International Journal of Science Education, 13*(1), 37–47.

Johnson, D. W., & Johnson, R. T. (1990). Cooperative learning & achievement. In S. Sharan (Ed.), *Cooperative learning theory and research* (pp. 23–37). New York: Praeger.

Jenkins, E. W. (2003). Guidelines for policy-making in secondary school science and technology education. UNESCO, Division of Science, Technology and Vocational Education; Section for science and technology education. Retrieved June 20, 2005, from http://portal.unesco.org/education.

Keller, E. F. (1989). The gender/science system: Or, is sex to gender as nature is to science. *Reflections on gender and science*. New Haven, CT: Yale University Press.

Kilbourn, B. (1980). World views and science teaching. In A.H Munby, G.W.F. Orpwood, & T. L. Russel (Eds.), *Seeing curriculum in a new light: Essays from science education* (pp. 34–43). Toronto: OISE Press.

Kinyanjui, K. (1985). Secondary school education for girls in Kenya: The need for a more science-based curriculum to enhance women's greater participation in development. *Working Paper No. 459*, IDS Nairobi, Institute for Development Studies, University of Nairobi.

Kinyanjui, K. (1993). Enhancing women's participation in the science-based curriculum: The case of Kenya. In J. K. Conway & S. C. Bourque (Eds.), *The politics of women's education: Perspectives from Asia, Africa and Latin America* (pp. 133–148). Ann Arbor: University of Michigan Press.

Knamiller, G. W., O-saki, K. M., & Kuonga, H. C. (1995). Tanzanian teachers' understanding of the science embedded in traditional technologies: A study to inform teacher education. *Research in Science & Technological Education, 13*(1), 67–76.

Kuhn, T. S. (1970). *The structure of scientific revolutions.* Chicago: University of Chicago Press.

Layton, D. (1991). Science education and praxis: The relationship of school science to practical action. *Studies in Science Education, 19*, 43–97.

Mazrui, A. A. (1978). *Political values and the educated class in Africa.* Berkeley: University of California Press.

Murfin, B. (1994). African science, African and African-American scientists and the school curriculum. *School Science Mathematics, 94*(20), 96–103.

Nyamnjoh, F. B. (2004). A relevant education for African development – some epistemological considerations. *African Development, 29*(1), 161–84.

Ocaya-Lakidi, D., & Mazrui, A. A. (1975). Secular skills and sacred values in Uganda schools: Problems of technical and moral acculturations. In G. N. Brown & M. Hiskett (Eds.), *Conflict and harmony in education in tropical Africa* (pp. 278–95). London: George Allen & Unwin.

Ogunniyi, M. B. (2005). The effect of a science module on in-service teachers' ability to implement an integrated science-indigenous knowledge curriculum. Paper presented at the National Association for Research in Science Teaching (NARST), Dallas, TX, April 4–7, 2005.

Ogunniyi, M. B., Jegede, O. J., Ogawa, M., Yandila, C. D., & Oladele, F. K. (1995). Nature of worldview presuppositions among science teachers in Botswana, Indonesia, Nigeria, and the Philippines. *Journal of Research in Science Teaching, 32*(8), 817–31.

Okebukola, P. A., & Ogunniyi, M. B. (1984). Cooperative, competitive, and individualistic science laboratory interaction patterns: Effects on students' achievement and acquisition of practical skills. *Journal of Research in Science Teaching, 21*(9), 875–84.

Pepper, S. C. (1970). *World hypothesis.* Berkeley: University of California Press.

Reiss, M. J. (1993). *Science education for a pluralist society.* Philadelphia: Open University Press.

Robertson, C. (1987). Developing economic awareness: Changing perspectives in studies of African women, 1976–1985. *Feminist Studies, 13*(1), 97–135.

Rogoff, B. (1984). Introduction: Thinking and learning in social context. In B. Rogoff and J. Lave (Eds.), *Everyday cognition: Its development in social context* (pp. 1–8). Cambridge, MA: Harvard University Press.

Rose, H. (1994). The two-way street: Reforming science education and transforming masculine science. In J. Solomon & G. Aikenhead (Eds.), *STS education: International perspectives on reform* (pp. 155–66). New York: Teachers College Press.

Schniedewind, N. (2004). Educating teachers for socially conscious cooperative learning. In E. G. Cohen, C. M. Brody & M. Supon-Shevin (Eds.), *Teaching cooperative learning: The challenge for teacher education* (pp. 47–64). New York: State University of New York Press.

Sertima, V. (Ed.). (1983). *Blacks in science: Ancient and modern*. New Brunswick, NJ: Transaction Books.

Sherman, S. J. (1994). Cooperative learning and science. In S. Sharan (Ed.), *Handbook of Cooperative Learning Methods* (pp. 226–44). London: Greenwood Press.

Solomon, J. (1994). Learning STS and judgment in the classroom: Do boys and girls differ. In J. Solomon & G. Aikenhead (Eds.), *STS education: International perspectives on reform* (pp. 141–54). New York: Teachers College Press.

Solomon, J., & Aikenhead, G. (Eds.). (1994). *STS education: International perspectives on reform*. New York: Teachers College Press.

Stamp, P. (1989). *Technology, gender and power in Africa*. Ottawa: International Development Research Center.

Sjøberg, S. (1998). The access of girls to science and technology. In M. B. Ogunniyi (Ed.), *Promoting Public Understanding of Science and Technology in Africa SSME* (pp. 233–60). University of Western Cape, South Africa.

Sjøberg, S. (2000). Science and Scientists: The SAS-study. Cross-cultural evidence and perspectives on pupils' interests, experiences and perceptions. Background, development and selected results. http://www.uio.no/sveinsj/SASweb.htm.

Sjøberg, S. (2001). A comparative and cooperative international study of the contents and contexts of science education. Retrieved December 7, 2005, from http://folk.uio.no/sveinsj/SASweb.htm.

UNESCO. (1999). Basic sciences for development of Eastern and Southern Africa. Retrieved December 20, 2005, from http://www.unesco.org/science/wcs/meetings/agr_arusha_99.htm.

UNESCO. (2004). *Connect, International Science, Technology and Environment Education Newsletter, 29*(3–4). Retrieved June 20, 2005, from http://portal.unesco.org/education.

UNESCO-CAMSTE. (2001). Science, technology and mathematics education for human development: Framework for action. Adopted at *The international Experts Conference on Science, Technology and Mathematics Education for Human Development*, Goa, India, February 20–23, 2001.

UNICEF. (1991). *The girl child: An investment in the future*. New York: UNICEF.

Urevbu, A. O. (1984). School science curriculum and innovation: An African perspective. *European Journal of Science Education, 6*, 217–25.

Urevbu, A. O. (1991). Impact of science and technology on everyday life: An African perspective. *Impact of Science on Society, 161*, 69–79.

Van Rensburg, P. (2005). Is the education fraternity ready for Thuto Le Tiro. *Mmegi, 22*, No. 186. Retrieved December 29, 2005, from http://www.mmegi.bw.

Vance, M. (1987). Biology teaching in a racist society. In D. Gill & L. Levidow (Eds.), *Anti-racist science teaching* (pp. 107–23). London: Free Association Books.

Warren, D. M., Slikkerveer, L. J., & Brokensha, D. (1995). Introduction. In D. M. Warren, L. J. Slikkerveer, & D. Brokensha (Eds.), *The cultural dimension of development: Indigenous knowledge systems* (pp. xv–xviii). Exeter, UK: The LEAD Programme of Leiden University in the Netherlands.

Wells, G., Chang, G.L.M., & Maher, A. (1990). Creating classroom communities of literate thinkers. In S. Sharan (Ed.), *Cooperative learning theory and research* (pp. 95–121). New York: Praeger.

Woodhouse, H., & Ndongko, T. M. (1993). Women and science education in Cameroon: Some critical reflections. *Interchange, 24*(1–2), 131–59.

World Bank. (2002). *Secondary Education in Africa: Strategies for Renewal. World Bank presentations at the December 2001 UNESCO/BREDA-World Bank Regional Workshop in Mauritius on the Renewal of Secondary Education in Africa. Document #25246.* The World Bank: Washington, DC.

Yakubu, J. M. (1994). Integration of indigenous thought and practice with science and technology: A case study of Ghana. *International Journal of Science Education, 16*(3), 343–60.

Notes

1   A "natural phenomenon" is defined as a physical event or experience that is apparent to the senses.

2   I use the term "African" to refer to a world view that may be prevalent within the African region, even as I am aware of the diversity and complexity of the numerous ethnic communities that make up African peoples. My position is that diversity should not negate the common threads of principles seen to guide African thought throughout the centuries (see Dzobo, 1975, p. 77, for a list of these principles).

3   African traditional cosmology refers to existing ways, over time, in which Africans have organized, explained, and understood the origin and structure of the universe.

4   Elsewhere, Hodson (1992) argues that unless *doing* science is linked to learning *about* science, then distraction and alienation may be the *real* outcomes of practical experiments.

3

REPRODUCTIVE HEALTH IN KENYA: A MATTER OF SOCIAL JUSTICE[1]

Jacinta K. Muteshi

ABSTRACT

In this chapter the argument is made that access to health services and to education is a human right yet to be realized by many Kenyans; these are issues that have a profound impact on the sexual and reproductive health of many women in Kenya. The author argues that the language used to write policy about these human rights should be illustrative of government commitment to access and should include stipulated measures of accountability. The author demonstrates the explicit connection between education and reproductive health that must be understood and incorporated into public policy so that women in both urban and rural African areas benefit from the knowledge. Furthermore, and most importantly, the chapter highlights how women from nations of the north and the south equally share profound challenges with regard to their reproductive and sexual rights and freedoms. The author ends by offering a discussion of these challenges and potential new directions for activism and policy initiation and implementation.

A 15-year-old girl was jailed for three years after she admitted throwing her newborn baby into a pit latrine in Nyahururu town. In mitigation the girl said she could not afford to look after two children. (*Daily Nation*, 2003, p. 6)

INTRODUCTION

In many African cultures childbearing is cause for jubilation, and the arrival of a new life is often a source of empowerment and status for women. Yet the cultural constructions of motherhood reinscribe inequality for women, for they also experience enormous burdens in their roles as mother; they are beleaguered by heavy workloads, deprived of access to adequate resources and exposed to laws and cultural values that increase their vulnerability.

In Kenya motherhood remains a high-risk activity. Current studies estimate a maternal mortality rate, which is the number of women who die in pregnancy and childbirth, to be 414 for every hundred thousand live births (Government of Kenya, 2003a). While the number of perinatal deaths in Kenyan is four per cent of births (Cook et al., 2003), no accurate figures are available for those infants who do survive birth but are killed or simply go missing within a few days of being born as a consequence of being unwanted. On the whole, births to unmarried or young adolescents are unintentional; however, one out of every two hundred adolescent girls is likely to die from complications of motherhood and unwanted pregnancies (Rogo, 1995). Compounding these issues is the fact that, even after a safe delivery, poor women are unable to provide their children the resources they need in order to live and have healthy lives.

Table 3.1 provides information about the reproductive health realities of women and girls in Kenya. Table 3.2 provides information about medically assisted births.

Table 3.1: Reproductive health information on Kenyan women and girls.

Estimated maternal mortality rates in Kenya, ages 15–49	414 for every 100,000 live births[a]
Number of unsafe abortions annually	300,000 (accounts for 30–40% of maternal mortality)[b]
Number of deaths from abortions annually	2,000[b]
Number of pre-natal deaths	40 out of 1,000 births[c]
Number of adolescent girls likely to die from complications of motherhood and unwanted pregnancies	4 out of 10[c]
Number of adolescents (single or married) who have already begun childbearing (15–24 years of age)	106 out of 1,000 (10.6%)[c]

Sources:
a = Kenya Demographic Health Survey (Government of Kenya, 2003a)
b = Advocacy Safe Motherhood (Reproductive Health Advocacy Project, 2004)
c = Kenya Demographic Health Survey (Government of Kenya, 1998).

Table 3.2: Percentage of assisted births in Kenya.
(Total = 3,464 births).

Doctor	12.3
Nurses/trained midwife	32.0
Traditional birth attendant	21.2
Relative/other	23.9
No one	10.2
Don't know/missing	0.4
Total	100.0

Source: Magadi (2002).

Health, in general, is defined and constructed within socio-cultural, political, and economic environments, which in turn affect health outcomes. Consequently, disadvantaged social, political, and economic environments affect the lives of Kenyan women and increase the harmful effects on women's reproductive health, which include unplanned births, early pregnancies, and experiences of life-threatening complications when giving birth or when terminating unwanted pregnancies. This chapter lays out the issues behind these serious threats to women's reproductive health and analyzes the place of reproductive health in its social, economic, and political contexts. The chapter also focuses on the language of human rights as necessary for interrogating what is said about the bodily experience of reproduction and the opportunities offered by the discourses of rights aimed at asserting and improving the reproductive and sexual health of Kenyan women.

SEXUAL AND REPRODUCTIVE HEALTH IN THE EDUCATION SYSTEM[2]

Formal education as presented in schools is often seen to have significant influence on how people make informed decisions about their lives, which includes making decisions about sexual behaviour. Historically, however, sexual and reproductive health has not been part of the Kenyan education curriculum. According to Brockman (1997), even though family life education sometimes addresses menstruation, anatomy, and so on, until 1997, sex education was not officially covered in the curriculum. Additionally, even if sex education was covered in the school curriculum, not everyone had access to this information through school because the education of girls was not seen as a priority in some rural communities.

With the rise of HIV/AIDS, however, there have been some attempts to deliver sexual and reproductive health education in schools. Boler et al. (2003) argue that these attempts have been faced with challenges emanating from the crisis in the education system (overcrowded classes, overstretched curriculum, and a shortage of training opportunities and learning materials) and, more importantly, from a long line of social disapprovals and taboos surrounding sex education. For instance, in the case of males, sex education, traditionally, is associated with initiation rights and the transition from boyhood to manhood. This happens partly because often parents are uncomfortable talking to their children about sexual issues; in fact, in some communities, it is considered shameful for parents to discuss sexually related issues with children. The role of talking to children about sexuality, varies by communities, but traditionally falls to the grandparents, or aunts, or those charged with the ceremonies of initiation into adulthood. For example, among the Kisii people, the grandmother is the children's source for learning about their sexuality. Brockman (1997) argues that taboos, traditional ways of teaching about sexual practices, and the fear of negative reactions from traditional families explain why teachers resist teaching sexual, reproductive, and health education.

Boler et al.'s (2003) study of educational response to the HIV/AIDS epidemic also documents teachers' reluctance to discuss sex and HIV/AIDS with students. The study found that teachers select the messages they want to give students, choosing to overemphasize scientific-based information and not make any direct reference to sex or sexual relationships. Like Brockman, the authors indicate that there are social and cultural constraints when it comes to teaching sex education and about HIV/AIDS. There exists a societal assumption that young people do not and will not have pre-marital sex. In sex education, traditionally, girls were taught to be docile and subservient, which was enforced through female genital cutting and the woman's role in marriage. Girls were also taught that to be married was of greater value than to be educated; as a result, many girls were married off early before completing compulsory schooling (Brockman, 1997). Therefore, even though there have been attempts to include sexual, reproductive, and health education in schools, these programs have been severely curtailed by the wider crisis in education and by social and cultural beliefs. These constraints are evident in health institutions such as clinics and in the behaviour of health personnel towards young people attempting to learn more about their sexuality and to access sex-related health resources such as condoms.

SOCIAL CONSTRUCTION OF GENDER AND
REPRODUCTIVE HEALTH OUTCOMES

Gender, defined as the different opportunities and attributes associated with being female or male, has a powerful influence on sexual and reproductive behaviour and outcomes. The views and practices of femininity and masculinity that reinforce female dependence, men's privileged status, and the inequity between women and men have meant that health is also experienced and defined within social relations of gender, which place women in subordinate positions. Throughout Kenya, women who face poor reproductive health do so because of poverty and other forms of marginality that can be located within gender inequalities. Conditions of inequity have limited females from accessing resources such as education, resulting in lower literacy rates which, in turn, lead to less frequent use of reproductive health services and less knowledge about the importance of reproductive health care.

Gender aspects also go a long way in helping explain the reluctance of women to seek reproductive health care. The heavy work burden that falls upon women provides them with little time or space to care for themselves, thus discouraging them from seeking health care because of the time it would take away from household, agricultural, and market work, as well as community obligations. Furthermore, for most rural women, the nearest health clinic tends to be a daunting six kilometres away. If and when women or men do get to the clinic, they face other disabling factors such as an inordinate amount of waiting time. In their study, "Integrating men into the reproductive health equation: Acceptability and feasibility in Kenya," Muia et al. (2000) concluded that structural constraints, including waiting time in clinics, decreases male participation. For employed men, time spent waiting at the clinic translates into wages lost. Furthermore, at the clinic, women often find themselves faced with discouraging staff attitudes and behaviours, which also discourage male participation.[3] One attitudinal example is that staff will provide very narrowly defined maternal and family planning programs and mainly offer these services to women who are married or to pregnant adult women; young unmarried girls are not seen as deserving such services.

The value placed on women also determines their health care practices. When less value is placed on females because of gender, they will not seek out health care if doing so requires payment. Among the poor, for example, if seeking health care requires spending family income, women's health will come second to other family needs requiring money. Concurrently, the low social status of women often means they lack autonomy over their own bodies. They are often denied the power to make decisions or negotiate with men on matters such as if and when they will have sex or even if contraception will be used. Thus, such issues of power prevent women not only from exercising their procreative power but also their sexuality. These unequal relations of power in sexual relationships expose women to sexual violence, sexually transmitted infections, and unwanted pregnancies.

Women's reproductive health is also challenged or unattainable if men are not involved in promoting women's health, or if men's own reproductive health needs remain unlinked to women's. Men are also a group affected by gender factors. Concepts of masculinity, which include risk-taking, unreasonable expectations that men should endure pain or ill-health, and the idea that reproductive health concerns are a woman's affair, hold men back from seeking reproductive health care; thus increasing the gravity of their illness, possibly even leading to death. Thus, while the burden of reproduction still falls upon women who lack decision-making power, concrete actions are yet to be taken that will encourage and enable men to shoulder responsibility for their sexual and reproductive behaviour, given the consequences this responsibility has on social and family roles. The outcome of gender disparities ultimately leads to an increase in ill-health for women, and often for men.

CULTURAL NORMS AND THE IMPACT ON REPRODUCTIVE HEALTH

The recognition of indigenous customs as the personal laws of the Kenyan ethnic communities has an impact on women's general and reproductive health. For example, among the Luo communities, wife inheritance is a traditional practice in which a widow is "inherited" by one of her dead husband's brothers. Traditionally, this was a way of ensuring resource support for the widow and her children, as well as to keep the children and the family unit together. Sexual activity was, among other things, expected in this arrangement as the "inherited" widow became the wife of her former brother-in-law. Complexities emerge in cases where the inheritor/new husband already had a wife as polygamous families may be characterized by inner-family tension and strife over issues such as access to resources, time spent with husband, number and sex of children in a wife's house, and a wife's individual capacities and opportunities.[4] Nowadays, wife inheritance presents an added threat of the widow contracting HIV/AIDS from the new husband, in the absence or lack of negotiating power and social support for women to insist on safe sex or reject sexual advances and the demands of inheritance practices may force her to engage in sexual activity. Inheritance laws among some Kenyan communities often leave widows impoverished, creating new vulnerabilities for women, at times forcing women and their young daughters into risky sex work or relationships placing them at risk of violence and sexually transmitted infections.

In addition to wife inheritance and its associated women-endangering practices, there are other forms of "adapted" polygamous unions that exist in present-day Kenya and other neighbouring countries. Researching these unions in Nigeria, Karanja (1986) referred to these women as "inside wives" and "outside wives." In these cases, polygamous marital arrangements are modified such that men may have "inside wives" that they have legally married and are publicly recognized and with clear marital rights and at the same time initiate relationships with other women, known as "outside wives," that will not be legally binding and thus unrecognized. Such marital transformations that often create legally unrecognized families not only pose risks to both inside and outside wives' access to marital wealth and resources, but also have an impact on women's reproductive and sexual health. Furthermore, such marital transformations challenge satisfying relationships and affect balanced family lives and the ability to safeguard one's reproductive-sexual health. For the majority of African women, HIV/AIDS infection is often in the context of marriage. For example, where rules of polygamy are changing, and/or where there is the frequent change of partners, sexual encounters increase. Such practices increase the risk of sexually transmitted infections such as AIDS and concerns leading to infertility and new-born diseases associated with these infections. Even though harmful customary practices such as female genital mutilation and early and forced marriages have been declared illegal under both the new Kenyan statutes and the recently adopted Children's Act (2001), they continue to be part of present-day Kenyan society. Thus, although statutes may legally enable Kenyan women to seek legal action, most women find that, culturally, they have no power to act against strong masculine values. The main reason is because the Kenyan state continues to give constitutional recognition to patriarchal customary laws, thus contradicting its own statutory prohibitions in favour of cultural traditions that harm the health of women. In this way, some cultural practices remain a key reproductive health concern for Kenyan women insofar as they determine or have influence over reproductive health decision-making and shape the context of reproductive behaviour in ways that are harmful to women.

ADOLESCENT ACCESS TO SEXUAL REPRODUCTIVE HEALTH SERVICES

Socio-cultural practices, including intolerance towards adolescent sexuality, continue to foster discrimination against female adolescents. Health service providers often fail or refuse to recognize that Kenyan adolescents are sexually active and in need of information and services. Other barriers that stand in the way of access to services can be the shyness and fear of embarrassment on the part of adolescents in undergoing medical examinations and the stigma associated with being sexually active as an adolescent (Daily Nation, 2006). Whereas studies show that it is common for young people in Kenya to start having sex in their early teens (World Health Organization, 2003), what is not so well known is that, unlike in Western nations, where sexually active adolescents are unmarried, in developing countries most are married and therefore face different challenges than their single counterparts (Population Council, 2001). For example, results from a study of youth sexuality and reproductive health, conducted by the Population Council (2001), reveals that 10.6 per cent of single adolescents in Kenya, mostly between ages fifteen and nineteen, are already having children. Their physical immaturity means they are ill-prepared for childbearing. There is also a belief among some Kenyan communities that sex with a young virgin will cure a man of AIDS. This belief suggests that young women and girls are much more at risk of being infected than their male counterparts. Furthermore, many young girls are also growing up at a time of increasing poverty in sub-Saharan Africa, which has compounded the risks they face. For example, girls growing up in poverty seek work earlier, which, given their age, places them in situations of risk of sexual abuse or exploitation. Child marriages and the fact that they are more likely to drop out of school given household-caring responsibilities or pregnancy means they have less access to information, and because they are young girls, they have less negotiating power to protect themselves against HIV/AIDS. Girls are also more vulnerable to HIV infections because, if not fully mature, their reproductive tracts are more susceptible to tearing, increasing their risk of sexually transmitted infections. In Kenya there is an increasing practice of older men, who would have had more partners and therefore be most likely to have been exposed to HIV, to have adolescents as sexual partners in a context where poverty can be the driving force towards the exchange of sex for school fees, support for families, or need for money.

Adolescent girls from poor families face a high risk of early marriage, sexual violence, HIV/AIDS, unplanned pregnancies, and unsafe abortions because of their socio-economic vulnerability. Yet these young, single women are not likely to receive reproductive health counselling support, family planning information, or access to all available family planning methods. Reproductive health staff members often impose age restrictions on information and resource access, depending on the types of women they feel should have such access (Population Council, 2001). Furthermore, as the epigraph to this chapter illustrates, custodial sentences handed out to young girls who kill their infants demonstrate a failure on the part of the Kenyan state and society to respond effectively to its vulnerable adolescents, especially those who are legal minors. Incongruously, the men responsible for the pregnancies remain untouched by law. Youth, therefore, remain ignored and vulnerable while politicians and secular and religious leaders continue to argue and disagree over the relevance or value of providing crucial services and life-saving information to adolescents.

POVERTY AND REPRODUCTIVE HEALTH NEEDS

Absolute poverty increased from 48 per cent to 53 per cent in rural areas of Kenya between 1992 and 1997, and poverty in urban areas increased by a much higher margin, from 29 per cent in 1992 to about 50 per cent in 1997 (Africa Population and Health Research Center, 2002). Rapid population growth has stretched infrastructures, which, combined with the Kenya government's inability to address infrastructural limits, means that the majority of households are becoming poorer. A large number of Kenyan women who live in households below the poverty line lack access to resources and opportunities, making it impossible for them to have healthy reproductive lives. For Kenyan women living in remote communities, pastoralist nomadic women, and internally displaced women, the demand and access to affordable, accessible, and quality reproductive health care remains difficult or unfulfilled even when health facilities exist. Maureen Mackintosh writes, "where systems have failed, that failure is experienced as a core element of exclusion ... contributing profoundly to people's experience of what it is to be poor" (cited in Freedman, 2003). In 1996, it was estimated that skilled health professionals attended to 45 per cent of births in Kenya (Cook et al., 2003). However, the likelihood of a Kenyan mother delivering her child in a hospital depends not only on her poverty status but also on where she lives. The importance of location is evidenced by the fact that only 30 per cent of children born to the rural poor are delivered in hospitals compared with 87 per cent of children born to the urban non-poor who are delivered in hospitals (Human Resources and Social Services Department and Central Bureau of Statistics, 2001). Freedman (2003) noted that 80 per cent of maternal deaths are caused by five direct obstetric complications: haemorrhage, infection, hypertensive disorders, obstructed labour, and unsafe abortions. Freedman outlines that, with the exception of deaths due to abortion, all the other four complications cannot be predicted or prevented. Emergency

Obstetric Care (EmOC) can, however, ensure that all births have a skilled attendant at hand to save lives and that all women with complications can get to it. Reproductive health risks are of course not the same for all Kenyan women; rather, risks are defined by where women live, their age, ethnicity, economic status, and educational levels. According to Graham et al. (2004), "women who died of maternal causes were more likely to have had no education and generally had worse dwelling characteristics than the women dying of non-maternal causes and those who were still alive" (p. 23).

POLITICS AND REPRODUCTIVE RIGHTS

In general, Kenyan women continue to confront strong political challenges in articulating reproductive health rights. In fact, Kenyan women now find themselves publicly censured and constrained when they seek transformations in gender norms and attitudes, or raise demands of their right to make informed decisions concerning their bodies, marriage, child-bearing, power to negotiate reproductive decisions, and the legal rights that safeguard reproductive and sexual health rights. Current constitutional review discussions and the opening up of political space to raise human rights issues has not enabled women leaders seeking to, for example, openly discuss issues of abortion. Rather, the provisional draft will constitutionally prohibit abortion and provide a new legal recognition of a foetus. In effect, the short-term political interests of policy-makers – who are predominantly men – and the need of men to retain control over women's sexuality and procreative roles often take priority over women's own reproductive health needs. As a consequence, there continues to be a lack of dialogue between leaders, policy-makers, service providers, and women clients on reproductive health issues. There is a need for these players to develop a deep understanding of how gender, culture, and health factors intersect and result in what are preventable maternal complications, deaths, and illnesses.

The cost of maternal illness, which often results in death, is that it threatens the health and survival of children, fathers, extended families, and the larger community. A mother's death means the loss of both her monetary and non-monetary contributions to all the afore-mentioned parties. A mother's death also increases the likelihood of economic, social, and psychological harm to her children, and it increases the burden on her survivors to take care for her children and home (UNFPA, 2000). If her survivors are unable or unwilling to assume these added responsibilities, the cost of support or assistance must surely fall upon the state. Raising the status of women by protecting and promoting their rights and empowering them so that they can make decisions, have choices, and exert control over their own lives is key to addressing the reproductive health concerns of women and the overall health and well-being of communities.

International human rights law and principles stipulate the responsibility of states to continuously take steps that improve people's enjoyment of these rights. Furthermore, these principles affirm that no state is too poor to meet basic needs, and that the services that governments provide must be guaranteed to all of its citizens equally; otherwise, the state is in violation of its duties. International human rights laws thus open the doors for a variety of actors – be they individuals, institutions, or groups – to process and articulate actions that are desirable to promote and protect the reproductive health and sexual rights of women.

Reproductive health rights imply the following:

- The freedom for girls, women, and men to decide if, when, and how to engage in sexual relations and/or to have children.
- The provision of information and services that enable girls, women, and men to meet their reproductive health needs.
- The provision of prenatal, post-partum, and post-abortion care, so that women can safely experience pregnancy and childbirth. (This is a matter of right to life and survival for all women, which depends on the fulfilment of two things: access to facilities that can provide emergency obstetric care, as noted in Freedman [2003]; and, access to affordable, effective, and safe methods of family planning.)
- Access to knowledge and care to enable awareness and prevention of sexually transmitted infections, including HIV/AIDS, as well as anti-retroviral treatment for pregnant women.

- Individual control over one's own sexuality.
- The right to liberty and security for women, which can only be ensured through strong support for the abandonment of cultural practices that harm women's health.
- The right to make decisions that are free from discrimination, violence, and coercion.
- The right to obtain the highest standard of sexual and reproductive health.

TOWARDS NEW INITIATIVES AND THE ROLE OF GOVERNMENT IN GUARANTEEING RIGHTS

One of the roles of government is to guarantee the human rights that entitle citizens to social arrangements that facilitate secure access to resources such as health care. Towards this end, Kenya has developed policies to help ensure the well-being and health status of all Kenyans. Spurred by the Program of Action that came out of the 1994 International Conference on Population and Development (ICPD), Kenya developed the National Implementation Plan for Family Planning Program, 1995–2000. Other specific Kenyan reproductive health care policies followed, such as the Reproductive Health and Family Planning Policy Guidelines (Ministry of Health, Government of Kenya, 1997) and the National Reproductive Health Strategy, 1997–2003 (Ministry of Health, Government of Kenya, 1999). There was also the National Development Plan (Ministry of Planning and National Development, Government of Kenya, 1997) and Poverty Reduction Strategy Paper, 2002–2003 (Ministry of Finance and Planning, Government of Kenya, 2002). These latter two prioritized the provision of health services that, importantly, emphasized the needs of Kenyan women and children. Such policies have brought attention to the discrimination faced by women by recognizing gender disadvantage as the source of Kenyan women's poor reproductive health. Of great significance is the government's mandate to ensure that women's rights are respected by all, as outlined in the Convention on the Elimination of All Forms of Discrimination against Women (CEDAW, 1979), to which Kenya is a signatory. Accordingly, "it is discriminatory for a State party to refuse to legally provide for the performance of certain reproductive health services for women." The CEDAW convention further states that "barriers to women's access to appropriate health care include laws that dehumanise medical procedures only needed by women and that punish women who undergo those procedures" (Kenya Medical Association and the Kenya Obstetrics and Gynaecology Society, 2004, p. 27).

There are also the United Nations Millennium Development Goals (MDGs) that, since 2002, have placed far-reaching responsibilities on governments around the world to ensure human development; four of the eight goals are health related.[5] Reproductive health is, therefore, an integral part of a country's development and under MDGs the Kenyan government has committed to reduce the maternal mortality rate by 75 per cent by 2015 (World Health Organization, 2003). This means that the Kenyan government must "offer total political commitment and provide capacity building for delivery of quality health care; provision of a minimum of 15 per cent of annual budget to health with at least 20 per cent of that to reproductive health; free delivery of services to women and a health system that is built around emergency obstetric care" (World Health Organization, 2002, p. 128).

All the aforementioned policies have tremendous implications because of what they can make possible; they also form a basis for putting pressure on the government in order to ensure that women's reproductive and sexual health becomes a reality. These policies are framed in ways that mandate initiatives to address women's reproductive health concerns and to provide for a multitude of services, thereby recognizing the interconnections between diverse reproductive health needs. Already, these policies have been instrumental in stimulating action that addresses women's health issues in concrete ways. For instance, policy initiatives addressing health needs helped launch the Safe Motherhood drive, a nationwide endeavour whose goal is to reduce the number of deaths and illness associated with childbirth. Additionally, the recommendations to strengthen district-level hospitals so that they guarantee reproductive health services for all women extend to all regions. These policies have further brought recognition to the important and positive role of men in ensuring reproductive health for themselves as well as for women. Thus, when governments ratify international human rights agreements, an enabling environment is created for women to attain good health.

However, because governments are predominantly male, structural, and attitudinal barriers to gender equality persist, compromising women's health status and well being.

International standards and policies notwithstanding, the Kenyan state has remained constrained in its ability to deliver on its reproductive health sector policies, thereby often failing to provide remedies against the human rights violations that persist. Policy instruments such as the Safe Motherhood initiative have made sporadic gains; however, their impact on reproductive health of Kenyan women will need time to be felt as, currently, high rates of maternal mortality and morbidity exist. Similarly, the needs of Kenyan adolescents remain unmet, while the dilemma of abortion rights continues to bedevil the Kenyan nation. The criminalizing of abortion has resulted in women and girls being subjected to unsafe abortions, contributing to an estimated three hundred thousand deaths per year or 30–40 per cent of maternal mortality rates (World Health Organization, 2002). Non-fatal resultant complications, in turn, place a very heavy burden on Kenya's health care system, whose obstetric budget is needlessly spent on attempts to remedy these avoidable consequences. In addition, the HIV pandemic continues to challenge the provision of health care, especially for Kenya's poor.

In general, the constraints that the Kenyan health sector face in deploying resources can be partially attributed to insufficient national funds, which is further compounded by government allocations when deciding priorities for the national budget. Even though Kenya subscribes to international recommendations and international human rights laws, the absence of national legislation undermines efforts that would enable affordable health insurance provisions for all Kenyans. At a different level, long-term government-supported ethnic marginalization, as manifested in the state's failure to serve all Kenyan communities equally—resulting in the concentration of resources in ethnically connected communities—has had devastating effects on the non-connected. Other related reasons for this failure within the health sector can be blamed on the moral bankruptcy of national officials, which has led to the mismanagement and theft of national resources, with little capital left to invest in women's reproductive health. Furthermore, there is a lack of awareness or disinterest and even fear on the part of some national leaders in taking measures to ensure women enjoy their reproductive health rights, given the divisiveness of reproductive health issues, the barriers of tradition with regards to sexuality, and the increasing size of the demand for reproductive health services.

Gender has not been a "core competence" of policy-making bodies (Kabeer, 2003); yet there is need to mainstream gender perspectives into the health care system because to have sustainable development with social justice requires the recognition of the social and economic costs that gender discrimination has on women and children. There is also the need to recognize the advantages of promoting gender equality such as the immediate gains it will bring to the national output. Additionally, it is important to note the cumulative nature of human rights and the ways that they could interactively be applied to advance interests in reproductive and sexual health (Cook et al., 2003). Consequently, out of this fundamental strategy flow three key interventions. First is reforming Kenyan laws to ensure compliance with human rights statutes. In this regard, this intervention is exemplified by the Reproductive Health Advocacy Project (RHAP), which is designed to review Kenya reproductive health policies and laws and seek changes, also to create awareness about unsafe abortions in Kenya. This project was initiated by collaboration between the Kenyan chapter of the Federation of Women Lawyers (FIDA) and the Kenyan Medical association. Additionally, Kenya is drafting a new constitution with a Bill of Rights that guarantees freedom from discrimination, recognizes and protects human rights and promotes social justice. Article 61 of the draft constitution brings a new recognition to the protection of rights to health and reproductive health care. However, challenges have emerged with new proposals from the religious right that is seeking a way to define, within the draft constitution, a statement that stipulates that life begins at conception. However a "no" vote on the Constitutional Referendum in November 2005 has meant that, for now, Kenya will have to wait for the process to restart. What is clear is that there remains a demand by Kenyans for a new constitution.

Second is creating accessible and equitable reproductive health care for all Kenyans. Seeds of change are present with regard to Post-Abortion Care (PAC), which is being successfully decentralized and democratized. Practitioners, especially nurses and clinical officers who were previously barred from rendering this care, are managing more PAC patients at lower levels of the health system (Onyango et al., 2003). The health sector is beginning to reach out to adolescents with programmes that will get youth to seek out reproductive health services through the establishment of "youth friendly health facilities". An Adolescent Reproductive Health and Development Policy is to be launched shortly. This policy will address the challenges of law, culture, poverty, and access to information and services that currently hinder reproductive health services for youth, by creating an enabling environment to improve the well-being and health status of youth.

Third is educating the public about the health aspect of women's rights, in particular, and human rights, in general, by establishing collaborative networks encompassing women, civil society organizations, health professionals, and policy-makers to disseminate needed information and monitor and enforce reproductive rights. Non-governmental organizations have initiatives to lobby, advocate, and raise awareness for a new constitutional order that will positively embrace women's reproductive health rights. Kenyan laws are also under review, and projects addressing gender responsive legal sector reform are underway. Women's non-governmental organizations are developing strategies for actions to influence legislation in favour of women's rights. More broadly, with regard to the Millennium Development Goals (MDGs), there are civil society organizations that have recently developed a campaign to input into government costing of the MDGs, as well as strategizing on actions that will roll out into villages across Kenya, targeting the poor, women, and the marginalized, with the intent to communicate the imperatives of the MDGs. At the same time this campaign is seeking to build the capacity of individuals and communities at the grassroots to hold the government accountable on the MDGs.

Fourth is understanding and responding to what women's named priorities are by taking into account the gendered dimensions of the socio-economic context, of service delivery and of decision-making within the health sector. Women's organisations already exist on the ground with clear understanding of the health issues of Kenyan women and are an important voice on these issues. Such organisations, together with gender experts must be present, represented and allocated with resources in the current reforms in the health sector to continue to provide services, carry out advocacy, as well as facilitate decision-making that will be responsive to mainstreaming gender into the health sector.

Kenya's *Economic Recovery Strategy for Wealth and Employment Creation: 2003–2007* recognizes the need to undertake corrective measures that provide for health insurance for the most vulnerable groups, rehabilitation of existing health facilities and wider coverage of quality health services, and improved affordability to improve the well being of the poor (Government of Kenya, 2003b). However, the discourses of gender equality have not sufficiently informed this key development strategy paper. It is clear, however, that the government must continue to undertake the implementation of measures that will strengthen good governance, enable economic justice, and expand democratic practices, thus setting the stage for the realization of social justice and gender equality.

REFERENCES

Africa Population and Health Research Center. (2002). *Population and health dynamics in Nairobi's informal settlements.* Nairobi: Africa Population and Health Research Center.

Boler, T., Ibrahim, A., Adoss, R.,& Shaw, M. (2003). *The sound of silence: Difficulties in communicating on HIV/AIDS in schools.* London: ActionAid.

Brockman, N. (1997). Kenya. In R. T. Francoeur (Ed.), *The International Encyclopaedia of Sexuality* (pp. 843–68). New York: Continuum, Vol. 2.

Cook, R. J., Dickens, B. M., & Fathalla, M. F. (2003). *Reproductive health and human rights: Integrating medicine, ethics and law.* New York: Oxford Press.

Daily Nation. (13th November, 2003). Girl jailed for throwing away baby. *Daily Nation.*

Daily Nation. (21st December, 2006). Advertising Feature: Adolescent Reproductive Health. Ministry of Health and Kenyan German Development Cooperation. *Daily Nation.*

Freedman, L. (2003). Strategic advocacy and maternal mortality: Moving targets and the millennium development goals. *Gender and Development, 11*(1), 97–108.

Government of Kenya. (2003a). *Kenya demographic health survey.* Nairobi: Central Bureau of Statistics.

Government of Kenya. (2003b). *Economic recovery strategy for wealth and employment creation: 2003–2007.* Nairobi: Kenya Government Printers.

Graham, W. J., Fitzmaurice, A. E., Bell, J. S., & Cairns, J. A. (2004). The familial technique for linking maternal death with poverty. *Maternal Mortality Lancet, 363,* 23–27.

Human Resources and Social Services Department and Central Bureau of Statistics. (2001). *Poverty policy briefing: Health GTZ social policy advisory services.* Nairobi, May.

Karanja, W. (1986). Outside wives and inside wives in Nigeria: A study of changing perceptions of marriage. In D. Parkins & M. Nyamwaya (Eds.), *Transformations of African Marriage* (pp. 247–61). Manchester: Manchester University Press.

Kabeer, N. (2003). *Gender mainstreaming in poverty eradication and the millennium development goals.* London: The Commonwealth Secretariat.

Kenya Medical Association and the Kenya Obstetrics and Gynaecology Society. (2004). Intervention to the National Constitutional Conference Technical Committee on the Bill of Rights – Article 32. *Daily Nation,* 30 January, p. 27.

Magadi, M. (2002). Maternal and child health. In Africa Population and Health Research publication, *Population and Health Dynamics in Nairobi's Informal Settlements* (pp. 95–118). Nairobi: Based on Kenya Demographic Health Survey data, 1998.

Ministry of Health, Government of Kenya. (1997). Reproductive health strategy, 1997–2010. Nairobi: Government Printers.

Ministry of Health, Government of Kenya. (1999). National reproductive health strategy: Implementation plan, 1999–2003. Nairobi: Government Printers.

Ministry of Finance and Planning, Government of Kenya. (2002). Interim poverty strategy paper for the period of 2000–2003. Nairobi: Government Printers.

Ministry of Planning and National Development, Government of Kenya. (1997). 8th National development plan, 1997–2001 Nairobi: Government Printers.

Muia, E., Olenja, J., Kimani, V., & Leonard, A. (2000). Integrating men into the reproductive health equation: Acceptability and feasibility in Kenya. Nairobi: Population Council.

Onyango, S., Mitchell, E., Nyaga, N., Turner, K., & Lovell, R. (2003). *Scaling up access to high quality post-abortion care in Kenya.* IPAS.

Population Council. (2001). Facts about adolescents from the Demographic and Health Survey – *Statistical tables for program planning: Kenya 1998 Population Council* (p. i). New York: Population Council.

Reproductive Health Advocacy Project. (2004). *Advocacy Safe Motherhood.* Nairobi: Reproductive Health Advocacy Project.

Rogo, K. O. (1995). Summary of research findings on women and health in Kenya: Developing an action agenda. In K. Kibwana (Ed.), *Women and autonomy in Kenya* (pp. 67–82). Nairobi: Claripress.

UNFPA. (2000). *The state of world population 2000: Lives together, worlds apart, men and women in a time of change.* New York: UNFPA.

World Health Organization. (2003). Family and reproductive health: Making a difference through the life span. Brazzaville: World Health Organization.

World Health Organization. (2002). Family and reproductive health: Making a difference through the life span. Brazzaville: World Health Organization.

Notes

1   The author is grateful to Musabi Muteshi for tirelessly reviewing drafts of this chapter and invaluable assistance in providing information. I also wish to recognize the late Dr. Katini Nzau-Ombaka for her review and insights of the first draft. I would like to thank Nombuso Dlamini for her assistance in strengthening the discussion on educational issues regarding the reproductive health concerns contained in this chapter.

2   I treat sexual health and reproductive health as one thing – reproductive health and rights because the questions and concerns under discussion in this chapter encompass actions and decisions regarding reproduction and sexual behaviour that cannot be separated if reproductive health conditions are to be understood. Such conflation does not pre-empt the new ground-breaking work in Africa on sexuality, sexual relationships, and sexual rights as a separate field of research.

3   I recognize that men's partnership is essential to advancing the reproductive and sexual health rights of women and gender equality; however, space does not allow for a realistic exploration of these joint responsibilities between women and men for assuring the health of women and families.

4   Because of inheritance laws, in many traditional Kenyan communities, male children are valued over female children.

5   United Nations Millennium Development Goals: (1) eradicate extreme poverty and hunger; (2) achieve universal primary education; (3) promote gender equality and empower women; (4) reduce child mortality; (5) improve maternal health; (6) combat HIV/AIDS, malaria and other diseases; (7) ensure environmental sustainability; and (8) develop global partnerships for development.

4

GENDER, POST-SECONDARY EDUCATION, AND EMPLOYMENT OPPORTUNITIES FOR WOMEN IN TANZANIA

Grace Khwaya Puja

ABSTRACT

This chapter discusses some of the many factors that contribute to women's low participation in post-secondary and technical education in Tanzania. The author explores how these limitations in education often mean women's employment opportunities in jobs that require technical skills and competencies are also limited. Historically, specifically during the colonial era, Tanzanian women were trained in home crafts, such as sewing, cooking, and cleaning. The author argues that Tanzania's postcolonial education policy structure and planning have played and continue to play significant roles in the systematic marginalization of women in post-secondary and technical education. Although many changes have taken place in education since Tanzania became politically independent in 1961, women continue to be under-represented in post-secondary education, especially in fields that offer technical skills and competencies. This chapter discusses the limitations in current research examining women and education in the country; the author attempts to explain why there has been limited change in this field. She also suggests strategic interventions at the policy and structural levels that are necessary to lead to change in access for Tanzanian women. The author concludes by discussing a few initiatives that have been implemented at the University of Dar es Salaam and discusses how these initiatives could be enhanced.

INTRODUCTION

This chapter examines the factors that contribute to women's under-representation in higher and technical education and their subsequent limited employment opportunities. It is also argued that a gender analysis of the education policy will reveal how, over the years, women's subordination has been structurally engrained. It stresses the need for research that looks for alternatives to these educational policies so that education better promotes equity and improves women's employment opportunities. Literature on education in Tanzania fails to examine how gender is mediated by social class, religion, ethnicity, regional diversity, and disability. Nor does this literature analyze how patriarchal, colonial, and Eurocentric capitalist ideologies have combined with traditional patriarchal African culture to establish the education system we find in Tanzania today. A close examination of this literature discloses that, more often than not, low participation of women in formal education is blamed on the so-called traditional African parents who are said to be more likely to educate their sons than their daughters. While this may still be true for many rural parents in Tanzania, it has to be understood within a context. These parental attitudes partly reflect the colonial patriarchal heritage that rewarded male-based ways and suppressed indigenous and female ways of knowing and structural participation. In general, women's educational subordination has resulted from the complex combination of the colonial heritage, traditional African practices, and external factors such as the International Monetary Fund (IMF) and the World Bank (WB), whose Structural Adjustment Programs (SAPs) define educational issues in Tanzania as they do in other African countries.

In Tanzania there is need for an approach that focuses on seeing the world from an African woman's perspective and that questions the way education is made available to women and men. This approach needs to be mindful of the intersection between gender and colonialism, underdevelopment, ethnicity, religion, and social class as sites that mediate African women's access to higher and technical education. Such an African-centred discursive framework validates African experiences and their histories and is conceptualized within an anti-colonial discursive framework as presented by Dei and Asgharzadeh (2001). According to Dei and Asgharzadeh, the anti-colonial standpoint affirms the reality of re-colonization processes through the dictates of global capital (popularly known as "globalization"). In his book, Rodney (1972) argued that Africa's underdevelopment state is a result of colonialism, the international capitalist system, and neo-colonial practices. Conversely, in colonial Africa, education was mainly designed to assist colonialists with the colonial process; consequently, it created stratification in the acquisition and valuing of resources in African society, and created conditions that led to unemployment, gender inequities, educational contradictions, and economic and political dependence. In order to be effective, the development process must begin by transforming the economy from its colonial externally responsive structure to one that is internally responsive. Accordingly, such a framework can also be utilized to examine and address issues of gender parity in Tanzanian education.

Writing from a North American context, Steady (1985) examines the subordination of Black women all over the world and advocates an overall cross-continental study of Black women in general. According to Steady, African women have, for centuries, experienced multiple oppression as a result of the intersection between gender, class, racial, cultural, and colonial experiences. She emphasizes that inequality between African women and men intensified during European colonialism, which, in itself was a direct product of the capitalist system introduced into Africa. Under the capitalist economic system, men's work is valued over women's work, which is seen as inferior and therefore unimportant.

WOMEN AND HIGHER EDUCATION IN AFRICA

According to UNESCO's 2003–2004 global monitoring report on Education for All (EFA), gender parity is better at the primary school level in the 128 countries that were involved in the survey (cited in Mugoni & Madziwa, 2004). A few African countries, including Botswana, Malawi, Mauritius, Namibia, the United Republic of Tanzania, and Zimbabwe, are said to have attained gender parity at the primary school level by 2000. The UNESCO report cites Swaziland as the only African country that had attained gender parity at the secondary school level by the year 2000. Factors that could contribute to this gender parity include Swaziland's small population (1.17 million), its boys-girls ratio, and labour migration of young men to South Africa. Overall, however, when compared to other countries, African countries, especially those in sub-Saharan Africa, still lag behind Europe, Asia, and Latin America in gender parity.

Girls' and women's under-representation in post-secondary education in Africa, especially in science-based and technological programs, and the related employment streams, has to be historically understood. For instance, in Tanzania Mainland, formerly Tanganyika,[1] at the time of independence in 1961, there were 490,000 students in primary school in the country's overall population of approximately 10 million (Omari, 2002). Discussing Tanganyika girls' access to education during this period, Malekela (1999) points out that in 1961 girls constituted 40 per cent of students in Standard 1 (first grade in elementary school) but only 23 per cent of students in Standard 7 (seventh grade). Due to the expansion of education after independence, these percentages slightly increased so that by 1971 girls constituted 42 per cent of the students in Standard 1 and 34 per cent of those in Standard 7. Increase in girls' enrolment became even more pronounced after the implementation of government initiatives designed to offer a more equitable education. Such initiatives include the 1974 Musoma Resolution aimed at offering Universal Primary Education (UPE) and the introduction of the Quota System, in mid-1970. By 1996 girls made up 49 per cent of students in Tanzanian primary schools (Ministry of Education and Culture, 1997).

Even though the percentage of female students has improved, especially at the primary and lower secondary school levels, girls' performance in secondary national examinations has been poor compared to that of boys. And, since secondary education is a ladder to post-secondary education, improvements in secondary school enrolments have not translated into the expected increase in candidates eligible for post-secondary education. Moreover, girls tend to drop out of secondary school due to hardships related to family income, pregnancies, or early marriages.

Examining access and equity in university education in Tanzania, Malekela (1999) points out that Tanzania Mainland has historically lagged behind Uganda and Kenya in higher education. While there were 374 Ugandan university students and 366 Kenyan university students between 1959 and 1960, there were only 185 Tanganyikan university students at Makerere[2] and overseas. Malekela cites the findings of a Manpower survey carried out in 1962, which indicated that 85 per cent of the jobs requiring a university degree in Tanzania Mainland were occupied by non-Africans: Europeans and Asians. Malekela agrees with Pratt that "there were only 12 civil engineers, no mechanical and electrical engineers, five chemists, one forester, nine veterinary doctors, eight electrical engineers and five telecommunication engineers, no geologists and only 38 out of 600 graduates were secondary school teachers" (Pratt, 1976, cited in Malekela, 1999, p. 36). While this breakdown does not indicate how many of these professionals were women, it is safe to conclude that they were probably all men.

The value of higher education is self-evident and is well discussed by Jones (1992), who points out that, due to the advanced technology prevalent in the world, the economic benefits of education are greater for those who are more educated and weaker for those who are less educated. Yet despite these widely acknowledged benefits of education, the situation for women in Tanzania has deteriorated as a result of so-called stabilization processes put in place by the World Bank (WB) and its associated Structural Adjustment Programs (SAPs). The WB introduced short- and medium-term loans, which force African governments to cut spending on social services. Furthermore, WB policies force African governments to spend less on education, resulting in the enforcement of systematic gender discrimination as girls and women were already denied access to post-secondary education.

When girls and women are denied full educational opportunities, they face limited employment opportunities and are consequently forced into low-paying jobs. The consequences are low social status and a poor quality of life, not only for women and girls, but also for their families and the societies from which they come. The World Bank has realized this drawback and is now partially funding the Primary Education Development Program (PEDP) and Secondary Education Development Program (SEDP) to address this problem. Nonetheless, this change comes a bit too late to effectively redress decades of gender inequity practices.

WOMEN'S EDUCATION IN TANZANIA

The Tanzanian formal education system follows seven years of primary school, four years of ordinary level secondary education, two years of advanced level secondary education, and a minimum of three years of university education. Pre-primary education was introduced in 1995 when it was formalized under the Education and Training Policy (United Republic of Tanzania, 1995).

Primary education was declared compulsory and universal as a result of the 1974 Musoma Resolution, which led to the enactment of the Education Act of 1978 in Tanzania. Although Universal Primary Education (UPE) has not yet been attained, the Musoma Resolution and other policy statements have led to increases in school enrolments at all levels. For example, compared to the 1971 statistics cited earlier, by 1988, girls made up 50.3 per cent of the total primary school enrolment, 36 per cent of public secondary schools, and 45 per cent of private secondary schools (United Republic of Tanzania, 1992b, p. 23).

In addition to these earlier efforts, in 2001 the Ministry of Education and Culture[3] started the implementation of the 1999 Education Sector Development Programme (ESDP). At the primary school level, the Primary Education Development Plan (PEDP) was developed to implement the ETP, which was in line with international agreements on Education for All (EFA) such as the Jamitien, Thailand, in 1990, and the Dakar, Senegal, in 2000 agreements. Tanzania signed these agreements. The PEDP aimed at attaining UPE in Tanzania by December 2006 (Ministry of Education and Culture, 2003). But, in her Budget Speech to the Parliament, the first female Minister for Education and Vocational Training, Margaret Sitta, in June 2006 states that in the 2005/2006 school year, only 74.6 per cent of the 7-year-olds were enrolled in Standard 1. She also discloses that the Ministry's target for 2006/2007 was to enrol 1,166,737 7-year-olds and all the remaining 8- and 9-year-olds. This implies that by December 2006, Tanzania had not attained UPE goals.

The selection procedures for secondary education are based on the students' results in the Primary School Leaving Examination (PSLE), which is done at the end of their seven years of primary education. Education records indicate that almost 50 per cent of primary school leavers in the country are selected annually for entry into first form (the first year of secondary education). Within the ESDP, this percentage is expected to increase. In the 1970s a quota system was introduced to address regional and district disparities as well as gender inequalities in the number of students entering secondary school.

The quota system involved using a selection procedure known as "cut-off points" for different districts and regions and for girls and boys in order to select diverse students for secondary schooling from various regional groups without competition. The quota system was criticized for claims of lowering the quality of education because, in some cases, students with low academic ability were selected from some economically disadvantaged regions, while others from privileged areas, who had better academic performance in the PSLE, were not selected. Although it was never officially stated, the quota system operated with the assumption that those from economically advantaged groups would go to private secondary schools. In addition to the latter academic standing controversy, and despite its good intent, the quota system was limited because it did not apply to the selection of students from Form Four to Form Five, which is based on the results of the National Form Four Examinations. Therefore, very few girls were selected for Form Five because their performance in the Form Four examinations was usually poor (Tanzania Development Research Group [TADREG], 1990; Tanzania Gender Networking Program, 1993). Such results indicate that there is a need to find out the conditions under which girls perform poorly in examinations and to suggest alternative strategies for change. This calls for a critical analysis of the schooling process, the cultural and external factors, and how the intersection of these factors contributes to women's low academic performance and, consequently, to their under-representation in post-secondary education.

It is worth noting here that initially, the quota system was introduced as a remedial program to minimize the historical regional inequality in education and would have served as a short-term solution while causes for poor student performance were being studied. Later, by the late 1980s, the government agreed with those who opposed the quota system and argued that it had outlived its usefulness; thus, the quota system was abolished (United Republic of Tanzania, 1995). This decision was very problematic, considering that the regional, gender, and religious inequities that the quota system sought to minimize still exist in the Tanzania education system.

As a Tanzanian educator, I am convinced that the unstated reason for abolishing the quota system was to move away from the philosophy of education for self-reliance (ESR). The education for self-reliance philosophy, which advocated equality in education, was replaced by new educational policies that are market-oriented, emphasize privatization, and advocate cost-sharing between students and government. This new focus upholds the capitalist ideals that underlie the Structural Adjustment Program (SAP).

In addition to the abolishment of the quota system, another factor that has been detrimental to girls' access to education in Tanzania is the paying of school fees. School fees were abolished in the 1960s to allow more Tanzanian children to participate in education. But school fees were reintroduced in the late 1980s as a result of cuts in government spending. Public spending on education at this time was reduced from 11.7 per cent in 1980/81 to 5.9 per cent by 1989/90 due to pressure from the World Bank (Ministry of Education and Culture, 1990). Decisions on school fees have been sporadic, since in 2001, as a strategy to implement the Primary Education Development Plan (PEDP), presumably with the support of the World Bank, the Tanzanian government once more, and unexpectedly, abolished schools fees at the primary school level. The government also reduced the secondary school fees by 50 per cent from forty thousand to twenty thousand Tanzanian shillings. In addition, as a move to promote post-secondary education, effective July 2005, the United Republic of Tanzania, through its Ministry of Science, Technology, and Higher

Education (MOSTHE), established the Higher Education Student Loan Board (HESLB), which is responsible for granting loans to qualified Tanzanians to pursue post-secondary education locally and abroad. While this move is positive, most of these loan recipients may not easily find employment after graduation. Payment of the loans is therefore in obvious jeopardy.

GIRLS' ACADEMIC PERFORMANCE

There is documentation indicating that girls' final results in the Primary School Leaving Examination (PSLE), the National Form Four, and Form Six Examinations have generally been poor in comparison with boys (TADREG, 1990; Tanzania Gender Networking Program, 1993; Malekela, 1999). In boarding schools, girls' performance has been noted to be much higher than in day secondary schools where girls go back home every day to help with family chores. The report of TADREG (1990) also found that the examination results of female students from girls-only boarding secondary schools were better than those of boys in co-education secondary schools. The TADREG study concluded that "girls' best chances of academic success are in the public non-growth boarding secondary schools and their worst chances are in the fast growing private secondary schools" (p. 12). The TADREG report was in tune with observations that girls' best chances of academic success was in boarding schools. In general, many of the Christian-affiliated private boarding schools for boys and girls have been leading in good performance in national examinations since early 2000. In the 1990s the situation was different because, during this period when private schools were being reintroduced, most of the students enrolled in private secondary schools were those who were academically poor, resulting in high student-teacher ratio, a high number of unprofessionally trained teachers, and most of the private schools were poorly equipped. As a result, most of the students in private secondary schools did not perform well in national examinations. But the situation had changed in many private secondary schools by early 2000. For instance, in the 2002 National Form Four Examination Results, 10.5 per cent of the girls who obtained Division

1 (first class grades) were from single-sex girls' boarding secondary schools (some of these were private secondary schools), while only 0.8 per cent of the girls who obtained Division 1 were from co-education secondary schools (United Republic of Tanzania, 2003).

Girls in private secondary schools

The private school system in Tanzania was abolished immediately after independence as a strategy for eliminating racial and religious discrimination in education. In the late 1980s, it was reintroduced on the condition that those who started such schools had to follow curriculum and staffing guidelines set out by the Ministry of Education. Yet, despite these guidelines, evidence indicates that many private secondary schools had limited fiscal and staffing resources. Most of them had few and untrained teachers, although student enrolments were high. The official teacher-student ratio in private secondary schools by mid-1994 was 1:28, but anecdotal information indicated that some single-teacher classrooms had as many as sixty students. In public secondary schools, the teacher student ratio was 1:17. Subject streams in private secondary schools were also very limited due to scarce resources, especially classrooms, technical equipment, and curriculum materials (Tanzania Gender Networking Program, 1993). While the situation has changed in some private Christian secondary schools, some private schools still offer poor quality education while charging very high school fees.

Moreover, private secondary schools and boarding schools (including those that are public) are only accessible to girls from rich families, especially those in the urban areas who can afford to pay the expensive school fees. This implies that girls from poor families are denied the right to a better quality of education. By implication the development of the private education sector is instrumental in class formation in the Tanzanian society. In order to minimize social differentiation through education, the Tanzanian government should provide quality education in public secondary schools: both single-sex boarding and the growing co-education community secondary schools should be adequately equipped and have facilities such as hostels to ensure high quality education for girls and boys.

Girls and school curriculum

In 1967, the Tanzanian government, under the leadership of Julius Nyerere, declared Education for Self-Reliance (ESR) as its new philosophy of education (Nyerere, 1967). Among other things, this philosophy emphasized that the purpose of education was to prepare the student for a productive and sustainable agricultural life. Nyerere argued that Tanzania was an agricultural country and was going to remain that way for many years. He reasoned that the majority of primary schools leavers would not be selected for secondary schools and saw no other options for these children but to prepare them for work in the villages where they came from. Such a view of the role of education has been widely criticized, but the discussion of the angles of criticism is beyond the scope of this chapter.

In part, ESR was a step towards designing an education that is based on the needs of African children. Nyerere's views of ESR were based on non-elitism and an education suitable for preparing students for life in rural Tanzania. He argued that ESR was committed to the ideals of an African socialist society, which were based on the three principles of "equality and respect for human dignity; sharing of the resources which are produced by our effort; work by everyone and exploitation by none" (Nyerere, 1967, p. 6).

In response to the declaration on ESR, four vocational streams were introduced into secondary education in the 1970s – the agricultural, commerce, technical, and domestic science streams with domestic science focused on girls (Hongoke, 1991). Although girls did study agriculture at the ordinary level, this specialization did not exist at the advanced secondary school level. To date, very few girls enrol in technical subjects at the secondary school level. In the early 1990s, the Ministry of Education, Culture, and Sports introduced a system in which girls are admitted to formerly boys-only secondary schools, through which select government boys' secondary schools were required to enrol girls in these traditionally male-dominated subjects. While this move was a positive one, girls faced problems such as sexual harassment and a hostile social and structural environment, which they were forced to tolerate in order to study in co-educational schools.

Another response to the ESR was the introduction of academic subjects, which were divided into the arts and sciences. In this academic stream, evidence indicates that girls are under-represented in the sciences, especially in the physics, chemistry, and mathematics (PCM) stream and in the physics, geography, and mathematics (PGM) stream. For example, in 1989, girls made up 11.2 per cent of the students enrolled in the PCM stream, but no girls were enrolled in the PGM stream. This was because there were no secondary schools designed to offer these subject combinations to girls (TADREG, 1990). This is just one example of the persistence of systematic structures that discriminate against the education of girls.

Another facet of girls' education is sexual and reproductive health education, which is a crucial component, partly because pregnancy is one of the reasons girls drop out of primary and secondary schools (Ministry of Education, 1984) or, as some have argued, the reason why they are expelled from schools (Makobwe, 1975; Kassimoto, 1987; Puja, 2003). Another reason why girls drop out of school is because of arranged marriages.

Sexual and reproductive health education is important in Tanzania because girls are also likely to be sexually harassed in the schools. Although sexual harassment exists in educational institutions, as it does in the rest of Tanzanian society, it was not adequately defined, studied, or addressed until 1998 when the Sexual Offences Special Provision Act was enacted (United Republic of Tanzania, 1998). Research indicates that girls' performance begins to deteriorate when they reach puberty since older boys, male teachers, and the public in general intimidate girls by focusing more on their sexual attributes than on their academic needs and performances (TADREG, 1990). I am not aware of any Tanzanian-based study that examines how girls' sexuality influences their academic performance and why Tanzanian educators and administrators spend more physical and monetary resources on how to control girls' sexuality and behaviour than in satisfying girls' needs for academic success.

WOMEN'S ENROLMENT AND SPECIALIZATION IN UNIVERSITY PROGRAMS

Despite the increases in participation of women at lower levels of education, according to government reports in the 1990s, the participation of women at higher levels, like at the University of Dar es Salaam (UDSM) has not changed appreciably (United Republic of Tanzania, 1992b). In 1990 women students represented 18.78 per cent of student enrolment at the University of Dar es Salaam and 15.4 per cent at the Sokoine University of Agriculture (SUA). Combined enrolment figures for two public universities, UDSM and SUA, show that women made up 18.38 per cent of the total student enrolment; that is, among the 3,210 students enrolled in these universities only 590 of them were women (United Republic of Tanzania, 1992b). Enrolment figures in various degree programs also consistently indicated that most women students were concentrated in the social science and arts programs and were under-represented in the technical and science programs.

In the academic year 1993–94, women made up 27.69 per cent of students in the Bachelor of Arts, Education program and 18.55 per cent in the Bachelor of Arts general program. These were two of the few programs in which women's enrolment was high at the UDSM. In the other programs, there were either very few women or women were absent altogether. For example, in the academic year 1993–94, there were only seven women in the Bachelor of Science, Computer Program, two in the Bachelor of Science Geology Program, and another two in the Bachelor of Science Agricultural Engineering Program (United Republic of Tanzania, 1994). Similarly, most of the women enrolled in SUA in 1993–94 were in the Bachelor of Science, Agriculture General Program, making up 18.39 per cent of the total enrolment. There were only three female students in the Bachelor of Veterinary Medicine Program, and only one woman was enrolled in the Bachelor of Science Horticulture Program. No woman was enrolled in the Bachelor of Science Agricultural Engineering Program, which is offered in collaboration with the Faculty of Engineering at the UDSM (United Republic of Tanzania, 1994). Figures also show that the same trend of women's under-representation in higher education continues at the Open University of Tanzania, established in 1992. The tendency for many women to be enrolled in the BA Education Program is also revealed in these figures, which indicate that there were 40 women among the 359 students (11 per cent) in the BA program.

In contrast to other Tanzanian universities during this era, the Muhimbili University College of Health Science (MUCHS) had the highest women's enrolment in the country with 34 per cent female students in various programs (United Republic of Tanzania, 1994). Women's enrolment in the Doctor of Medicine program was the highest for all university programs in Tanzania, totalling 36 per cent in 1993–94, and, since medicine in seen as a male profession, it is interesting to note that the percentage of women in the Doctor of Medicine program at Muhimbili rose from 22 per cent in 1989–90 to 36 per cent in 1993–94. Therefore, there is a need to explore and effectively use the factors that have contributed to an increase in female undergraduate enrolment in this program. Overall, however, data from degree programs confirm that women are under-represented in most university programs and that this under-representation is more serious in the science and technological programs. According to the Ministry of Education and Culture (2003), women represented less than 5 per cent of students enrolled in engineering programs in Tanzania by the 2001–2002 academic year.

WOMEN IN TECHNICAL EDUCATION IN TANZANIA

Technical education in Tanzania has historically excluded women. While men were taught such skills as carpentry and masonry, women were taught sewing, cooking, washing, and ironing skills, which, at best, would prepare them to be housewives. This systematic gender-based discrimination is perpetuated by the educational policy-makers and planners in Tanzania, who give lip service to gender equity in the provision of technical education. An analysis of statistical data from the three technical colleges in Tanzania (Dar es Salaam, Arusha, and Mbeya) confirms that systematic gender discrimination continues to exist in technical education.

Statistical data for the periods of 1989–90 and 1993–94 show that women were not enrolled in some programs, including the Full Technician Certificate (FTC) in Mechanical and Civil Engineering. Women were only enrolled in FTC Electrical and Telecommunication and in FTC Laboratory Technology. The total enrolment for

Dar es Salaam, Arusha, and Mbeya Technical Colleges for the 1993–94 academic year was 1,826 students, of which only 118 (6.5 per cent) were women (United Republic of Tanzania, 1994), which confirms the dominant view that technical education in Tanzania is a "male subject" and is unsuitable for women.

Many factors contribute to gender inequity in post-secondary and technical education. One factor has to do with Tanzania's social and cultural practices. In Tanzania, women's voices are devalued and their problems are not seen as a priority; hence, their low social status. This perception of women is also reflected in the sexual division of labour, the pervasiveness of sexual harassment, and the type of educational policies and programs that are designed for female students. The sexual division of labour at home denies women students time for studies; consequently, most of them perform poorly in school examinations and are not selected for post-secondary education. These factors influence the way female students see themselves and their educational expectations and performance. There is a need for detailed studies that examine the extent to which girls' participation in household chores affects their academic performance. This research should also examine how other factors such as early marriages interact with participation in household chores as well as with performance.

In Tanzania, girls are expelled from school if they are married early or become pregnant. In 1991, 45,487 primary school children dropped out of school and 48 per cent of them were girls. Among those who dropped out of school, 2,046 of them did so due to pregnancy (Tanzania Gender Networking Programme, 1993). Furthermore, although girls are sexually harassed at all levels of schooling, the effects of sexual harassment on their academic performance have not been adequately analyzed. Although Mosha (1991) established that sexual harassment exists at the UDSM, she did not explore how experiences of sexual harassment affect female students' participation, their academic performance, or their future employment opportunities. Elsewhere, I argue that, unlike male students, female undergraduates in Tanzanian university campuses live and study under a very hostile environment, especially those enrolled in male-dominated programs such as engineering. They are also likely to experience four types of violence on campus: physical, structural, symbolic (including psychological violence), and everyday violence (Puja, 2003). It is apparent that there is an urgent need to study how sexual harassment influences girls' educational and career opportunities at all levels of education in the labour market.

EDUCATIONAL POLICY FACTORS

To begin, some policy initiatives like the quota system that were aimed at improving girls' access to and success in higher education ended up producing the direct opposite results in that girls' performance in secondary school examinations did not improve and, in some regions, deteriorated. The basic problem with the quota system was that it was based on a deficit model, which viewed students as a problem to be managed. Streaming, or the vocationalization of secondary education, in the 1970s also contributed to the current gender inequity in higher and technical education by denying female students certain subject combinations and by streaming many girls into the Domestic Science/Home Economics or Human Nutrition, which did not prepare them for either higher or technical education. In cases where streaming allowed for entry into higher education, such as in the case of Home Economics and Human Nutrition at the Sokoine University of Agriculture, girls who specialized in this degree program had fewer and limited employment opportunities when compared with those who specialized in other science fields such as engineering and medicine.

Teaching resources in science and technology are also based on boys' or men's experiences. For example, the use of machines in teaching mathematics and physical sciences is based on boys' interests, further marginalizing female students who already feel alienated by the educational system. The absence of female role models and female mentors is yet another problem. Apart from the Teacher Assistance in Mathematics and Science (TEAMS) Project at the University of Dar es Salaam that was funded by the Dutch government, whose major goal was to increase the number of science teachers in Tanzanian secondary schools, most science and technical subjects in schools are taught by male teachers. Put differently, gender-blind policies deny female students opportunities to learn from positive female role models. At the University of Dar es Salaam, for example, there are very few female academic staff members in senior positions, and the few that are on staff are mainly working in the social sciences. Information unveils that in 1993–94 there were only two female full professors at the University of Dar es Salaam, both of whom were in the social sciences. By the year 2000–2001, the situation had not changed considerably because there were only five female full professors compared to forty male full professors. But the number of female academicians slowly rises as one goes down the ladder from full professor to assistant professor to lecturer to tutorial assistant levels. In 2000–2001, for instance, there were twenty female lecturers compared to 169 male lecturers but there were only nine female assistant professors while there were 103 male assistant professors (University of Dar es Salaam, 2001).

EMPLOYMENT IMPLICATIONS FOR WOMEN IN TANZANIA

There is a direct link between education and employment for women. The 2000–2001 Integrated Labour Survey Analytical Report (United Republic of Tanzania, 2001b) states, among other things, that, in general, males in the country have higher average monthly incomes compared to females. The same report indicates that more men than women are employed in the Legislators/Administrators/Managers occupation category, a high-paying and high-status category that requires post-secondary education. Women's poor economic status has to be understood in light of their low level of education and their under-representation in post-secondary education. Galabawa (2005) clearly points out that women's economic benefits from education are limited by, among other things, the "unequal education opportunities at all levels of education system … and those who receive education tend to choose areas of study which reflect the breakdown of occupations into male and female sectors" (p. 62). Consequently, the end results are labour-market earnings that are differentiated by gender.

The overall illiteracy rate for women in Tanzania is higher than that of men, and it contributes to the types of work done by women and the incomes they earn. According to the 1988 Tanzanian Census report, only 0.06 per cent of employed women had an education and, of those employed, 0.3 per cent had a university education. The census report also shows that 55.88 per cent of the employed women had never been to school, while 33.25 per cent of the employed men had never been to school. Women's poor education translates into their annual cash earnings. In 1984, women's annual cash earnings in regular employment (public and private) were Tanzanian Shillings 1,091.7 million, compared to Tanzanian Shillings 6,275 million for men. The situation has not changed because, based on the findings of the Integrated Labour Survey Analytical Report for the years 2000–2001, the mean monthly income of males is higher than that of females (United Republic of Tanzania, 2001b). For instance, data on mean monthly income of paid employees by occupation and gender in 2000–2001 in the Professional occupation category was Tanzanian Shillings 94,606, while the mean monthly income of males in the same occupational category was Tanzanian Shillings 148,253.

NEW DIRECTIONS

Tanzania is cited as one of the African countries that has attained gender parity at the primary school level (Mugoni & Madziwa, 2004). This observation is supported by primary education statistics, which indicate that in 2004 girls were 50 per cent of the children enrolled in Standard 1 (first grade) in government primary schools (Ministry of Education and Culture, 2004). However, the transition rate from primary to secondary education is higher for boys than it is for girls. The existence of fewer secondary schools for girls than for boys, early and often arranged marriages, pregnancies, and many other factors all play into the difficulties faced disproportionately by women. For instance, in 2003, although girls were 50 per cent of the candidates who sat for the Primary School Leaving Examination, only 32.55 per cent of them passed (Ministry of Education and Culture, 2003). This gender gap in school performance calls for new strategies examining and addressing factors that contribute to girls' poor performance in national examinations to ensure quality education for girls aimed at increasing their chances to pursue secondary and post-secondary education and expand their chances of employment.

Similarly, efforts should be made at the secondary school level to ensure that there are career-counselling services to enable girls to make informed decisions about subject choices leading to better career opportunities such as in high-paying professional jobs typically requiring science and technology expertise.

It is anticipated that, with the implementation of the Education Sector Development Programme (ESDP), especially through the Secondary Education Master Plan (SEMP), the Higher Education Master Plan (HEMP), and the Technical Education Master Plan (TEMP), which were launched by the Tanzanian government in 2003, there will be a new emphasis on the need to pay attention to mainstreaming gender at all levels of education.

One of the Tanzanian educational institutions that has made progress in taking gender into account is the UDSM, which has since the early 1990s taken special measures to alleviate the gender gap that exists at the university. As a result of a female student committing suicide at the UDSM in 1990 because of sexual harassment and other gender-specific issues, a Gender Dimension Task Force (GDTF) was formed in 1996. Among other things, the GDTF carried out a gender analysis of students' enrolment, staff recruitment, and gender awareness among the university community. Based on the findings of the study, gender issues were included in the University of Dar es Salaam Institutional Transformation Programme (ITP) known as UDSM 2000, which lasted from 1994 to 2000. Under the ITP, the Gender Dimension Task Force was upgraded into a Gender Dimension Program Committee (GDPC) that is chaired by the male UDSM Chief Academic Officer, who appointed a female academician to be the "Desk Officer." The GDPC has initiated and carried out a number of gender-specific initiatives, including the following:

1. The establishment of the Female Undergraduate Scholarship Program (FUSP);
2. The extension of the Pre-entry Program (PEP) that was originally meant for female science teachers to include female engineers and female undergraduates in medicine;
3. Gender-mainstreaming at the University of Dar es Salaam; which is "a commitment to ensure that all

women's as well as men's concerns and experiences are integrated to the design, implementation, monitoring and evaluation of all legislation, policies and programs so that women and men benefit equally and that inequality is not perpetuated... Gender mainstreaming is integral to all development decisions and interventions; it concerns the staffing, procedures and cultures of development organizations as well as their programs and it forms part of the responsibility of all staff" (Leach, 2003, p. 12).

4. The establishment of the Anti-Sexual Harassment Policy of the University of Dar es Salaam in 2004 (University of Dar es Salaam, 2006a);
5. The implementation of a proposed UDSM Gender Policy (University of Dar es Salaam, 2005); and
6. A proposed UDSM Gender Centre (University of Dar es Salaam, 2006b).

Another initiative of the UDSM aimed at increasing the number of female students is the lower "cut-off points" for female undergraduate applicants in various degree programs. This procedure implies that female applicants who meet the admission criteria but have one point less than male applicants, especially when there is high competition for places of admission, are admitted into the degree programs for which they qualify.

While these efforts of the UDSM are highly commendable, most of them are externally funded. For instance, the Female Undergraduate Scholarship Program is funded by the Carnegie Foundation of New York and the Pre-entry program and others are supported by the donor community with minimal financial commitment from the Tanzanian government and the University of Dar es Salaam. This implies that the sustainability of such promising efforts is in jeopardy once the external funding sources withdraw. In addition, these efforts should be linked to addressing how primary and secondary education play an important role in preparing students for university.

Moreover, the application of the lower cut-off points for female students should be used with care, and it should be viewed as temporary so as not to create an impression that girls' poor performance in national examination is either natural or permanent. Instead, efforts should focus on examining the root causes of girls' poor performance at the lower grades and suggest ways to eliminate or minimize them. There is also a need to address gender issues in post-secondary education and employment opportunities in relation to other sites of differentiation in education that include regional variation (rural versus urban), religion, ethnicity, and the economy. Finally, the Ministry of Education and Culture should put in place a recruitment policy aimed at ensuring gender equity in employment, especially in areas where women are under-represented.

This discussion of gender, post-secondary education, and employment opportunities for women suggests that gender inequity in Tanzania exists at all levels of education but that it is more pronounced in higher and technical education. Gender inequity that exists at the lower levels of education lays the foundation for gender inequity in higher and technical education. In Tanzania, like in many African countries, the role of education, especially higher and technical education, in empowering women has not been well examined. Yet, existing literature indicates that factors contributing to gender inequity in higher and technical education are partly rooted in societal norms, colonial heritage, traditions, and beliefs about woman's role in society. These value systems are often not questioned, although they are reflected in the planning and provision of education in Tanzania at all levels, particularly at the post-secondary and technical education. Societal and historical factors interact with external factors such as the implementation of the Structural Adjustment Programs (SAPs) designed by the World Bank in collaboration with the International Monetary Fund and African governments.

These SAPs translate into educational policy reforms aimed at decentralization, privatization, and/or liberalization. Consequently, provision of education in Africa is directed not by the desire to promote social equity but by market forces whose major focus is economic benefit of international, regional, and local financial organizations.

There is need for further research on factors that inhibit women's participation in post-secondary and technical education from a gender perspective. Such a study would examine educational policy, planning and administration of education, the curriculum, and classroom processes. Such a study would also explore how power is negotiated as well as how issues of sexuality and gender roles are handled. Research has indicated that, in the Tanzanian social structure, women and girls are considered the inferior group with few or no economic resources, while boys and men are considered the superior group with wealth and power (Mushi, 1999). To break this cycle, further research has also to focus on gender relations and the economic structure and how these two factors limit the education of girls from an early age. The research should also suggest alternative strategies to overcome structural barriers that limit women's participation in post-secondary education in Tanzania. The initiatives made by the UDSM should be emulated at the lower levels of education in order to examine factors that inhibit girls' and women's active participation in post-secondary education programs. There should be a more serious commitment by the Tanzanian government in terms of allocating resources and in ensuring gender is mainstreamed in education policy, planning, and administration.

REFERENCES

Dei, G.J.S., & Asgharzadeh, A. (2001). The power of social theory: Towards an anti-colonial discursive framework. *Journal of Educational Thought, 35*(3), 297–323.

Galabawa, J.C.J. (2005). Returns to investment in education: Startling re-evaluations and alternatives before Tanzanians. *Professorial Inaugural Lecture Series No. 45,* Dar es Salaam: University of Dar es Salaam.

Hongoke, C. (1991). Consequences of educational planning on the future careers of girls in Tanzania. In B. Brock-Utne & N. Katunzi (Eds.), *Women, Education, Development (WED) Report No. 3: Twelve papers from a conference,* September 1990 at the Institute of Development Management (IDM), Mzumbe in Collaboration with the Women's Group, IDM. Dar es Salaam: Women Education Development, pp. 64–77.

Jones, P. W. (1992). *World Bank financing of education.* Washington, DC: World Bank.

Kassimoto, T. J. (1987). Attitudes of parents, students and ex-pregnant school girls on the expulsion of pregnant girls from school. A case study of selected schools and areas in the Dar es Salaam and Mbeya regions. MA thesis, University of Dar es Salaam, Tanzania.

Leach, F. (2003). *Practicing gender analysis in education. Oxfam skills and practice.* London: Oxfam GB.

Makobwe, K. M. (1975). *Towards family life education in Tanzania schools, possibilities and constraints.* MA thesis, University of Dar es Salaam, Tanzania.

Malekela, G. A. (1999). Access to equity in university education in Tanzania, *Perspectives in Education, 15*(1), 34–36.

Ministry of Education and Culture. (1990). *Basic education statistics in education.* Dar es Salaam: Ministry of Education and Culture.

Ministry of Education and Culture. (1997). *Basic education statistics in education.* Dar es Salaam: Ministry of Education and Culture.

Ministry of Education and Culture. (2003). *Basic education statistics in education*. Dar es Salaam: Ministry of Education and Culture.

Ministry of Education and Culture. (2004). *Basic education statistics in education*. Dar es Salaam: Ministry of Education and Culture.

Mosha, E. (1991). "Sexual harassment and other problems for girls in Tanzania," In: Brock-Utne B. and N. Katunzi (Eds). *Women and Education in Tanzania: Twelve papers from a seminar*. WED Report No.3:116–123.

Mugoni, P., & Madziwa C. (2004). *Gender parity in education: Count down to 2005*. Gender and Development Newsletter for Southern Africa.

Mushi, S. L. (1999). Preparing Tanzania's young children for the economic world: Possibilities for collaboration with other countries. ERIC Document (ED436463).

Nyerere, J. K. (1967). *Education for self reliance*. Dar es Salaam: Government Printer.

Omari, I. (2002). Editorial: Education in Tanzania since independence. *Papers in Education, 22*, v–xiii.

Puja, G. K. (2003). Gender violence in Tanzanian university campuses. *Papers in Education, 23*, 110–26.

Rodney, W. (1972). *How Europe under-developed Africa*. Dar es Salaam: Tanzania Publishing House.

Steady, F. C. (1985). African women at the end of the decade. *Africa Report, 30*(2), 4

TADREG (Tanzania Development Research Group). (1990). *Girls' educational opportunities and performance in Tanzania*, Dar es Salaam: Research Report No. 2.

Tanzania Gender Networking Program. (1993). *Gender profile of Tanzania*. Dar es Salaam: TGNP.

United Republic of Tanzania. (1992a). *Population census, national profile: Basic demographic and socio-economic characteristics*. Dar es Salaam: Bureau of Statistics, Presidents' Office, Planning Commission.

United Republic of Tanzania. (1992b). *Women and men in Tanzania*. Dar es Salaam: Bureau of Statistics, Presidents' Office, Planning Commission.

United Republic of Tanzania. (1994). *Higher and technical statistics, 1989/90–1993/94*. Dar es Salaam: Ministry of Science, Technology and Higher Education.

United Republic of Tanzania. (1995). *Education and training policy*, Dar es Salaam: Ministry of Education and Culture.

United Republic of Tanzania. (1998). *The sexual offences special provision act, 1998*. Dar es Salaam.

United Republic of Tanzania. (2001a). *Education Sector Development Programme: Primary Education Development Plan (PEDP)*. Dar es Salaam: Ministry of Education and Culture.

United Republic of Tanzania. (2001b). *Integrated labour force survey 2000/01: Income of employed population-analytical report*. Retrieved January 3, 2006, from http://www.nbs.go.tz/publications/index.htm.

United Republic of Tanzania. (2003). *Basic statistics in education, 1999–2003*. Dar es Salaam: Ministry of Education and Culture.

United Republic of Tanzania (2006). *Hotuba ya Waziri wa Elimu na Mafunzo ya Ufundi, Mheshimiwa Margaret Simwanza Sitta (Mb). Kuhusu Makadirio ya matumizi ya fedha kwa mwaka 2006/2007*. Dar es Salaam: Government Printer.

University of Dar es Salaam. (2001). *Institutional Transformation Programme, PMU/ UDSM 2000: Facts and figures 2000/2001*. Dar es Salaam: University of Dar es Salaam Transformation Programme Management Unit.

University of Dar es Salaam. (2005). *Study report on the establishment of gender centre at the University of Dar es Salaam*. Gender Dimension Programme Committee.
University of Dar es Salaam. (2006a). *University of Dar es Salaam anti-sexual harassment policy*. Dar es Salaam: UDSM Gender Dimension Programme Committee.
University of Dar es Salaam. (2006b). *University of Dar es Salaam Gender Policy*. Gender Dimension Programme Committee.

ABBREVIATIONS

BA Education	Bachelor of Arts with Education
EFA	Education for All
ESDP	Education Sector Development Programme
ESR	Education for Self-Reliance
FUSP	Female Undergraduate Scholarship Program
GDPC	Gender Dimension Program Committee
GDTF	Gender Dimension Task Force
HEMP	Higher Education Master Plan
HESLB	Higher Education Student Loan Board
IDM	Institute of Development Management
IMF	International Monetary Fund
ITP	Institutional Transformation Programme
MOEC	Ministry of Education and Culture
MOEVT	Ministry of Education and Vocational Training
MOSTHE	Ministry of Science, Technology and Higher Education
MUCHS	Muhimbili University College of Health Sciences
PCM	Physics, Chemistry and Mathematics
PEDP	Primary Education Development Plan
PEP	Pre-entry Programme
PGM	Physics, Geography and Mathematics
PSLE	Primary School Leaving Examination
SAPs	Structural Adjustment Programs
SEMP	Secondary Education Master Plan
TADREG	Tanzania Development Research Group
TEAMS	Teacher Assistance in Mathematics and Science
TEMP	Technical Education Master Plan
TGNP	Tanzania Gender Networking Program
UDSM	University of Dar es Salaam
UPE	Universal Primary Education
WB	World Bank

Notes

1 By 1961 Zanzibar was a British protectorate ruled through the Sultan of Oman. In 1963 Zanzibar became independent from the British but continued to be ruled by the Sultan of Oman until 12 January 1964 when there was a revolution. In the same year Zanzibar and Tanganyika joined to form the United Republic of Tanzania. The author has not come across the primary and secondary education statistics for Zanzibar for 1961. Moreover post-secondary education is a union matter. Therefore students in post-secondary institutions are either from Zanzibar or Tanzania Mainland.

2 Makerere in Uganda was the only existing university in the region serving the needs of mainly Kenya, Uganda, and Tanzania.

3 Effective December 2005, the "Ministry of Education and Culture" was renamed and changed to the "Ministry of Education and Vocational Training" (MOEVT) under the new Tanzanian government that came to power following the 14 December 2005 general elections.

5

INFORMATION TECHNOLOGY AND THE CURRICULUM PROCESS: STUDENT PARTICIPATION AND THE CHANGED ROLE OF THE TEACHER

Selina L. P. Mushi

ABSTRACT

This chapter discusses students' free and unlimited access to an ever-expanding information base in North America in comparison to limited student access and use of IT in Tanzania. The author demonstrates that in North America, where IT is highly advanced, a major challenge is to make IT accessible to all segments of the population, thus reducing what has been termed the digital divide. The author analyzes the organizational, cultural, and educational values of the Tanzanian society, and shows that emerging IT needs have to be contextualized. She argues that the need for and development of IT expertise must target skills useful for solving practical problems in society, and at the same time, be mindful of practical applications globally. In presenting new directions for IT development in Tanzania, the author argues that teachers in both industrialized and developing countries need to engage in professional development workshops to hone their skills to empower students in the use of IT for meaningful and independent problem-solving within the curriculum. She also warns that these problem-solving skills must function effectively in the context of the current global society. Then she outlines new directions for Tanzania and other developing countries for determining contextual needs of IT in order for these countries to become active participants in both the production and consumption of IT globally.

INTRODUCTION

Information Technology (IT) has made tremendous amounts of information accessible through computer networks within the industrialized world. The quantities of information available through IT networks continue to increase and the information being accessed by students has changed the traditional ways of school learning while casting important questions on the curriculum process. The traditional perception of students as mere recipients of pre-planned curricula has changed over time to the perception that students are active participants in their own learning. Advancements in IT have made students even more active, self-motivated learners who are explorers of the Internet in search of information of their liking. Students of all ages browse the Internet, websites, CDs – some of which come free of charge, and use e-mail to communicate worldwide. Access to information exposes students to different ideas and notions, which are related both to the curriculum and to everyday life. It is now obvious that IT will continue to influence major decisions made in the school system and in society in general.

More than a decade ago, Cummins and Sayers (1995) predicted that: "In the world of the twenty-first century, decision-making and problem-solving in virtually all spheres – business, science, community development, government, politics – will depend on electronic networks that span diverse national and cultural boundaries" (p. 12). Today, teenagers and college students in North America are experiencing "life online" (Rainie, 2005) as they easily access and use IT in e-mailing, downloading music files, remixing and sharing music, etc. Discussing the special world of teens and college students and implications for learning contexts, Rainie points out that these students "see the Internet as a virtual textbook and reference library, virtual tutor and study short cut, virtual study group, virtual guidance counsellor, virtual locker, backpack and notebook and a trusted, smart friend" (slide 12).

The fast pace of IT advancements seems to speed up the life of knowledge. While knowledge was measured in decades and probably even in centuries due to the slow pace of its transmission, this is no longer the case in the twenty-first century. According to Gonzalez (2004), the amount of knowledge in the world has doubled in the past ten years, and the life of knowledge is shrinking more and more, meaning that knowledge is being created and simultaneously fading faster than ever before. This evolution in the use of IT calls for new skills at the workplace, and in turn the school system ought to feel the pressure to incorporate IT skills into the curriculum.

Although schools, teachers, and curriculum planners have generally embraced IT as a formal part of learning, it seems the education sector has been slower than other sectors in incorporating IT in the organized curriculum. For example, reviewing Michigan State's Five Year Technology Plan, Fitzpatrick (1994) saw education as the last major labour-intensive industry to begin to use technology in its day-to-day business. Expressing concern for the State of Michigan, Fitzpatrick pointed out that out of the state's 524 K–12 school districts only six had a direct connection to the Internet, and of the fifty-seven Intermediate School Districts none had direct Internet connectivity. Eleven years later, White (2005) notes that while information technologies have greatly transformed the practice of business, manufacturing, administration, finance, and the provision of other services, IT has yet to impact on the delivery of education and training in a similar way. Peha (2005) concurs with White's conclusion and points out that schools have been slow to adopt technology as part of conducting everyday business.

Given the speed of growth of IT, it is close to impossible to determine what changes will be in place five years from now. At the moment, students in Canadian and American schools, like students in other industrialized countries who have easy access to the Internet at home and at school, are becoming increasingly conversant with various information storage and retrieval systems without formal school curricula having to include those skills. This unlimited exposure to IT interacts with students' experiences in the curriculum process, yet the consequences of this interaction on students' learning and their ability to evaluate and critique what they learn are not well known to teachers and curriculum planners. Classroom teachers, who function as links between the planned curriculum and its actual implementation and evaluation, are challenged by this situation where students' exposure to, and use of, IT may exceed that of their teachers.

While top-down curriculum planning predetermines the goals of schooling in general, bottom-up curriculum processes provide opportunities to examine IT classroom needs at local levels, so that students can get more challenging learning activities at school. In many developing countries, including Tanzania, the top-down approach to curriculum planning is the norm, thus making it challenging to determine IT needs at local levels. As a result of the high accessibility to IT by students, in industrialized nations, studies need to focus more on how IT is affecting student learning. In developing countries, such as Tanzania, the major task involves introducing bottom-up approaches to the curriculum process so that teachers can determine contextual needs for IT at local levels to supplement the dominant top-down curriculum process. What follows is a discussion of the digital divide found within a given country as well as between different countries. As well, there is discussion of the IT lessons that developing countries can learn from the industrialized world. A more important discussion centres on the need to contextualize IT needs for Tanzania while ensuring that Tanzanians are both active consumers and producers of IT.

DIGITAL DIVIDE WITHIN NORTH AMERICA

The education industry versus the business sector

Effective teaching is not "delivering education"; rather, it involves providing students with opportunities to create, own, develop, and use knowledge to solve problems in their school learning activities as well as in their daily lives. Students have to be given opportunities to connect learned IT skills to problem-solving in real life contexts. Siemens (2004) suggests *connectivism* as a learning theory for the digital age. There are no pre-packaged solutions that can be delivered intact to students or teachers and work for all students in all situations. While there is a big push to make the education industry adopt technology quickly and in similar ways as the business sector, effort needs to be spent on why and how the education industry is different from other sectors where the goods processed are not human beings. Furthermore, the education sector needs to be considered in its own right rather than in comparison to other sectors where uniformity among goods is assumed. Teachers need to develop appropriate and conducive opportunities for students to seek out new ways of creating contextual knowledge, skills, and dispositions that will enable students to learn effectively as individuals while collaborating with other members of society in the effort to improve the quality of human life. Effective learning and use of IT skills within the curriculum cannot be mass-implemented since teachers' knowledge of individual students' learning patterns and utilization of IT skills is necessary. Due to the nature of the education sector, therefore, teachers need to be effectively involved in making decisions about teaching and learning processes that can make IT a positive experience for students. In the United States, the effects of the digital divide in the curriculum include discrepancies between the education sector and business sectors, student accessibility to computers, and assessing the learning of IT skills, among others.

Student accessibility to computers

Children in their teen years and younger constitute the generation that has grown up with computers in their households in most parts of North America. This generation is embracing IT as a normal part of life. However, there seems to be a considerable discrepancy between IT skills offered and utilized in school curricula and IT skills that children already have when they begin school. There is need for the organized curriculum to realistically assess and include students' already acquired IT skills in their learning, in order to close the gap between what students learn at home and what they learn in classrooms.

Secondly, computers are not evenly distributed in North American schools. In the United States, while most students in some communities own MP3 players and engage in constant instant messaging and downloading from the Internet (Tetlegah & Hunter, 2006), and while students from higher family income levels have early access to computers and show significantly higher levels of full-spectrum technology use (Ching et al., 2005), other students from lower income families lag behind (Kalyanpur & Kimani, 2005; Chinget al., 2005). School boards and districts strive to provide appropriate IT access to all educators and students. However, it is evident that a significant digital divide still exists in the United States. Poor communities in urban areas are often poorly equipped when it comes to digital media (DiBello, 2005).

Since schools are organized into school districts, parents' choices of schools where they can send their children are limited, as they are determined by the school district to which they belong. If the families cannot afford home computers, then the children will be lagging behind because their schools will most likely not have enough computers either, since the socio-economic status of an area tends to predetermine the economic situation of the school. In other words, children of poor families go to poorly equipped schools, which then limit students' chances of accessing and developing IT skills, thus threatening the efforts to narrow the digital divide within the same country that is technologically advanced. Other factors such as age, gender, disability, and culture also determine the extent to which students in the United States access and utilize computer technology (Ching et al., 2005; Kalyanpur & Kimani, 2005).

Assessing the learning of IT skills

In the United States and Canada, assessment and evaluation of learning outcomes are typically done in a bottom-up fashion where internal evaluation may carry more weight than external evaluation. In standardized testing, however, schools are evaluated according to pre-established goals and strict standards. It is unlikely that children in poor neighbourhoods will achieve the pre-determined IT standards if their homes and schools have few or no computers. To evaluate students more effectively, student and family input is necessary so that the entire context of living and learning is evaluated, rather than just the products of school learning.

Where the curriculum includes IT skills as standards to be achieved by students after a prescribed program, anecdotal information indicates that, on the one hand, some students come to the IT programs already proficient in most of those skills, while, on the other hand, other students cannot even achieve the expected skills by the end of the program, due to lack of, or limited access to, computers outside school. Research has indicated that some families cannot afford to buy home computers, leading to their children only getting exposure to IT at school. This has led to what some researchers refer to as the "digital divide" (Graham, 2002; Campbell, 2001; Looker & Thiessen, 2003). The effect of this "divide" will be long-lasting in individual learners, families, and communities if the problem is not addressed seriously and in a timely manner.

THE DIGITAL DIVIDE BETWEEN INDUSTRIALIZED AND DEVELOPING COUNTRIES

In developing countries, the situation is very different from that of industrialized countries in that mere communication through electronic mail, for instance, is still a new phenomenon in many schools today. E-mail use, which is widely accepted because of its time-saving nature, is only common in cities. People can use it to arrange meetings, or even discuss important issues, therefore cutting down meeting times. However, only a few people have easy access to e-mail such as, in the case of Tanzania, professors in universities and other high-ranking professionals in government offices.

In Tanzania, computer literacy is rare in primary schools and teacher preparation colleges. In fact, traditionally, if a college or university student was not being prepared to work as a secretary, there was no perceived need for that student to acquire typing skills and, more recently, computer literacy, including word-processing. In Tanzanian academic communities, it is still generally perceived that mental work or thinking skills are superior to the how-to knowledge of using tools like calculators or computers to simply ease the operational tasks. A scholar is seen as someone whose role is to engage in mostly mental work; that is, reason and think in order to create new knowledge relevant for problem-solving in his or her area of specialty. Those people who are charged with less thinking responsibilities can then utilize the knowledge created by the "thinker," using any tools available to them, including computer technology. In the recent years, however, these "thinkers" have begun to develop computer interest and are acquiring computer skills such as word processing and use of statistical packages and graphics. Time will tell what impact the growing reliance on technological skills will have on these traditionally powerful academic minds.

The introduction of general technology tools such as calculators and computers has left parents concerned about the education their children receive in schools. For instance, in some cases, parents have shown concern for their children doing mathematical operations using calculators, rather than processing the arithmetic mentally in order to understand the reasoning behind the mathematical operation. Teachers and parents believe that students have to understand the reasoning first, before they strive to make the task easy to carry out. Once the thinking and rationale are in place, then the student can use shortcuts like the calculator or the computer to get the answer. Moreover, in lower levels of schooling, availability as well as the utility of specific IT skills determines the emphasis put on learning those skills. The utility of IT is one major factor that will determine the needs for learning IT skills in Tanzania. At the post-secondary level, such as at the University of Dar es Salaam, students have access to fully equipped computer labs, and they select the tools they need to do their academic work. Most students teach themselves how to use e-mail because of its utility, i.e., efficient communication. Worth noting is that most of these computers were obtained from industrialized countries such as Sweden, Norway, the Netherlands, and the United States; therefore, sustainability of IT access is an issue worth immediate attention.

As a result of the limited number of computers, it is quite possible for a Tanzanian student to go through primary school, secondary school, and university education without learning IT skills such as word processing and e-mail, which are taken for granted in industrialized countries. When students from Tanzania come to study in North American universities, they face the centrality of IT and its challenges in both their intended disciplines and as a necessary means for enhancing their learning in order to successfully complete their programs of study. Interestingly, Tanzanian students as well as other students from developing countries quickly catch up with the computer skills needed to successfully complete their programs of study, since they immediately realize there is high utility in learning those skills.

When I began my doctoral program in 1990, I sat in front of a computer for the first time in my life. I had gone through the system of education in Tanzania, had successfully completed a master's degree, and I had been teaching at the University of Dar es Salaam for three years. At the University of Toronto, I had to cope with the technology environments just like other students who had had opportunities to use computers from childhood. My program of study involved participation in online credit courses, thus the need to successfully pass those courses resulted in high energy and motivation to acquire the necessary IT skills.

For international students, financial sponsorship is intertwined with academic success; the consequence of failing a course is scholarship withdrawal. The challenges that international students face are much more intense than those faced by native students, who often have alternative financial resources. Furthermore, the need to catch up with the technological world is overwhelming for international students because of the pressure to succeed due to the sacrifices made by family in the country of origin to create an opportunity to study abroad. Therefore, it would be useful for the hosting universities to put resources in place that will help students arriving from developing countries around the world. Such resources will help the students to acquire at least proficient word-processing skills before they start their academic programs.

Recent curricular changes have been planned to introduce, at the primary and secondary levels, a new subject, TEAHAMA (short for "Teknolojia ya Habari na Mawasiliano;" which translates to "Information and Communication Technology" (Ministry of Education, 2005, p. vi). This new subject will help Tanzanian students learn computer skills for their everyday activities, as well as provide them with opportunities to use technology in advanced educational programs. This is a positive move that deserves effective implementation and evaluative follow-up.

SOME LESSONS FROM INDUSTRIALIZED COUNTRIES

The growth and spread of IT in industrialized nations provide some useful lessons for developing nations. Countries like Tanzania can draw important lessons at their early stages of embracing and using IT at different levels of the school system. The lessons include: how unlimited access to information relates to the curriculum process, the way some philosophical issues in teacher preparation are modified by the use of IT, the changed role of the teacher, the funding and management of IT programs in schools, and changes in ways of assessing students' performance.

Information access and school learning

The search for knowledge and new information has always been an integral part of school learning. The classroom teacher as the traditional primary source of knowledge was always looked up to for the provision of pre-sorted, well-organized information that was directly related to the school curriculum. Oftentimes, the information was related directly to portions of the curriculum on which evaluation of performance in the form of examination questions was likely to focus. Oftentimes teachers face the challenge of choosing between teaching for the standardized examination on which the quality of teaching and students' learning are judged and teaching to help students learn how to function in everyday life and professional situations. It is difficult to make a reasonable and completely acceptable choice between these two functions since one would facilitate the students' immediate survival (to the next stage of schooling) and the other would increase the students' chances of being productive members of society.

It takes careful screening and selection of information to sharpen the focus on the prescribed curricula geared towards achieving good grades. There is a gap between learning in school and learning how to interpret one's reality in order for an individual to function in self-relevant ways and at the same time contribute to society's well-being. School learning is often based on experiences of past generations of students, teachers, researchers, writers, and curriculum planners; therefore, it becomes a challenge for students to fulfill this interest and to focus on the *here and now – and the probable*. Until school learning becomes relevant and informs students how to adjust to, evaluate, and critique society, it will not be of immediate interest to students; thus, it will always lag behind IT in capturing students' interests. Teachers will have to continue to motivate students to learn in school, and one way to do so is to selectively incorporate IT into day-to-day problem-solving classroom practices, which in turn requires teachers' high competence in IT.

Philosophical issues in teacher preparation

When information technology started booming in the 1980s, teacher education in industrialized countries had been in place for about a century. In traditional teacher education, the school curriculum goals and objectives and the means for achieving them were predetermined and rigidly defined. Needless to say, it was difficult to dynamically reflect and take advantage of IT within the design of teacher preparation programs, due to the uniqueness of the industry. Providing more bottom-up opportunities for needs assessment and implementation of the curriculum goals and objectives has prompted changes in the way teacher education is evolving in Canada and the United States. There is no universal set of standards that teacher preparation programs can impress on new teachers to make them teach effectively at all times and in all places. However, Tanzania and other non-industrialized countries can learn from this factor and begin to open up for more bottom-up opportunities for teacher candidates and their educators to determine their IT needs locally and link them to the national curriculum. Importing technology from industrialized countries without modification will be a big mistake, since there is no package that can work out of context.

As discussed by Willis and Mehlinger (1996), within teacher education, computer-mediated learning has erroneously been perceived as a behavioural approach to teaching and learning. The behavioural approach to teaching and learning tends to condition the learner by use of reinforcements, both positive and negative, for specific behaviours. Positive reinforcements are rewards that encourage the learner to engage in certain behaviours, while negative reinforcements distinguish behaviours that are not preferred by the teacher, instructor, or program. The behavioural approach is problematic in that it overlooks the learner's intrinsic motivation to learn, namely, internal drive to learn and personal standards that the learner might want to achieve, in favour of often standardized teacher or institutional goals for learning. Utilization of present-day IT should look beyond these behavioural models, which resulted from the wave of programmed learning in the 1960s and 1970s (Willis & Mehlinger, 1996). Several computerized instruction packages have been developed that assume that teaching is a systematic process of solving problems. Schon (1991) referred to this as the "technical rationality" model. Developing IT needs locally will be more time-consuming but more effective in the long run. Contextually appropriate IT skills have to not only encourage higher-order critical thinking, but also call for, help develop, and support analytical skills to define and solve problems as part of the learning process.

Funding and management of IT

In the past decade, Information Technology was fraught with management problems such as deciding who is to maintain and update information in a timely manner and who will create standards (Langenberg, 1991). While this problem may no longer exist in North America, the problem of screening the information accessible to young children is a growing one. It is now an undisputable fact that there are unwanted types of exposures and information easily available to students at a young age. In some cases, for example, youngsters have learned on the Internet how to commit crime. It will be irresponsible for teachers, parents, and curriculum decision-makers to assume all information accessible on the Internet by young learners is constructive.

Funding has been identified as one of the most important problems facing the use of IT in teacher education (Willis & Mehlinger, 1996). Teacher education was (and still is in many cases) typically the least funded of professional programs in higher education in the United States. The old assumption was that teacher education did not require specialized laboratories, computers, and modern equipment available to other professional training programs. Willis and Mehlinger (1996) noted that some public schools were better equipped than the colleges in which their teachers had been trained. It is interesting to see that teacher education, irrespective of the nation's level of industrialization, has been lagging behind in terms of funding, and whenever it is necessary to cut funding, teacher education becomes the first victim. This tendency to cut funding in teacher education is also common in Tanzania and probably in other African countries as well. There is a Kiswahili proverb that explains this tendency. The proverb goes: "*ivushayo mbovu,*" meaning, after using the means to cross over to safety, that same means is deemed useless (or broken). Government officials and funding agencies need to keep in mind that each and every bureaucrat in a funding decision-making position must have been given at least some of the foundation for success by the school system which is nurtured by teacher education.

There are two major reasons to reasonably increase funding to teacher education programs. The first is to facilitate high quality teacher education programs with up-to-date access to computer and other IT equipment, so as to adequately prepare IT-competent teacher candidates who are capable of providing students the IT knowledge they need in order to have meaningful life opportunities. The second reason is that schools are now faced with a challenge to graduate students who have IT skills to use in everyday life. At the beginning of the twenty-first century, more and more individuals find IT skills a necessary tool for survival in, for example, running their own businesses. Concerns of funding are always a feature in discussions of improving education at all levels in Tanzania. However, it is now evident that the Government of Tanzania and the Ministry of Education need to step up and fund programs that aim to prepare the young population for life-sustaining IT skills. More and more primary, secondary, and university graduates in Tanzania are likely to engage in small businesses since the government sector can no longer absorb most graduates into the already saturated work force. It is important to study the core causes of differential funding, and the resulting consequences and possible appropriate approaches narrowing the technological gaps at the different levels need to be explored.

Validity of assessments

The purpose of conducting assessments is to use the resulting data to make informed decisions about learning needs, credentialing, and funding. Information collected for the purpose of determining how well learning outcomes have been achieved presupposes successful teaching. The teaching involves opportunities to interact with ideas, notions, materials, equipment, and guidance in order to achieve the intended learning outcomes. If certain groups of learners have not had these opportunities for learning, then, obviously, the learning outcomes have certainly not been achieved. Testing such groups of learners for the sake of comparing performance to that of other learners who have had rich learning opportunities is actually an ineffective way to test the effects of teaching since it fails to uncover the deprived students' learning contexts and is therefore invalid.

Secondly, there is a need to distinguish between assessment of students' competence in using IT skills and assessment of students' competence in the core content learned with or without IT. Ignoring this important distinction will render assessment data invalid for decision-making. Such considerations are important for developing countries as they introduce IT into the curriculum and, at the same time, aim to minimize the digital divide.

The changed role of the teacher

The teacher's role has changed and will continue to change as technologies advance and as the younger generation of students joins the profession. The fact that students are already accessing information based on their own interest has necessarily changed the role of the teacher, and teachers are likely to find themselves in tricky situations if they stick to the old curriculum that does not match students' ways of learning within context. Students can access information from their homes (sometimes under parents' supervision), in libraries, in cyber-cafes in search of enjoyable information that often does not relate to the homework they are expected to do in a timely fashion. This suggests that teachers must provide structures for processing the information that interest students and relate it to classroom content in interesting ways, which will result in effective learning. There is a need for the teacher to develop and constantly adjust structures for understanding the information accessed by students in ways that lead to coherent learning.

To guide students to learn, teachers themselves need to be informed about IT. North American teachers attend workshops and training in the use of different types of software, which helps hone their IT skills and develop the confidence they need to guide learners. Teaching and learning therefore go hand in hand and this is more so now due to IT advances. It is very unrealistic for teachers to assume they can continue teaching students who are much more technologically advanced than themselves, without engaging in IT in-service training.

Teachers who have, for the most part, been implementers of school curriculum will now assume the role of curriculum designers – a curriculum that addresses the needs of their local communities and students. This is not the same as narrowing down a topic or teaching according to the level of difficulty, as teachers have always done. It is a process of continually blending learning experiences with technological advances, while at the same time focusing on the important aspects of the school curriculum and on students' IT skills.

Core curriculum documents used by teachers are prepared by curriculum planners who need feedback from schools in order to revise the curriculum from time to time. The feedback will no longer be the teachers' personal comments on the process of implementing the curriculum; rather, it will be the teachers' suggestions for modifications based on the actual classroom process, in response to students' individual learning and relationships with technology. The teacher will need to continually moderate the curriculum to satisfy students' learning desires, and to incorporate changes curriculum planners see as necessary nation-wide. In these instances, the teacher becomes an important curriculum moderator, not just an implementer.

Teachers have always evaluated students' learning processes. However, what needs to be evaluated is changing. Instead of trying to judge who remembers more of last week's lesson, it might be more useful to ask what has been learned, how useful has it been, what other facts have been found, and what knowledge needs to be updated. In order for students to participate in such discussions, they have first to evaluate their own perceptions and understandings of previous learning experiences. The teacher will have to encourage learners to search, share, and evaluate information related to class content. Factual information will have to be continuously updated as students present their findings. The teacher's role as an evaluator of classroom learning thus will involve overseeing students' discussions and exchange of ideas, and the synthesis of these ideas, as well as the evaluation of their own learning processes. The teacher, in this sense, becomes a meta-evaluator.

TANZANIA: ORGANIZATION, CULTURES, AND THE EDUCATION SYSTEM

African societies have demonstrated different ways of life, compared to western societies. First, the typical African family is not defined by two parents and their offspring; rather, it is defined by a larger network of relationships and mutual understanding that is constantly being negotiated. In Tanzania a "family" can include up to three or four generations in the same homestead, different religious beliefs (especially through intermarriages), and also individuals from other bloodlines who have been accepted into the "family." Every member of the network has a role to play, and that role gives the individual a place and usefulness in the network, which creates unique relationships that are difficult to globalize. The ways in which IT is evolving in African countries, and in Tanzania in particular, are different from the ways it evolved in industrialized countries. Individuals see IT as a way to help them connect more strongly with their family members and society, on the one hand, and as a tool for connecting with the outside world academically, professionally, or in businesses, on the other.

Some African societies are highly organized from the grassroots to the national level. Tanzania offers an example of a highly organized society, where it is literally feasible for each individual to be well known starting at the family level throughout the hierarchy to the national level. This structure is a modification of traditional societal organization typical of pre-colonial times. The communication technology then ranged from mouth-to-ear to drumbeats or other kinds of sound-making devices, depending on the distance being covered by the communication. These information technologies kept societies connected and informed as was necessary for survival. Beginning in the 1960s, the Tanzanian rural society, which is about 64 per cent of the entire population of 36 million (United Nations Population Fund, 2003), has been organized according to a "Ten Cell" leadership, the village level, the communities, the district, regional, zonal, and national levels.

Every ten families make up a ten-cell unit of leadership with a leader known as a *balozi* (ambassador). The balozi is responsible for keeping order, resolving conflicts, communicating necessary information, and providing advice and general leadership within the unit. In this sense, any unwanted act in this unit is easily identified and acted upon accordingly. The dominant level of information technology used here is person-to-person, made possible by physical proximity. Radio and telephone are common outside media – not used to communicate from person to person within the ten-cell unit. Television sets are only additional and considerably rare tools used for *bringing in* information. There is no ten-cell-based radio broadcasting. Computer technology falls in this category of one-way, incoming information. This situation calls for developed IT skills to reciprocate communication.

Several of the ten-cell units make a village that operates under a village chairman, the *Mwenyekiti wa kijiji*, who keeps close contact with the ten-cell leaders. Information technology at this level includes mouth-to-ear (one-on-one, village meetings, leadership meetings, etc.), radio for news from higher levels in the organizational hierarchy, and sometimes telephones. At this level some villagers may have relatives who live in cities or in foreign countries and have learned how to communicate by e-mail with their family members who, in very limited cases, may also have a computer at home (in the village) and know how to retrieve and send e-mail. However, such communication from outside the village, and especially from a foreign country, is usually not about the village; it is about the outside world, outside culture, and outside values, which are, understandably, of secondary importance to the villagers.

Several villages make a *kata*, while several kata make a *tarafa*. At these levels of the organizational hierarchy, schools, health centres, security services, adult education programs, etc., are managed. Current information technologies at these levels include telephones, radio, e-mail (in rare cases), and television. It is common to see on national television that a certain tarafa has the highest harvest of corn, rice, wheat, or any other food or cash crop grown in that area. Information *originating* from the kata and tarafa is valuable in the sense that it is *owned by the people* of those places and also *shared with other Tanzanians* and beyond. The people are therefore not mere consumers of information, but also originators and communicators. It is important to note that information coming from a kata or tarafa will actually be from a specific village and maybe even a specific family. The organizational unit at this level needs to keep abreast of the functioning of schools within the area and maintain continued communication with all teachers. Some important decisions are made at this level regarding the running of schools; therefore, computer technology needs to be available both at the organizational unit and in the schools.

The districts and regions are much higher levels in the organizational hierarchy. Several districts report to one region. These levels include cities, schools, colleges, businesses (local and international), hospitals, police forces, etc. Districts are considerably self-managing in some areas, while in other areas they report to the region. Information technologies at these levels are mainly telephones, e-mail, some access to websites, internal computer networks, the Internet (typically a receiving-only utility), national television (a receiving and sending utility) external television (a receiving-only utility). There is relative anonymity of individuals living in large cities like Dar es Salaam, Morogoro, Dodoma, Arusha, Moshi, Mwanza, Mbeya, etc. This "weaker" internal connection between individuals makes it more likely to connect to the outside world through modern IT, where they become *consumers* of IT, mainly from the western world. To strengthen use of IT skills at these levels, the focus needs to be on schools and colleges. Due to city culture and the relative anonymity, Internet cafes are likely to be currently available where students and the general population learn some e-mail and word-processing skills. Individual cities and schools will have different needs, depending on what is already available.

There are seven zones in the hierarchy of the Tanzanian system of education. Each zone has several regions. Zones report to the national level, mainly in terms of educational decision-making involving secondary schools and colleges of teacher preparation. Since highly qualified professionals work at this level (secondary school teachers, high school teachers, college professors, doctors in referral hospitals, etc.), the need for, and likely use of, highly developed IT is unquestionable. Zones are also key units for teacher training in Tanzania. Currently, computer technology is available to differing extents, and equipment and training are provided by different organizations from some industrialized countries like Sweden, Norway, and Germany. There is need to train more educators in schools and colleges in order to strengthen IT skills for teachers and students. Training can be done locally and from external sources, where available and appropriate.

The national level is the highest organizational structure in Tanzanian society. Most sectors are highly centralized – education, agriculture, policing, etc., and bottom-up reporting is required. The need for advanced IT at this level is evident. Universities have advanced equipment for internal and external communication through computer networks. Universities are considered national and international institutions; therefore, the IT within these institutions is comparatively highly developed to the extent that even students have access to fully equipped and up-to-date computer labs.

These six organizational levels provide important contexts for analyzing the need, utility, and growth of IT in Tanzania. The Tanzanian society is very purpose-oriented from the individual level up to the national level. The utility of IT, as seen by the individual and also as seen in relation to that individual's level of functioning in the organizational hierarchy, will drive the need and priority for IT access and use.

NEW DIRECTIONS FOR TANZANIA

As pointed out by Mushi (1996), the classroom teacher will most likely remain central in educating students, despite developments in IT. Teaching is influenced by many factors, some of which are the classroom, the type of students (some more knowledgeable and some less knowledgeable than the teacher), and the location of the classrooms and the nature of facilities within and outside classrooms. Among all these factors, the teacher is the classroom authority who can work to make students appreciate learning. To bring about effective learning and use of IT skills, teachers must engage in IT-based professional development workshops to make learning interesting and meaningful for students.

There are certainly significant positive developments in the availability and use of computer technology, such as academicians being more computer literate and efficient users, and administrators using computer skills in their daily work activities (word-processing, e-mail communication, etc.). Another major trend taking shape now is the use of e-mail communication among the younger generations, even in the non-academic endeavours. E-mail users are motivated by the high utility value of sending and receiving information efficiently.

The name of the Ministry of Education and Culture has also changed to "The Ministry of Education and Vocational Training" to signal more emphasis on vocational and technical education than in past years. The Ministry of Education and Vocational Training needs to work closely with institutions of higher learning in the country (colleges and universities) and information technology experts in order to embark on a strong footing in making modern computer technology an integral part of learning at all levels. One hindrance that has repeatedly occurred is the donation of old computers and outdated technology by foreign countries to Tanzania. Old computers and outdated technology only drag back Tanzania's efforts to build a modern, computer-literate society. In some cases the government pays a lot of money to ship the old computers and the accompanying "expert" to install them, instead of using the money to buy up-to-date computers (no matter how few) and use local experts to install them. The Government of Tanzania needs to make sure this practice of dumping old computers and outdated technology into the country while using up the little money available for technology improvement does not continue.

In order for Tanzania to embark on contextually meaningful ways of making IT a tool for effective school learning and practical problem-solving in society, the Ministry of Education and Vocational Training has to initiate discussions at different levels of the school system about the IT needs to be incorporated into the curriculum. There is need for a clear policy commitment on the part of the Tanzanian government to promote and develop research on IT needs, starting with the infrastructure and reliable supply of electricity. A clear policy of self-reliance and better allocation of available resources will help Tanzanians begin to realize IT goals that are planned realistically, instead of relying on foreign aid and donations that are not necessarily matched to the most burning internal IT needs. The following questions are suggestions about the issues that should be considered in these discussions, which will help Tanzanians focus IT contextually:

1. What level of IT is currently in use, where, and for what purpose?
2. How is the IT in use making life better for the people using it?

3. What are the strengths and weaknesses of the current level of IT being used in schools, colleges, and universities? How can these be addressed from within, and what supplemental help can be obtained from other countries?
4. In what creative ways can IT be used to advance self-identities, communities, and the entire Tanzanian society?
5. What mechanisms can be put in place for schools to make IT part of their daily functioning and problem-solving?
6. How can Tanzanian youth be guided and nurtured to be producers of IT rather than mere consumers?

Given the challenges of funding, Tanzania needs to start on the right footing by encouraging zonal, regional, district, and lower organizational units to develop short-term and long-term plans for acquiring computer equipment on their own and motivate the development of IT specialists and leaders by providing additional computers as well as training. Minimizing the digital divide right from the beginning is extremely important because if not addressed the problem can quickly accelerate to unmanageable discrepancies. All levels of the organizational hierarchy need to work to come up with the most important IT needs and ways to obtain computer equipment and get trainers. It will be a challenge for the Tanzanian government to provide computers and training professionals to all schools in all organizational units; therefore, self-reliance is an invaluable way to motivate people to start defining and solving their own problem and only ask for help when they have established a base.

The Tanzanian education system puts a lot of emphasis on learning of content, with or without IT skills. While IT skills make learning of content easier, they may not and should not take the place of specific content areas such as mathematics, language skills, physics, chemistry, biology, history, geography, etc. If the content area of focus is Information Technology, then IT skills should dominate the evaluation procedures. However, if another content area is being assessed, care should be taken not to confuse myths with facts regarding the role of IT in school learning.

The following table lists some myths and facts that can be used in making decisions about managing IT in Tanzanian schools:

	MYTH	FACT
1.	Anything to do with IT is useful learning.	IT is only a tool to facilitate useful learning – one must first know what he/she wants to learn.
2.	Ability to browse through the Internet is in itself high-level learning.	Ability to browse the Internet is one way to look for information, which may or may not be useful for intended high-level learning.
3.	A primary school child who can use the computer to do math or science projects is gifted.	A primary school child who can use the computer to do math or science projects may or may not be gifted – the child has only learned to click in the right places.
4.	A word-processed essay has superior content to that of a hand-written essay.	A word-processed essay is easier to read – it may have lower, equal, or superior content to that of a handwritten essay.
5.	E-mail makes communication easy.	E-mail makes communication easy among computer-literate parties.
6.	Students in schools that have enough up-to-date computers experience more effective learning of intended content than students in schools without any computers.	Students in schools that have enough up-to-date computers *may* experience more effective learning *of computer technology – depending on their motivation* and probably intended content – than students in schools without any computers.
7.	Computers are the highest priority in today's schools because they make students smarter by providing easy access to information.	Computers may be the highest priority in today's schools that consider information surfing and use of software as "smartness."
8.	Teachers have to learn IT fast to catch up so that they can be ahead of their students and teach IT to their students.	IT grows and changes so fast that any teacher focusing on being ahead of her students will have to spend her lifetime doing just that, with little success. Teachers have to provide carefully developed structures to guide their students in using IT, where appropriate, as a tool for effective learning.
9.	African students are lagging behind in learning school content because they do not have any computers in their schools.	African students are lagging behind in surfing the Internet for easy access to information, so they are forced to think of other creative ways of problem-solving in learning school content.
10.	African schools need computers as a matter of emergency so that the schools can begin to reduce any disadvantageous division of learners because of their access to digital IT.	African schools need computers in addition to the high quality content teachers as a matter of emergency so that teachers can use those computers as tools, where appropriate, to provide contextually relevant education for problem-solving and advancement of self-identity at personal and societal levels.

The Tanzania Institute of Education (TIE), the Ministry of Education and Vocational Training, the National Examinations Council, and the Faculty of Education of the University of Dar es Salaam need to work together to find effective ways to: (i) monitor validity of assessments in light of the IT era versus learning of content; (ii) motivate Tanzanian software engineers to develop varieties of relevant software for Tanzanian students to self-assess in content mastery and in competition for higher levels of education; and (iii) sustain interest and motivation for Tanzanian software engineers working in foreign countries to participate in enhancing IT learning and utilization in Tanzanian schools and communities.

Information technology is a tool for learning, problem-solving, and making life better at individual and societal levels. It is extremely important to ensure that use of IT in Tanzania serves the needs of the Tanzanian people, as perceived and evaluated by the Tanzanian people. The organizational hierarchy of the Tanzanian society has held the fibre of the different cultures together so successfully for so many years because of the interconnectedness of families and cultural groups. The hierarchy facilitates transparency throughout the education system, empowers individuals with a sense of belonging and a sense of purpose, and also provides mechanisms for academic, professional, political, and societal upward mobility, depending on one's effort. Motivation for schooling and for working hard (in small businesses) to advance one's academic and economic/professional life is intense.

To make IT relevant to the day-to-day lives of villagers, the village organizational unit has to embrace IT as an additional tool to better understand and define their problems and develop local solutions. The Mwenyekiti wa kijiji has to have access to a computer and have the skills to retrieve and act on relevant information. As a leader, he or she will need to communicate with other village leaders and his or her own people for informed joint decision-making on matters concerning their village. Schools are important units within villages. Some decisions about the functioning of schools are made at village levels, as long as they do not contradict higher levels in the organizational hierarchy. Accessibility to IT must involve both the schools and the village leadership. Tanzanian schools and communities must use IT as a means to strengthen this organizational hierarchy. Among other questions, schools, villages and communities need to ask: "who are the possible individuals, private sectors, companies or non-profit organizations that can work with our schools and community to help in conducting IT needs assessment, guidance, and, where possible, financial support?" One way to motivate the organizational units to work towards wiring schools and obtaining computer equipment is to hold annual competitions. If villages, Kata, Tarafa districts, regions, and zones compete in starting, sustaining, and advancing use of IT skills, major milestones can be achieved. Even though 38 per cent of the Tanzanian population lives below the Basic Needs Poverty Line (National Bureau of Statistics, 2002), the Tanzanian government, starting with the school system, needs to set the direction for realizing the technological advancements necessary for the twenty-first century, albeit gradually.

REFERENCES

Campbell, D. (2001). Can the digital divide be contained? *International Labour Review, 140*(2), 119–41.

Ching, C., Basham, J., & Jang, E. (2005). The legacy of the digital divide. *Urban Education, 40*(4), 394–411.

Cummins, J., & Sayers, D. (1995). *Brave new schools*. Toronto: OISE Press.

DiBello, L. C. (2005). Are we addressing the digital divide? Issues, access, and real commitment. *Childhood Education, 81*(4), 239.

Fitzpatrick, J. (1994). Concept paper on technology and education reform. Retrieved January 28, 2004, from http://www.merit.edu/mail.archives/mjts/1994-02/msg00021.html.

Gonzalez, C. (2004). The role of blended learning in the world of technology. Retrieved January 16, 2005, from http://www.unt.edu/benchmarks.archives/2004/september04/eis.htm.

Graham, S. (2002). Bridging urban digital divides? Urban polarization and information and communications technologies (ICTS). *Urban Studies, 39*, 33–56.

Kalyanpur, M., & Kimani, M. H. (2005). Diversity and technology: Classroom implications of the digital divide. *Journal of Special Education Technology, 20*(4), 9–18.

Langenberg, D. N. (1991). The lonely scholar in a global information environment, In G. R. Boynton and S. D. Creth (Eds.), *Proceedings from the Symposium on Scholarly Communication: New Technologies and New Directions* (pp. 27–40). Westpoint, CT: Meckler Corp.

Looker, E., & Thiessen, V. (2003). The digital divide in Canadian schools: Factors affecting student access to and use of information technology. Halifax: Atlantic

Research Data Center. Retrieved December 28, 2003, from http://www.statcan.ca/engl/rdc/pdf.

Ministry of Education. (2005). *Mwongozo wa Ufundishaji/Ujifunzaji somo la TEHAMA katika Shule za Msingi Tanzania.* Dar es Salaam: Ministry of Education.

Mushi, S.L.P. (1996). ESL student teachers' observed abilities to reflect on practice teaching in Tanzania: An experiment on explicitly taught and spontaneous reflection. PhD dissertation, Ontario Institute for Studies in Education, University of Toronto.

National Bureau of Statistics. (2002). *Tanzania Socio-Economic Database* (TSED). Dar es Salaam: National Bureau of Statistics.

Peha, S. (2005). Slow adoption of technology in schools. Retrieved July 5, 2006, from http://www.larta.org/lavox/articlelinks/2005/050411_paper.asp.

Rainie, L. (2005). Life Online: When everyone connects to everyone and everything connects to everything. Paper presented at the ECAR meeting, Carefree, Arizona, December 8, 2005.

Siemens, G. (2004). Connectivism: A learning theory for the digital age. Retrieved July 18, 2006, from http://www.elearnspace.org/Articles/Connectivism.htm.

Schon, D. A. (1991) *The Reflective Turn: Case Studies In and On Educational Practice*, New York: Teachers Press, Columbia University.

Tetlegah, S. Y., & Hunter R. C. (2006). *Advances in Education Administration, Volume 8: Technology and education issues in administration, policy and applications in K–12 Schools.* Greenwich, CT: JAI Press.

United Nations Population Fund. (2003). *United Republic of Tanzania.* Retrieved March 7, 2006, from http://www.unfpa.org/profile/tanzania.cfm.

White, G. (2005). Beyond the Horseless Carriage: Harnessing the potential of ICT in education and training. Retrieved September 5, 2005, from http://www.educationau.edu.au/jahia/webdav/site/myjahiasite/users/root/public/papers/horseless_carriages_GW.pdf.

Willis, J. W., & Mehlinger, H. D. (1996). Information technology and teacher education. In J. Sikula, T. J. Buttery & E. Guyton (Eds.). *Handbook of research on teacher education* (pp. 978–1029). New York: Prentice Hall International.

6

ENVISIONING AFRICAN
SOCIAL WORK EDUCATION

Uzo Anucha

ABSTRACT

American and British models of professional social work that have been exported to Africa have been critiqued as unable to address the unique issues and cultural characteristics of the majority of Africans. Such critiques have increased as the social work profession in the Western world has failed to come up with answers to many of its own most vexing social problems. African social work educators are therefore questioning the borrowing of such "problematic" Western social work knowledge. This paper critically reviews the challenges for Africa presented by the Western-influenced social work legacy that is largely remedial in nature and underpinned by the charity and casework model that locates problems within individuals and their families. The author builds on recent scholarship as well as her experiences of schooling and working in Africa and the West, to explore how Africa, with particular reference to Nigeria, can begin a process of re-visioning and transforming its social work education and training programs.

With all the major social problems facing Africa, social work cannot continue to fiddle with minor problems. (Shawky, 1972, p. 6)

INTRODUCTION

At the start of the twenty-first century, the social work profession in the Western[1] world, particularly in North American countries such as Canada and the United States, faces unprecedented challenges. Changing demographic, political, and social trends have ushered in a practice environment that is increasingly complex, demanding, and diverse. Rossiter (1996) rightly points out that social work's foundation has been shaken and shattered by historical, social, and intellectual currents of the past two decades that have left the profession in a state of disarray and its epistemic traditions' credibility under scrutiny. While the profession grapples with these profound changes, failures of social welfare programs aimed at addressing homelessness, welfare dependency, neglect, and abuse of children, alcohol and substance abuse, crime and mental disorders are being laid on the profession's doorstep (Lindsey & Kirk, 1992).

Some have questioned Western social work's professional capability to respond effectively to these urgent demands, noting that other professionals such as social and political scientists who are unschooled in traditional social welfare concerns are providing decision-makers with most of the data they use (Howard & Lambert, 1996). These external criticisms have been paralleled by debates among social work providers that have polarized the profession. These criticisms and debates have led to an examination of the role of social work; that is, questions have been asked whether the role of social work is to change people or to change the systems that govern society. Another question that has arisen is how should it best enter the discourse of social reform? Further, questions have been asked about the contributions social work has made to epistemology and of how the profession builds the knowledge it uses to solve social problems.

The social work profession in developing[2] countries also faces un-relenting and mounting critique, particularly of its continued reliance on Western social work knowledge when such borrowed knowledge has been found problematic even in the environments for which it was developed. Walton and Abo El Nasr (1988) summarize the basic argument that justifies this criticism, "if the social work profession in the exporting countries fails to achieve its aims in solving the main problems in these countries, such as discrimination, unemployment, poverty, etc., how can we agree to indigenize or adapt a weak profession to the local needs and problems in the importing countries?" (p. 140). Warning of the need for caution in the borrowing of Western social work knowledge by developing countries, Hammoud (1988) also points out that social work education in developed countries is in disarray and far from consensus because of conceptual deficiencies and practical difficulties. Consequently, these difficulties raise theoretical and practical problems with the unabridged adoption of Western social work knowledge by developing countries.

American and British models of professional social work that have been exported to developing countries have been criticized for imposing Western-based practice theory in contexts where they do not fit and for reinforcing hegemony and cultural imperialism in which Western social work values, knowledge, and skills are positioned as elite and superior (Midgley, 1981). In Africa, social work education has been particularly critiqued for retaining its colonial heritage even though the critical problems and challenges the continent faces today could not have been imaginable during the colonial era. Consequently, such Western social work knowledge frequently fails to address the unique issues and cultural characteristics of the majority of Africans.

Despite the awareness of the mismatch between Western social work knowledge and the local realities of African countries, not much curriculum change has occurred to address these concerns. Therefore, a key challenge that arises from these critiques is how to transform and re-vision social work education and training in the African continent to better meet current social realities. A central question is, how can social work education in Africa develop and adopt new approaches that can support the transformation of social work practice from one that Shawky (1972) derided as "fiddling with minor problems" to social work practice that tackles the "major social issues" of twenty-first-century Africa such as large-scale poverty, unemployment, and the social consequences of the HIV/AIDS pandemic? Related questions that have been asked by others include: what is to be done with the current Western-influenced theories and practices of social work; how best can schools of social work in Africa enter the ongoing discourse on the necessity of shifting from remedial social work to developmental social work; and, what should be the content of social work education when this shift is made? (For further questions and concerns, see Bak, 2004; Osei-Hwedie, 1993.)

This chapter contributes to the debates about the nature of social work in Africa by critically reviewing the challenges for Africa of a colonial social work legacy that is largely remedial in nature and underpinned by the charity and casework model that locates problems within individuals and their families. The chapter also examines the possibilities that a developmental social work perspective as well as indigenous knowledge might offer for re-visioning social work education and training for Africa with particular reference to Nigeria, Africa's most populous country.

HISTORICAL OVERVIEW OF SOCIAL WORK IN NIGERIA

As the old adage of all meaningful educational theorising and best practices posits, moving from the "known to the unknown" is the best way to go about educating. (Jagusah, 2001, p. 123)

Although the *idea* of social working in Nigeria and other African countries predates colonialism, formal social work packaged as a profession with well-articulated theories began with colonization and, in some countries, after independence (Adepoju, 1974, cited in Odiah, 1991). Burke and Ngonyani (2004) point out that historically, in Africa, social welfare needs were more commonly met using resources within the community at different levels – the tribe, clan, and family systems. Odiah (1991) notes that "kinship system in the traditional Nigerian society provided for family welfare, child welfare, health, mental health, care for the aged, informal education, recreation, social planning and development" (p. 11). Not only did the extended family meet social welfare needs but it also dealt with problematic behaviours that the community regarded as deviant by involving the wider kin, and it was not uncommon for restitution penalties to be imposed (Adepoju, 1974, cited in Odiah, 1991). Although this traditional reliance on the extended family has been considerably weakened by industrialization and urbanization, when compared with the Western world, the reciprocal obligations of family members towards one another still operate quite strongly in many Nigerian communities.

When social work as a profession was introduced in Nigeria in the 1950s and 1960s, it completely replicated the social work systems that existed in Britain and was underpinned by a colonial mentality that worked to promote the belief that anything that came from the West was superior and therefore was worthy of inclusion in Nigeria's social and economic system. Asamoah and Beverly (1988) note that upon gaining independence from colonial powers a vast number of countries in Africa emerged with formal welfare systems similar to their erstwhile colonizers. These welfare systems differ according to the respective colonial power involved. For example, in former British colonies like Nigeria, remedial social services similar to those in the United Kingdom were established. Asamoah and Beverly further point out that it is imperative that welfare systems be examined according to their historical context so as to understand how present social welfare systems are shaped and influenced by external forces imposed before, during, and after colonization. They conclude that within the African context, modern social work practices are influenced by a mix of influences that range from early activities of missionaries, voluntary organizations, tribal societies, traditional customs and practices, pre- and postcolonial economic, political, and social realities, to social welfare policies implemented during colonial periods.

In an extensive review of the historical context of social work in Nigeria, Odiah (1991) traces the evolution of social work during colonialism and after Nigeria's independence in the early 1960s and links it to Nigeria's quest for modernization and industrialization, which it pursued in an attempt to emulate the successes that the Western world had experienced. This quest shaped the social welfare priorities that the country undertook, which were tilted towards programs that benefited a newly emerging urban middle class. Odiah points out that increased government expenditure that was directed towards the provision of public housing, education, and health primarily benefited an urban elite minority.

For example, despite allocating over 20 per cent of Nigeria's revenues to education, little progress was made in rural education because the majority of the education budget funded the creation of universities and government subsidies to private education, which only benefited an urban middle class. The public housing agenda that the government pursued also failed to address the housing needs of the urban poor but favoured the urban middle class (civil servants, teachers, etc.) who could afford the high rents that the government charged in an effort to recover capital investments. Odiah further describes how the neglect of the needs of the rural majority was also felt in the provision of health care where the government chose to spend the greater proportion of the health care budget on the provision of modern hospitals in urban areas, which curtailed its ability to provide basic health services to the rural majority. The provision of health care and the curricula in the newly funded universities was modelled on Western practices.

During the transition to independence, Nigerian social welfare officials were sent to the West (Britain and America) to study and acquire the necessary skills to assume control of the administration of social welfare services when the colonial social welfare officials disengaged post-independence. The social workers who were sent to the West studied Western social work theories and methods and the administration of Western social welfare systems. Odiah points out that, despite concerns that some raised that such Western-based education and training was irrelevant to what these Nigerian social work students needed to know to practice at home, many disagreed, arguing that developing countries would eventually develop their social welfare service to Western standards. However, this reliance on Western social work knowledge did not change even after training facilities were set up in Nigeria.

Despite the widely differing issues, limitations, and opportunities that confront social workers in the West and in Africa, the legacies of Western social work education still permeate social work education and practice in Nigerian, more than four decades after independence. Jagusah (2001) confirms the challenges that previously colonized

African countries face in casting off the legacies of imperialism. In a review of the pre-colonial, the colonial, and the postcolonial periods in African education (with specific references to Nigeria and South Africa), Jagusah mocked as naïve some African intellectuals who believe that "the colonists are gone, yet they do not give heed to the colonizing structures and marginality left behind that still influences the African discourse of power and knowledge of otherness" (p. 123).

Midgley (1990) summarizes the challenges of developing countries adopting Western theories and practice approaches as including: limited relevance to the needs of developing countries; human services that are largely remedial, urban-centred, limited in scope, and informed by practice models that are inappropriate; and, social workers who have been trained in the traditions of casework but who lack the needed resources to effectively address clients' needs.

THE CURRENT CONTEXT OF SOCIAL WORK PRACTICE AND EDUCATION IN NIGERIA

Today, in Nigeria and many other African countries, social work is not well-recognized or valued as a profession (Burke and Ngonyani, 2004). This may be related to the fact that Nigeria has no formal social welfare system, making it difficult if not impossible for social workers to draw on any resources to assist clients whose problems are often related to or compounded by poverty. Writing for the National Institute for Social and Economic Research (NISER), Adeola aptly summarized this mismatch between what social workers have to offer and what clients really do need: "The majority of those who seek social work assistance in Nigeria are in dire need of material resources; many are destitute; unemployed, homeless, landless, illiterate, in poor health, and hungry ... the scale of absolute poverty in the society defies remedies which rely on professional counselling" (NISER, 1980, quoted in Odiah, 1991, p. 48).

Similarly, in 1980, in a very vivid and haunting description of the social situation of many of Africa's poorest countries, the Independent Commission on Development Issues noted:

Many hundreds of millions of people in the poorer countries are preoccupied solely with survival and elementary needs. For them work is frequently unavailable or when it is, pay is very low and conditions often barely tolerable ... permanent insecurity is the condition of the poor. There are no public systems of social security in the event of unemployment, sickness or death of a wage-earner in the family ... the combination of malnutrition, illiteracy, disease, high birth rates, underemployment, and low income closes off the avenues of escape. (Brandt, 1980, quoted in Estes, 1995, p. 43)

More than two decades after the Independent Commission painted this dismal picture of the social development of Africa, considerable underdevelopment still remains, although some slight improvements have been made in reducing infant, child, and adult mortality and increasing literacy and adult life expectation (Estes, 1995).

The plight of Nigeria and its people may be one of the best contemporary examples of how historical, political, economic, social, and environmental problems can converge in severe threat to the well-being of an entire nation. According to the United Nations, Nigeria is one of many developing countries that is impeded by a vicious circle linking poverty, insecurity, and vulnerability in a context of growing inequalities (United Nations, 2003). Nigeria, Africa's most populous country and the tenth largest country by population in the world, is confronted with large-scale social deprivation. Located in West Africa, the boundaries of the country set by the British colonial powers cut across different cultural and physical spaces. Because of this arbitrary setting of boundaries, Nigeria is made up of more than 250 ethnic groups of Christian and Islamic faiths who have not always managed to co-exist peacefully. Immediately after independence in 1960, Nigerian was beset by ethno-religious conflicts, which degenerated into years of civil war when the southeast attempted to secede as Biafra. The end of civil war in 1970 coincided with the start of the oil boom years in which Nigeria became a major oil exporter.

As the world's thirteenth largest producer of crude oil and the sixth largest oil producer in the Organization of Petroleum Exporting Countries (World Bank, 2002), Nigeria derives enormous income from exporting oil. It also has significant reserves of mineral and agricultural resources as well as human capital. Despite these endowments that should ensure that Nigerians enjoy one of the highest global living standards, the majority of the population live in extreme poverty. With per capita income falling significantly to about $300 between 1980 and 2000 (well below the sub-Saharan average of $450), approximately 90 million of Nigeria's 133 million people are living in absolute poverty (Nigerian National Planning Committee, 2004).

The country has no state-supported social welfare system; therefore, most people must depend on their extended families to meet the exigencies of life such as unemployment, ill-health, and sustenance during old age. Although medical care is provided to government employees and to most workers in large industrial and commercial enterprises, the rest of the population does not have this basic right. Despite several attempts at reform, the majority of Nigerians in the rural areas lack access to primary health care, in large part because the great majority of treatment centres are located in large cities. Facilities are often understaffed, under-equipped, and low on medications and other medical supplies. Patients must generally pay user fees and buy their own supplies and medications, which they often cannot afford.

The result of this lack of access to health care by the majority of the population is devastating: Nigeria has an infant mortality rate of 105 per thousand live births and a life expectancy of fifty-one years. UNICEF (2004) estimates that, at present, about one in five Nigerian children die before the age of five – the implication being that a baby born in the country is thirty times more likely to die than one born in any industrialized country. Similarly, the risk of maternal death in Nigeria is a hundred times higher than in an average industrial country. Other preventable illnesses that the government has been unable to halt include measles, whooping cough, polio, cerebrospinal meningitis, gastroenteritis, tuberculosis, bronchitis, waterborne infectious diseases, and sexually transmitted infections. Infection with the human immunodeficiency virus (HIV) that causes acquired immunodeficiency syndrome (AIDS) is on the increase and becoming more prevalent. In 2001, 3.5 million Nigerians were estimated to be infected with HIV and 170,000 Nigerians died of AIDS. In 2000, the World Health Organization rated the health system at 187 out of 191 countries in the world.

In 1999, Nigeria ended fifteen years of military rule by electing Olusegun Obasanjo as president and again re-elected him in 2003. At the beginning of his presidency, President Obasanjo admitted that reducing Nigeria's endemic poverty was one of the most challenging tasks that confronted his government. His administration launched what has been touted as a comprehensive home-grown poverty alleviation program – the National Economic Empowerment and Development Strategy (NEEDS) – and has promised to reduce by half the number of Nigerians who live in poverty.

In addition to the social consequences of widespread poverty, Nigeria also faces other social issues such as gender inequity. Article 1 of the United Nations Convention on the Elimination of all Forms of Discrimination against Women (CEDAW) (United Nations, 1979) defines discrimination against women as: "any distinction, exclusion or restriction made on the basis of sex which has the effect or purpose of impairing or nullifying the recognition, enjoyment or exercise by women, irrespective of their marital status, on the basis of equality of men and women, of human rights and fundamental freedoms in the political, economic, social, cultural, civil or any other field." Nigeria became a signatory to the convention on April 23, 1984, and also signed both the 1985 and 2001 ratifications. Despite being a signatory to CEDAW and the existence of national protections, Nigerian women still face barriers to their full participation in society. Many of the challenges facing them emerge in the context of gender-based power differences that create disparities in resources, social capital, and options for action.

Gender-based status differences create special difficulties for Nigerian women in three main areas: vulnerability to poverty through reduced access to, and control over, property and financial assets (Okeke, 2000; Pierce, 2003); increased exposure to risk for HIV/AIDS and other STDs (Adeokun et al., 2002; Eltom et al., 2002); and trafficking in women (Bamgbose, 2002). The empowerment of Nigerian women is the key goal for interventions that seek to mitigate these negative consequences for women and girls. Experience in Nigeria and other developing countries has demonstrated that increasing the empowerment and resources available to women is an effective strategy for improving social outcomes not only for women but also for their families and communities (Uduigwomen, 2004). These social issues that confront Nigerians – structural threats to the equality of women, poverty, large-scale unemployment, lack of access to basic health care and others – require social work practice that is not focused on personal deficiencies, rather, on deficiencies in societal structures and systems that have to be remedied to allow people to develop their human potentials to the fullest capacity (Bak, 2004).

The social work profession, with its long tradition of empowering and working with marginalized people through multi-level interventions and collaborations with community-based organizations, is well positioned to contribute significantly to women's empowerment and gender equality in Nigeria. Ideally, social work programs in Nigeria should produce social work practitioners who have the skills and knowledge to develop and implement community-based interventions that address the social problems faced by Nigerian women, their families, and communities. The next section describes why social work education in Nigeria that embraces a social developmental perspective rather than a remedial focus can train a new generation of professional social workers with the necessary skills and knowledge to address the priorities of Nigerian women through prevention and intervention projects that are founded on the principles of empowerment and long-term social change. A strengthened social work education sector can better educate, prepare, and position future social workers to contribute significantly to Nigeria's national and local initiatives that address these pervasive social issues.

CHALLENGES OF A REMEDIAL SOCIAL WORK-BASED CURRICULUM FOR NIGERIA

> African social work must proceed from remedial social work – foreign by nature and approach – to a more dynamic and more widespread preventive and rehabilitative action which identifies itself with African culture in particular and with socioeconomic policies of Africa in general. (ASWEA, 1982, p. 11)

The last three decades have witnessed a growing uneasiness reflected in the above call by the defunct Association of Social Work Education in Africa (ASWEA) about the dilemmas of remedial social work and the urgent need for social work education and training programs in Africa to move away from this problematic approach. Remedial social work – a legacy of colonization and the influence of Western social work – has it roots in the Charity Organization Society model of social work that emphasized individualized social services. According to Young and Ashton (1956/1963), the Charity Organization Society movement that began in 1869 in England viewed poverty as a character and moral deficiency of the poor and the solution to poverty as reform or rehabilitation of the individual. The Charity Organization Society's focus on individual reform was in sharp contrast to that of the Settlement House Movement that began in 1884 in England. The Settlement House Movement viewed capitalism as the cause of poverty and therefore saw the solution as reform of society. Mullaly (1997) points out that the two major competing views of society and social welfare within social work emerged from these two traditions.

From the Charity Organization Society emerged a conventional social work perspective of society and social welfare that understands and links social problems to personal difficulties or, at best, immediate environmental issues. This conventional social work perspective, which Mullaly argues is the dominant/mainstream social work perspective, sees the role of social work intervention as helping people cope and adjust to existing institutions or, if necessary, modify existing policies in a limited fashion. The contribution of the Charity Organization Society to social work is a remedial model that emphasizes casework with individuals and families and focuses on the coping, adjustment, and restoration of the poor rather than the changing of social conditions. In contrast, the progressive/critical social work perspective that emerged from the Settlement House Movement argues that present social institutions are not capable of adequately meeting human needs and points to worsening social problems; growing gap between rich and poor; worsening plight of disadvantaged groups; and resurrection of conservatism in many developed countries as evidence that the present set of social arrangements does not work for large numbers of people. The contribution of the Settlement House Movement to social work includes a self-help model of community organizations that focuses on participation of the poor, community development, and social action.

The remedial model of social work focuses on personal deficiencies instead of societal deficiencies and has been increasingly criticized by scholars in the developing world, and Africa in particular, as inappropriate and irrelevant to the needs of their societies (Midgley, 1990). Burke and Ngonyani (2004) rightly point out that, though

Africa's social problems might be similar to those of developed countries (child and wife abuse, divorce, sexual assault, etc.), they are worsened and compounded by poverty as well as an unequal international economic system. The authors also note that there are certain social problems, such as inadequate food distribution, lack of access to education and health, and the prevalence of STDs and HIV/AIDS, which are unique and peculiar to developing countries. These large-scale problems demand more than a remedial social work approach. A remedial social work approach has also been criticized for being costly and using resources inefficiently. Pointing out these shortcomings in the case of South Africa, Bak also argues that individualized social work is unable to address or change the "unequal power balance and the pressure towards conformity" (2004, p. 92) that is inherent in this approach.

In an analysis of the curriculum of social work education and training programs in Nigeria, Odiah (1991) concluded that they were framed by a remedial social work approach that was based primarily on Western theories with little emphasis on courses that are relevant to the country's realities. Odiah found that less than 10 per cent of the course materials had local content. For example, teaching of social administration and policy seldom referred to local social welfare policies but focused on British social policy and administration. Courses on the history of social work similarly focused on the history of social work in Europe and North America. The curricula in the majority of the schools emphasized a remedial approach and were dominated by casework courses that were almost entirely based on American theories. Odiah points out that "curriculum content only serves to widen the gap and perpetuate the very condition of inappropriate training practices" (1991, p. 113).

The influence and unsuitability of this remedial approach of social work education and training programs in Nigeria can be clearly seen in the findings of a cross-sectional survey conducted by the country's National Institute of Social and Economic Research.[3] This survey sought to understand the extent of professional social work in Nigeria by seeking the views and perceptions of forty-one social workers on various aspects of their education in Nigeria. All the respondents were employed as field workers by the Ministry of Social Development, Youth, and Culture. Despite the caveats that should accompany the findings because of sample size issues and age of data, three of the findings of the survey reported by Odiah (1991) are particularly germane to this chapter's discussions as they emphasize that social work education and training programs in the country have not modified their curricula to adequately and appropriately address the major social problems of contemporary Nigeria.

Firstly, when asked how best the social work profession in Nigerian could positively contribute to development and poverty – two of the country's endemic social issues, a majority of respondents (60%) felt that the profession could do so by pursuing practices at the macro level such as community development, self-help, co-operatives and other micro-businesses that increase people's income. While acknowledging that social workers did not seem to have much power to influence government welfare policy, the majority of respondents (60%) felt that the profession could contribute to these issues by engaging in social planning activities. Although 80 per cent of respondents were employed as caseworkers, only 30 per cent of respondents believed that casework could adequately address the basic needs of clients while only 10 per cent agreed that casework and group work were appropriate for addressing the social problems of developing countries like Nigeria.

Secondly, when respondents were asked how effective their social work practice was with clients, considering the limited resources they had to draw from, an overwhelming majority (80%) of respondents thought the remedial social work they were engaged in where they provided help on an individual basis to clients was a band-aid that did not address the root causes of their clients' problems. For example, social workers in probation and family welfare were quite doubtful and negative in their assessment of how effective and adequate their interventions could be in addressing the underlying causes of their client's needs when such problems stemmed from pervasive poverty. The social workers who worked as probation officers reported that a majority of their clients were from economically disadvantaged communities and had become involved in criminal activities such as petty theft out of poverty. Social workers in family welfare reported that a majority of their clients lived in the poorest sections of town in inadequate housing and had very low incomes and education and faced chronic unemployment, poor health, and malnutrition. The respondents believed that a lot of the social problems their clients faced were consequences of poverty.

Finally, an overwhelming majority (80%) of respondents felt that social work as it existed in Nigeria – with no resources and framed by the remedial approach that focuses on individual casework – was incapable of contributing solutions to clients' problems. However, a majority of respondents also said that social work had the potential of contributing to the country's programs by engaging in developmental activities.

THE POSSIBILITIES OF A SOCIAL DEVELOPMENTAL PERSPECTIVE

The shortcomings of a remedial-based curriculum have stimulated the search and exploration of new theoretical models that might be better suited to the consequences of underdevelopment. More recently, increasing numbers of African social work educators, scholars, and practitioners are turning to a social work developmental perspective to re-vision and transform this remedial social work legacy to one that speaks to their own unique social realities. Mupedziswa (2001) argues that, if social work is to move from remedial social work to preventative and rehabilitative action, it must transform its programs within a social developmental approach starting from social work education and training. South African-born James Midgley, who has written extensively about social development and social welfare, defines social development as a "process of planned social change designed to promote the well-being of the population as a whole in conjunction with a dynamic process of economic development" (1995, p. 25). Expanding on the necessity to link the promotion of human welfare to economic development, Midgley (1997b) emphasizes the need for "policies and programmes that enhance people's welfare and at same time contribute positively to economic development" (p. 11).

South Africa's experience with a social developmental perspective can provide Nigeria and other African countries with important observations on the challenges and possibilities that a developmental approach offers for social work practice that is responsive to poverty, large-scale unemployment, and other big social problems. After liberation in 1994, South Africa embarked on a re-visioning of its social welfare system informed by a developmental perspective that has involved a transformation of service provision and policy formulation, as well as a review of curricula of professional social work education (Drower, 2002). Drower reports that the White paper for Social Welfare published in 1997 by the Ministry for Social Welfare and Population Development departed from South Africa's history of a remedial and rehabilitative approach to embracing a developmental approach. Bak (2004, p. 82) points out the White Paper outlined "principles, guidelines, recommendations, proposed policies, and programmes for developmental social welfare in South Africa." Drawing from Midgley's definition of a social developmental perspective as well as the UN World Summit on Social Development that was held in Copenhagen in 1995, the White Paper emphasized the importance of linking social development and economic development.

Mupedziswa (2001) proposes benchmarks/criteria that social work education and training institutions in Africa can utilize in evaluating whether their programs are oriented towards the promotion of a social work developmental perspective. They fall into two broad categories – curriculum-related or extra-curricular activities. Curriculum-related activities involve rigorous curriculum review exercises to ensure the horizontal and vertical integration of courses. These activities may include regular field workshops and practical field work that are oriented and consistent with a developmental perspective, such as rural placements resulting in a demonstration by faculty and students of an understanding of developmental concepts such as indigenization, authentication, and social development. Further, these activities require the use of innovative teaching strategies such as seminars, role plays, guest lecturers, and self-directed projects/assignments that are consistent with a developmental orientation. Extra-curricular activities that are related to promoting a developmental perspective include the development and use of indigenous teaching materials, generation and use of local research, localization of a significant proportion of staff, employment of graduates in developmental oriented positions, and participation in national social policy development and monitoring.

BEGINNING THE PROCESS OF RE-VISIONING
SOCIAL WORK EDUCATION IN NIGERIA

The challenges facing twenty-first-century Nigeria, including large-scale unemployment, poverty, the AIDS pandemic, lack of access to basic health care and structural threats to the equality of women, demand a social developmental model of educating and training of social workers to better meet these major challenges. The extensive benchmarks for transforming curriculum and unlearning pedagogical practices that are more compatible with remedial social work than a developmental model described by Mupedziswa and others (Estes, 1994; Gray, 1996; Mamphiswana & Noyoo, 2000; Midgley, 1990; and Odiah, 1991) offer some concrete pragmatic frameworks that the social work profession in Nigeria can draw from to begin a dialogue on re-visioning its social work education and training programs. In addition to the important and pragmatic strategies suggested by these scholars, informed by my experiences in the Nigerian educational system in the 1980s acquiring undergraduate and graduate degrees in psychology; my experiences in the late 1990s in the Canadian educational system acquiring undergraduate and graduate degrees in social work; and a recent visit back to Nigeria in the summer of 2004 on a collaborative research project with colleagues in a Nigerian university, I tentatively suggest three core issues that this dialogue might focus on as well. I also suggest two curriculum issues that current social work programs in Nigeria can focus on to strengthen the training of a new generation of professional social workers with the necessary skills and knowledge to address the priorities of Nigeria.

First, social work education in Nigeria needs to rediscover and tap into the wealth of indigenous knowledge that abounds within local communities and integrate these into the curricula. The concept "indigenous knowledge" is sometimes used synonymously with "traditional" knowledge and "local" knowledge to differentiate the knowledge developed by a given community from that developed in formal educational institutions. To problematise these definitions an editorial from the July 1998 issue of *Indigenous Knowledge and Development Monitor* focused on three definitions of indigenous knowledge; the second and third definitions are particularly useful to my discussions. The author discusses the definition given by

Grenier (1998) that describes indigenous knowledge as "the unique, traditional, local knowledge existing within and developed around the specific conditions of women and men indigenous to a particular area" (p. 7). The other definitions incorporate and expand Grenier's definition:

> Indigenous knowledge is the sum total of the knowledge and skills which people in a particular geographic area possess, and which enable them to get the most out of their natural environment. Most of this knowledge and these skills have been passed down from earlier generations, but individual men and women in each new generation adapt and add to this body of knowledge in a constant adjustment to changing circumstances and environmental conditions. They in turn pass on the body of knowledge intact to the next generation, in an effort to provide them with survival strategies. (Birmingham, 1998, p. 3)

Social work education in Nigeria must harness and adapt these resources that exist within communities as a base for enhancing development. Izugbara et al. (2003) provide evidence of the possibilities of drawing from indigenous knowledge to address some unique social problems in Nigeria such as communal conflicts. The authors describe how they relied on the indigenous cultural and knowledge systems and values to restore peace and normalcy to two warring Nigerian local communities. Their success with this case highlights the potentials of indigenous knowledge outside areas where research has already proved beneficial such as in health, agriculture, and the environment.

Mathias (1995) provides a detailed framework that Nigerian social work educators can draw from to begin the process of increasing available information on indigenous knowledge and encouraging their application in developmental activities. This framework lays out key tasks and activities that are necessary for these two objectives to be achieved. Examples include conducting in-depth research that involves local people and focuses on recording and analyzing indigenous knowledge in order to find out how this knowledge can be applied to relevant projects addressing social needs. Mathias also suggests several ways that indigenous knowledge could be disseminated to communities such as: providing information on indigenous knowledge success stories to the media, packaging it for policy-makers and development planners, developing manuals and case studies that demonstrate the applicability of indigenous knowledge, integrating indigenous knowledge modules into courses, and developing educational materials based on or including indigenous knowledge.

The dialogue to re-vision social work education and practice must also embrace the concept of indigenization. In contrast to the concept of authentication, which argues that social work in Africa and other developing countries needs to completely repudiate all Western influences, indigenization cautions against throwing the baby out with the bath water, arguing that Western models can be modified to suit local conditions. Walton and Abo El Nasr (1988) describe indigenization as a process that involves taking Western social work models and modifying them to suit a different cultural environment. Sometimes, this adaptation might also require consideration of both the political and socio-cultural context of the importing country.

Midgely (1981) emphasizes that the key idea in indigenization is ensuring appropriateness – of both professional social work roles and social work education – to the expectations of social work practice in a particular environment. Midgely (1990) points out that some social workers from developing countries have recognized the significance of indigenous religion and cultural beliefs and are incorporating these into their social work models. Burke and Ngonyani (2004) describe how casework is being indigenized in Tanzania to incorporate values like group self-determination with family and community involvement. These values are more appropriate in an African culture than individualistic Western values such as confidentiality and self-determination.

An important part of the dialogue on re-visioning social work education and practice in Nigeria is willingness and openness to sharing experiences with applying indigenous knowledge to contemporary problems and indigenizing Western knowledge to local conditions with international colleagues. Mamphiswana and Noyoo (2000) point out that social work education that is properly located and contextualized within indigenous African culture, tradition, and civilization will enable African scholars to contribute original products within the intellectual global village. In the current quest for internationalization of social work, driven primarily by globalization but with remnants of imperialism, exchange of best practices, theories, and resources have usually been unidirectional from the

West to developing countries. In what Midgley (1990, p. 300) correctly terms "the one-way international flow of ideas and practices," these exchanges have frequently cast social work educators and scholars from developing countries as potential recipients, and social work educators and scholars from the West as potential donors of knowledge.

This positioning needs to be challenged by both sides actively working together to ensure that experiences of developing countries social workers are visible on the international arena. Midgley pointed out several areas in which Western social workers could learn from social workers in developing countries, despite the vast differences in the demographic, economic, and cultural characteristics of the two. The experiences of social workers in developing countries who cope and manage with scarce resources and have long experience with working across cultures, as well as extensive experience dealing with social consequences of widespread and persistent poverty, can greatly inform and enrich social work practice in Western countries.

Stressing this point, Yan (2005) suggests that Western social work educators and scholars need to "empower colleagues from the developing world and de-centre the leading role of the developed world. We need to let the voices, ideas, experience, and theoretical conceptualizations of our colleagues from the developing world be heard, not only in their own countries as an indigenous knowledge, but also in the Western world as an alternative perspective" (p. 13). Yan offers several pertinent suggestions on how social work educators and scholars from both developed and developing countries can work towards learning from each other, taking into consideration unequal access to resources. Concrete suggestions include that journals should have reviewers and editorial boards from both developed and developing countries and conferences should provide incentives that encourage developing countries' participation such as special panels and fee waivers.

In addition to dialoguing about the three core issues discussed above, Nigerian social work education programs, at both the diploma and bachelor levels, need to focus on two pragmatic issues. The first is curriculum review using participatory research methods to identify gaps such as an overemphasis on academic content and minimal practical, culturally relevant, and community-based content and practice. This curriculum review will inform the development of critical course components identified as missing or deficient in the programs. Examples of missing course components include: gender and development, working with rural adults, community development, and family- and community-based social work practice. Strengthening the curriculum will enable the social work education sector in Nigeria to train a new generation of professional social workers with the necessary skills and knowledge to address the priorities of Nigeria through prevention and intervention projects that are founded on the principles of long-term social change.

The second issue is the establishment of an effective field education office to better support student practicum and field work. There is a broad consensus in social work literature that field education is critical to effectively prepare students in professional programs such as social work and teaching. While in the field, students assume the dual role of learner and practitioner and are expected to take over the responsibilities accordingly. Students carry out agency assignments, observe agency policies, preserve confidentiality, provide written reports and records, and otherwise behave in an appropriate professional manner. Field education is essential in helping students integrate theories learnt in the classroom with practice.

One of the great challenges facing universities around the world is how to move from the confines of the institution into the fields, streets, and villages of their nation. Nowhere is this truer than in Nigeria, where the universities, modelled after colonial British institutions of the period, are often physically and programmatically removed from the needs of the poor and marginalized. While such separation is regrettable anywhere, in the context of Africa, where so much is needed and there is so little infrastructure and expertise available, it is simply unacceptable. An effective field education program will help social work students build a bridge between the academic world and the real world inhabited by the vast majority of Nigerians.

In conclusion, the challenges facing twenty-first-century Nigeria demand a re-visioning of Nigeria's social work education from a remedial model towards a social developmental one. To begin re-visioning social work education and training programs, Nigerian professionals need to draw on new dialogues. Particularly, professionals must seek to integrate some of the extensive benchmarks for transforming curriculum and pedagogical practices to be more compatible with remedial social work in Nigeria. These advances described by several authors offer concrete pragmatic frameworks that the social work profession in Nigeria can draw from. In addition to these, I have suggested three core issues that this dialogue might focus on. First, social work education in Nigeria needs to rediscover the value of indigenous knowledge and integrate these into the curricula. In addition to recognizing the value of indigenous knowledge, social work education must also embrace the concept of indigenization of Western knowledge. Finally, Nigeria must be willing to share its experiences with applying indigenous knowledge to contemporary problems and indigenizing Western knowledge to local conditions within the international community. I have also suggested two pragmatic issues that current social work programs need to focus on. The first is a curriculum review using participatory research methods to identify gaps. The second is establishment of an effective field education office to better support student practicum and field work.

REFERENCES

Adeokun, L., Mantell, J. E., Weiss, E., Delano, G. E., Jagha, T., Olatoregun, J., Udo, D., Akinso, S. (2002). Promoting dual protection in family planning clinics in Ibadan, Nigeria. *International Family Planning Perspectives, 28*(2), 87–95.

Adepoju, A. (1974). Rural-urban socio-economic links: The example of migrants in south west Nigeria. In S. Amin (Ed.), *Modern migrations in West Africa* (pp. 127–37). London: Oxford.

Asamoah, Y., & Beverly, C. (1988). Collaboration between Western and African schools of social work: Problems and possibilities. *International Social Work, 31*, 177–95.

ASWEA. (1982). *Survey of curricula of social development training institutions in Africa.* Addis Ababa. Association of Schools of Social Work in Africa.

Bak, M. (2004). Can development social welfare change an unfair world: The South African experience. *International Social Work, 47*(1), 81–94.

Bamgbose, O. (2002). Teenage prostitution and the future of the female adolescent in Nigeria. *International Journal of Offender Therapy and Comparative Criminology, 46*(5), 569–85.

Birmingham, D. (1998). Learning local knowledge of soils: a focus on methodology. *Indigenous Knowledge and Development Monitor, 6*(2), 1–3.

Burke, J., & Ngonyani, B. (2004). A social work vision for Tanzania. *International Social Work, 47*(1), 39–52.

Drower, S. J. (2002). Conceptualizing social work in a changed South Africa. *International Social Work, 45*(1), 7–20.

Eltom, M. A., Mbulaiteye, S. M., Dada, A. J., Whitby, D., & Biggar, R. J. (2002). Transmission of human herpesvirus 8 by sexual activity among adults in Lagos, Nigeria. *AIDS, 16*(18), 2473–2478.

Estes, J. (1994). Education for social development: Curricular issues and models. *Social Development Issues, 16*(3), 68–90.

Estes, J. (1995). Social development trends in Africa 1970–1994: The need for a new paradigm. *Social Development Issues, 17*, 18–47.

Gray, M. M. (1996). Towards the understanding of developmental social work. *Social Work Practice 1*, 9–12.

Grenier, L. (1998). *Working with indigenous knowledge: A guide for researchers.* Ottawa: IDRC.

Hammoud, H. R. (1988). Social work education in developing countries: Issues and problems in undergraduate curricula. *International Social Work, 31*, 195–210.

Howard, M. O., & Lambert, M. D. (1996). The poverty of social work. In P. R. Raffoul & C. A. McNeece (Eds.), *Future issues for social work practice* (pp. 270–92). Needleham Heights: Allyn and Bacon.

Izugbara, O., Ugal, A., & Ukwayi, J. (2003). Indigenous knowledge and communal conflict resolution: Evidence from Nigeria. *African Journal of Indigenous Knowledge Systems, 2*, 1–14.

Jagusah, O.I.W. (2001) Educational policy in Africa and the issue(s) of context: The case of Nigeria and South Africa. *International Education Journal, 2* (5), 113–25.

Lindsey, D., & Kirk, S. (1992). The continuing crisis in social work research: Conundrum or solvable problem? An essay review. *Journal of Social Work Education, 28*(3), 370–81.

Mathias, E. (1995). Framework for enhancing the use of indigenous knowledge. *Indigenous Knowledge and Development Monitor, 3*(2) 17–18.

Mamphiswana, D., & Noyoo, N. (2000). Social education in a changing socio-political and economic dispensation: Perspectives from South Africa. *International Social Work, 43*(1), 21–32.

Midgley, J. (1981). *Professional imperialism: Social work in the third world.* London: Heinemann.

Midgley, J. (1990). International social work: Learning from the third world. *Social Work, 35*(4), 295–301.

Midgley, J. (1995). *Social development: The development perspective in social welfare.* Thousand Oaks, CA: Sage.

Midgely, J. (1997b). Social work and international social development. In M. C. Hokenstad & J. Midgley (Eds.), *Issues in international social work* (pp. 17–26). Washington, DC: NASW.

Mullaly, R. (1997). *Structural social work: Ideology, theory and practice.* Don Mills, ON: Oxford.

Mupedziswa, R. (2001). The quest for relevance: Towards a conceptual model of developmental social work education and training in Africa. *International Social Work, 44*(3), 285–300.

Nigerian National Planning Committee. (2004). *Meeting everyone's needs. National Economic Empowerment and Development Strategy.* Communications Development Incorporated: Nigeria

Odiah, C. A. (1991). Identification of gaps in social work education on Nigeria. PhD dissertation, University of Toronto.

Okeke, P. E. (2000). Reconfiguring tradition: Women's rights and social status in contemporary Nigeria. *Africa Today, 47*(1), 49–63.

Osei-Hwedie, K. (1993). The challenge of social work in Africa: Starting the indigenization process. *Journal of Social Development in Africa, 8*(1), 19–30.

Pierce, S. (2003). Farmers and 'prostitutes': Twentieth-century problems of female inheritance in Kano emirate, Nigeria. *Journal of African History, 44*(3), 463–86.

Rossiter, A. B. (1996). A perspective on critical social work. *Journal of Progressive Human Services, 7*(2), 23–40.

Shawky, A. (1972). Social work education in Africa. *International Social Work, 15*(3) 3-16.

Uduigwomen. (2004). A critical assessment of the retributive theory of punishment. *Global Journal of Humanities, 3*(1&2): *9-13*

United Nations. (2003). *Report on the World Social Situation, 2003.* United Nations General Assembly: New York.

United Nations (1979). Convention on the Elimination of all Forms of Discrimination against Women. Retrieved January 26, 2007 from: http://www.un.org/women-watch/daw/cedaw/

UNICEF (2004). *State of the World's Children.* United Nations: New York.

Walton, R. G., & Abo El Nasr, M.M.A. (1988). Indigenization and authentication in terms of social work in Egypt. *International Social Work, 31,* 135–44.

World Bank. (2002). *Health Systems Development Project Document.*

Yan, M. C. (2005). Searching for international social work: A reflection on personal and professional journey. *Reflections: Narrative of Professional Helping, 11*(1), 4–16.

Young, A., and Ashton, E. (1956/1963). *British social work in the 19th century.* London: RKP.

Notes

1 The term "Western" refers to countries with advanced industrial development, for instance, the G7. However, very often in social work literature, "developed countries" are used interchangeably with "the West" or "Western countries" or "the North." Very often these terms are loosely defined. Since it is not the intention of this chapter to define these terms, I will use them interchangeably to signify a group of Anglophonic industrial countries.

2 Some people use "Third World" or "the South" to describe countries that are economically underdeveloped. In this paper, for consistency, "developing" is used to signify the process of development.

3 For an extensive description of survey methodology, see National Institute of Social and Economic Research, 1982, in Odiah (1991).

7

A COMPARISON OF INSTITUTIONAL DISCRIMINATORY PRACTICES AGAINST PEOPLE WITH DISABILITIES IN NORTH AMERICA AND AFRICA: CASES IN ZIMBABWE AND CANADA

Zephania Matanga

ABSTRACT

This chapter makes a cross-disability discussion of institutional discriminatory practices against people with disabilities in Zimbabwe and Canada. The author explores the negative attitudes toward people with disabilities in economic, social, political, and intellectual structures in these societies. This analytical comparison between Canada and Zimbabwe demonstrates that discriminatory practices against people with disabilities are not confined to the developing world; rather, they are global. The chapter provides deeper insight into the challenges facing people with disabilities and offers a discussion of current policy developments and institutional initiatives that are working to address these challenges.

INTRODUCTION

Since time immemorial people with disabilities have been isolated, ostracized, and relegated to charity, medical, psychological, rehabilitation and, recently, to a few integrated institutions. These austere institutions are administered by able-bodied professionals who are, in most cases, insensitive to the needs of their clients. Also, until recently, public policies have not reflected the interests of handicapped people. Yet even the current policies that attempt to incorporate the interests of people with disabilities are designed and implemented by able-bodied professionals in ways that force the handicapped to try and fit themselves into the able-bodied world. This chapter is based on data collected from Canada and Zimbabwe about the challenges faced by the disabled in these two countries. This analytical comparison yields interesting results, which demonstrate that discriminatory practices against people with disabilities are not confined to developing countries, rather, they percolate throughout the economic, social, political, and intellectual structures of any society, regardless of its development status. The data further indicate that the challenges faced by people with disabilities in these two different contexts are similar and that they are not isolated; rather, they cross national and cultural boundaries. These findings also challenge the notion that discriminatory practices committed against people with disabilities are either self-inflicted by the disability itself or dismissed as isolated incidences and localized problems, which are especially prevalent in and mostly confined to developing countries. Such notions of disability often strip the disabled of their fundamental rights and basic humanity. The assertion here is that, just as slavery, the holocaust, and other forms of oppression are universally considered unacceptable, the ill-treatment of people with disabilities should also be viewed as a universal inequity.

BACKGROUND AND THEORETICAL FRAMEWORK

Although a number of policies have been enacted, both in Canada and Zimbabwe, to alleviate the challenges experienced by people with disabilities, there have been few progressive initiatives since people with disabilities continue to experience discriminatory practices. For instance, in 1982, the Government of Canada formalized disability rights in the enactment of the *Charter of Rights and Freedoms*, particularly in Section 15 of the Canadian Constitution. According to Section 15 of the *Charter*, every individual is equal before and under the law and has the right to equal protection and equal benefit of the law without discrimination and, in particular, without discrimination based on race, national or ethnic origin, colour, religion, sex, age, or mental or physical disability. Over the years, some steps have been taken to ensure that people with disabilities experience the basic human rights as stipulated by Section 15 (Government of Canada, 1982). Yet, to date, such rights have been slow in coming, as indicated by the 2004 Speech from the Throne, in which the Government of Canada stated:

> Many Canadians with disability are ready to contribute but confront different obstacles in the workplace and in their communities. Too often families are left on their own to care for a severely disabled relative. Here too, the government of Canada has a role. We want a Canada in which citizens with disabilities have the opportunity to contribute to and benefit from Canada's prosperity – as learners, workers, volunteers, and family members. Canada can not afford to squander the talents of people with disabilities or turn its back on those who seek to provide care and a life of dignity for family members with severe disabilities. (Citizenship and Immigration Canada, 2004, p. 1)

Therefore, despite stipulated policies such as stated in the *Charter of Rights and Freedoms*, Canadians with disabilities continue to struggle against discrimination and live in poverty. The discrimination faced by Canadians with disabilities is further demonstrated by the employment gap between Canadians with disabilities and able-bodied aged twenty-five to fifty-four years, which has significantly increased despite the economic boom of the 1990s. More significantly, according to a Labour-force Participation Survey (Service Canada, 2001), youths with disabilities face challenges in making the transition from school to the labour market, with only 45.7 per cent of youths with disabilities being employed compared to employment rates of 56.6 per cent for youths without disabilities. In general, youths with disabilities are more likely to be unemployed than youths without disabilities (11.2 per cent, compared to 8.5 per cent). The difficulties faced by youths with disabilities in the transition to employment are also apparent in the labour-force participation rates of young people no longer in school. Among youths with disabilities, 53.0 per cent who are out of school are employed and 13.7 per cent are unemployed; the remaining 33 per cent were unaccounted for in the survey. In contrast, among youths without disabilities who are no longer students, 72.3 per cent are employed and 9.1 per cent are unemployed; again, 18.6 per cent of respondents made no response on their employment status (Service Canada, 2001). It is also important to note that according to Statistics Canada (2001), during the working-age years fifteen to sixty-four, persons with disabilities experience great challenge. The employment rates range from 45.7 per cent for youths with disabilities to 51.2 per cent among core-working ages, to 27.3 per cent among older workers with disabilities. These rates are all substantially lower than those of persons without disabilities. As well, 51.3 per cent of working age Canadians with disabilities are not in the labour force at all versus only 20.6 per cent of those without disabilities (Statistics Canada, 2001).

Literature on the plight of the physically disabled in Africa is lacking. What is known is from the United Nations Population Information Network, which indicated that of the almost 800 million people living in the continent, 50 million are disabled. Given the fact that the definition of disability in Africa is very conservative, it is surprising that these statistics are pointing that one in every sixteen Africans has a disability. Moreover, only 2 per cent have access to any form of rehabilitation, 90 per cent of children with mental disability die before age five, and 70 per cent of disabled adults are unemployed and live in poverty. Additionally, in Africa there are factors such as wars, land mines, malnutrition, diseases, poverty, and so on that make disability more widespread than in other parts of the world. As recently as 2005, the United Nations Secretary General Kofi Annan, marking the International Day for Persons with Disabilities, noted that:

Persons with disabilities make up the world's largest minority group. They are disproportionately poor, are more likely to be unemployed, and have higher rates of mortality than the general population. All too often, they do not enjoy the full spectrum of civil, political, social, cultural, and economic rights. For many years, the rights of persons with disabilities were overlooked. (United Nations Enable, 2005, p. 1)

This statement comes fifteen years after the United Nations declaration of a decade for persons with disabilities and sixty years after the Holocaust.

Lifton (1986) has documented how Nazi physicians killed those who were disabled or sick before the Nazis undertook the mass killing of Jews. Yet, compared to the Jewish Holocaust, and to other atrocities of a similar nature, the killing of the disabled did not receive much public outcry when the atrocities were discovered after the war. Commenting on the unequal treatment of the disabled, Woodil (1992) argues, "While much of the study of persons with a mental or physical disability has resulted in less drastic treatment than death, many persons with a disability have been confined, subjected to treatments without their consent, and abused with the tacit or explicit approval of professionals trained in scientific research" (p. 19). Similarly, McGee et al. (1991) state:

In reviewing the programs in more than 200 institutions in the United States and other countries, we have witnessed a pattern of punishment practices such a beatings, isolation, persistent administration of electric shock to parts of the body, the use of psychoactive drugs for chemical restraint, using helmets that emit irritating noise called white sound, masked helmets locked at the neck, persons tied like animals to metal bed frames, turn-of-century straitjacket, and noxious substances squirted in the face and eyes. (pp. 24–25)

In many developing countries, including Zimbabwe, the treatment of the disabled is also serious, especially regarding access to schools, workplaces, and other public institutions. Not providing access to these places is viewed by the able-bodied public as natural, unavoidable, and justifiable. Acquiescence is tantamount to publicly accepted neglect. For example, in Zimbabwe in 1986, the Ministry of Education suspended the recruitment of visually handicapped teachers, citing the public's negative attitude as a concern. Actually, in one school in Zimbabwe, the head of the school rallied teachers, parents, and students to stage a demonstration against a female visually handicapped teacher. Parents were unwilling to allow this teacher, regardless of her qualifications and excellent teaching experience, to teach their children. Instead of defending the teacher, as it often does with other employees who, in some cases, are corrupt and incompetent, the Ministry of Education quietly removed her from the school and sent her to work at another school designated for blind students. In 1991, Canada witnessed a similar incident involving a visually impaired teacher. A colleague of mine, Patti Simmons, despite his honours degree from McMaster University, his degree in education from the University of Toronto's Faculty of Education, and his excellent record of practice teaching, encountered formidable resistance from Ontario school boards in his employment search. In the end, he was hired at Fort Frances High School as a replacement teacher for one year.

Incidents of discrimination against the disabled are likely to take place almost every day throughout the world and are always dismissed as isolated and insignificant. Since these incidents take place in both developed and developing countries, one can safely argue that discrimination against people with disabilities is not economically based; rather, it is based on negative attitudes and intolerance. This perspective is articulated by Smith (1985) when stating that the general public's typical assumptions about a person with a disability are that he or she is lazy, stupid, unmotivated, and doesn't care. Developing this point further, Beezer (1991) states that in discussing the problem of a visually handicapped job applicant one court made the following observations, which could apply equally to other handicapped persons: "The blind person in our society seems burdened with a double handicap: The first handicap – loss of physical sight – does not appear, however, to present as great an obstacle as the second – society's lack of vision as to the capacity of a blind individual to enjoy a full and a meaningful life despite the loss of physical sight" (*Hoffman v. Ohio Youth Commission*, 13 FEP, case 30, Ohio, 1975).

In 1988 the Zimbabwe Ministry of Education reluctantly changed its discriminatory policies against visually handicapped teachers. Its reluctance was best demonstrated by the non-committal statement in its policy that a "blind teacher may be hired." Under this policy visually handicapped teachers were expected to persuade heads of schools to hire them, which meant that the heads of schools had the choice to either accept or reject a visually handicapped applicant. Even though the Ministry changed its discriminatory policies, working conditions for visually handicapped teachers continue to be intolerable as teachers are still required to pay their marking assistants from their meagre salaries. More importantly, promotional prospects for the visually handicapped are still very remote.

In Ontario, the prospects for visually handicapped teachers are also bleak, which is demonstrated by the absence of visually handicapped teachers in Toronto public schools. The only places to have hired visually handicapped teachers are Hollywood and Bradford schools in Scarborough, which are residential schools for visually handicapped students. Although the visually handicapped teachers' rights are protected under the Ontario Human Rights Code, discriminatory practices are still exercised in very subtle ways. For instance, on a job application, if an applicant indicates that he or she is blind, he or she is automatically disqualified and never receives a response. If one does not indicate on the application form that he or she is handicapped and this is noticed by the interviewers, chances of employment are narrowed. In the United States, visually handicapped teachers have had to request the intervention of the court to redress this situation.

Teachers' negative attitudes are dangerous to children with disabilities in mainstream schools, as demonstrated by a study conducted by Colman et al. (1987). This study investigated whether or not regular classroom teachers and resource-room teachers systematically differ in their perceptions of the behavioural adjustment of mainstream handicapped pupils in the primary grades in the Washington school district. They found that "regular classroom teachers rated the handicapped pupil sample as significantly more maladjusted than did resource room teachers on the WIPBIC total score on four of the five scale scores" (1987, p. 34). Colman et al. further argue that teacher expectations are powerful determinants of teacher-child classroom interactions. Their study uncovered that approximately one-third of teachers formulate differential expectations of students' classroom competencies and then act upon them in their instructional and management interactions. In other words, handicapped and disadvantaged pupils usually comprise the membership of the less competent group, for whom teachers hold drastically lowered expectations. "As a result, teachers who fit this profile are very likely to behave in ways that maximize the achievement of the high expectation, more competent pupils and minimize it for the low expectation, less competent pupils. Mainstreamed handicapped pupils are especially at risk for this process" (1987, p. 38). Writing from personal experiences, Martinez (1990) confirms that disabled people face institutional risks in the very early stages of their lives: "Most of the people I have met who work in this field don't believe that I could have a good quality of life or that I could even live on my own. When I was little, the doctor told my parents that I would never be able to take care of myself and that they should put me away" (p. 3).

In a study about the impact of inclusion in schools, Smith and Smith (2000) uncovered that many teachers were reluctant to work in inclusive ways that accommodate people with disabilities. Inclusion here is defined as the practice in which schools and other public institutions put in place resources in order to accommodate the needs of the disabled population. Smith and Smith reveal a troubling trend, in which teachers are supportive of inclusion in the abstract but argue that they find it unrealistic in their daily dealings with the disabled. Smith and Smith (2000) went further to point out "prior research has indicated that classroom teachers may be very sceptical of inclusion and that they strongly expect that the practice will present inherent problems" (p. 165). In Nova Scotia, Sadhu (2002) conducted a study in which she examined teachers' perceptions of the conditions under which they provide appropriate education to students with special needs. In this study, teachers' views on inclusion rendered results similar to those of Smith and Smith, indicating that many teachers found the inclusion of physically disabled students a challenge. Sadhu states that teachers identified inclusion as a challenge because of lack of adequate professional development, material, and human resources.

Another study by Brackenreed (2004) investigated teachers' perceptions of testing accommodations to the Ontario Secondary School Literacy Test for students with special needs. One of the major findings of this study was that:

> Items that drew disagreement from the respondents tended to cluster into a distinct group of items that appears to be concerned with alternate test formats such as: extended time limits, reading

a test aloud, reducing the number of items on a page, rewording questions, and teaching test-taking skills. It would appear that most of the teachers perceive that these accommodations do change the nature of what is being assessed, or do contaminate the validity of the testing instrument, which negates the advisability of making comparisons between students with special needs who write the test with these accommodations and students without special needs who do not use these accommodations to the test. (p. 15)

In this regard, inclusion has still retained the fundamental principle of integration. Through integration a student with special needs has to accommodate the school or work activities instead of the activities being adjusted to meet his or her disabling conditions. All these studies indicate that, while in developed countries inclusion has become a politically correct notion, its practical application has not yet served well students with special needs.

In developing countries the trend has been more towards integration as opposed to inclusion, resulting in an increase in special schools that care for the disabled separately from able-bodied students. Devereux and Sabates-Wheeler (2004) argue that the continuing separation of the disabled is in tune with "traditional beliefs among many Zimbabweans, which consider a disabled child inherently different from other children. For this reason, *inter alia*, it made sense to develop separate education systems" (p. 48).

The above are examples of larger problems facing people with disabilities in all spheres of their lives. There is a general absence of acceptance from teachers, professors, students, and the society at large to accommodate people with disabilities. The premise of this chapter is that the perpetuation of discriminatory policies is largely driven by stereotypic attitudes rather than the technical and economic development status of communities and countries. Additionally, this chapter argues that the public's silence on these issues of discrimination is tantamount to gross neglect and mistreatment.

Attitudinal problems were clearly demonstrated in the two studies set in Zimbabwe and Canada. The Zimbabwean study focused on the integration of visually handicapped teachers into mainstream schools. In this qualitative study, I interviewed twenty-one education officers about the problems visually handicapped teachers face in mainstream classrooms. Although this study dealt with a lot of issues, in this chapter I have focused on five potential problems: marking, classroom management, involvement in extra-curricular activities, use of audio-visual aids, and community attitudes. The study in Ontario focused on the involvement of people with disabilities in a research organization. This case study examined issues of power and how the staff mediated decision-making processes, economic reward, and the relationship between the researchers and the disabled participants. The study also examined elements of social organization in research, specifically, the social and cultural factors that impede or promote full participation of persons with disabilities in research studies.

The results yielded from these two studies were generally similar in that both studies pointed to negative perceptions as key factors in the way researchers and education officers viewed people with disabilities. The issue is how competent people with disabilities are overshadowed by the negative attitudes of those who work with them.

CURRENT REALITIES OF THE DISABLED IN CONTEXT

To further explore the inequities facing people with disabilities described by Waxman (1990) and others, I decided to take a close look at how people with disabilities are treated in two countries – Canada and Zimbabwe. Canada is an attractive site because of its location in a highly developed part of the world and because it was declared by the United Nations as one of the best countries to live in (Edwards, 2000). Moreover, Canada is well known internationally for promoting and exercising human rights. Zimbabwe was the second choice because it is located in southern Africa and is considered one of the least developed countries in the world. Moreover, like many other African countries, until 1992, Zimbabwe did not have a law safeguarding the interests of disabled people. It therefore provided an opportunity to examine the struggles developing countries face in their efforts to address human-rights issues. Overall, however, the results from these two studies should not be taken as representative of how people with disabilities are treated throughout the world. Broader generalizations require broader sources of comparison; however, it is hoped that the information provided by these two studies will lead to a wider examination of discrimination in the international community.

The Canadian study, which was based in Toronto, demonstrates how researchers perpetuate handicapped people's dependency by, for example, encouraging them to volunteer their time to projects funded by the government. In contrast, able-bodied researchers receive huge salaries. The idea that people with disabilities should volunteer their time and energy to publicly and privately funded projects and not receive compensation has become an acceptable institutional practice in Canada. People with disabilities are encouraged and convinced to volunteer because researchers argue that the research projects for which they volunteer are intended to benefit the disabled community. The relationship between the disabled volunteer and the able-bodied researcher is euphemistically described as a "partnership" between consumers and researchers; yet, in reality, it is a partnership of the unequal. Writing from a North American perspective, Ysseldyke et al. (1992) argue that research organizations' main motives are to receive funding by pretending that they are promoting the interests of the handicapped. However, 80 per cent of research budgets are spent on salaries for able-bodied people, management activities, and conducting endless meetings hosted in expensive hotels. Ysseldyke et al. further point out that "assessment and decision-making require as much as thirteen to fifteen hours of professional time. If we estimate an average charge of 15 dollars per hour by each professional then the costs of assessment are obviously high" (1992, p. 127). Actually, the main issue is not the exorbitant cost of assessing handicapped persons but the information gained from the assessment. They also observe that, "It costs as much as 1,800 dollars to assess and make decisions for one student and the practical knowledge gained from such activities is marginal at best" (p. 127). In the Canadian context, a report written by Burt Perrin Associates for Evaluation Services, Evaluation and Data Development for Human Resources Development Canada (1999) states:

> While the full costs of disability to society are not known, the estimated cost to the federal government of income support programs and provision of goods and services is more than $6 billion annually. This does not take into account the costs of provincial programs and private sector insurance plans, or the lost income

and foregone taxes from people who are capable of work but who face barriers which prevent them from employment. (p. 1)

In Zimbabwe, using disabled people as fundraising objects is common. The Ministry of Education, as well as schools and churches, capitalize on, for example, the plight of visually handicapped students as a way to secure funding from donor agencies. For instance, one school in Zimbabwe solicited and received funds for building a school dormitory that would house handicapped students, yet not one blind student is a resident of that dormitory. Subjecting human beings to this sophisticated exploitative practice is dehumanizing.

Africa needs to pay special attention to disability issues because, at the moment, it is fertile ground for an uprising of the disability population. Over the last three decades, Africa has experienced numerous civil wars, political unrest, armed struggles against colonialism and apartheid, natural disasters such as droughts, and diseases such as HIV/AIDS, which have produced a higher percentage of people with disabilities, especially among the working-age population. For example, following national independence, Zimbabwe was embroiled in a thirteen-year civil war that left over one million people disabled. The disabled population in Angola and Mozambique, which are countries that were engaged in armed struggles against colonialism and later civil wars for over fifty years, is estimated to be higher than that of Zimbabwe. Survivors of these wars not only suffer from permanent physical disability and other injuries, they also suffer from war trauma. The anti-humane land mines, which were planted during the wars and subsequently forgotten about, continue to maim and kill people in Angola and Mozambique. Such violent realities have resulted in a large percentage of young people who could potentially contribute to the economy of the country becoming disabled, uneducated, and dependent on welfare systems or international handouts. Above all, many African countries have very limited resources for welfare or other social-support programs. As a result, disability in Africa is not only a moral, social, and charitable issue but also an economic one. The major initiative currently taking place in Africa is the African Decade for Persons with Disabilities. This initiative is administered by the Secretariat for African Decade for Persons with Disabilities, which is a pan-African disability organization whose purpose is to facilitate development processes linked to the Continental Plan of Action for the African Decade (1999–2008). The Secretariat is located in Cape Town, South Africa, and derives its legitimacy from the Consultative Conference Delegates (CCD), the Africa Rehabilitation Institute (ARI), and a representative of the South African Government. The Decade Management Committee is composed of two representatives from the following regional Disabled People's Organizations:

- African Union of the Blind (AFUB),
- Pan-Africa Federation of the Disabled (PAFOD),
- Inclusion Africa and Indian Ocean (IAIO),
- Pan-Africa Federation of Users of Psychiatric Services (PANUPS),
- Africa Branch of World Federation of the Deaf (WFD/Africa), and
- Africa Branch of World Federation of the Blind-Deaf (WFBD/Africa).

The secretariat is implementing the Continental Plan of Action in Ethiopia, Mozambique, Kenya, Rwanda, and Senegal to serve as a sample that can be replicated in other African countries in the future.

A LOOK AT CANADA'S SERVING ORGANIZATION

The Canadian research organization, which was the subject of this study, was established to examine and develop appropriate assistive devices that would improve the quality of life and promote integration of people with disabilities into society. It was a partnership between several universities and research institutes and was funded by the Ontario Ministry of Health.

The funding was granted on the understanding that people with disabilities would have direct, timely, and meaningful input into the many and varied activities of the research organization. Input included the selection of projects that were to be undertaken and the selection of methods through which the projects were to be evaluated. Such input and process-related ideas were inserted at the proposal stage, but the proposal itself did not stipulate how they would be implemented. Even though the Ministry of Health and the research organization insisted that they valued the input of people with disabilities, they did not have a clear plan stipulating how and where these inputs fit into their agenda. Hence, the implementation was left in the hands of the researchers. Also, there were no checks and balances to ensure that the organization did actually include people with disabilities. Therefore, it was clear from the very beginning that the Ministry of Health and the researchers were simply paying lip service to the involvement of people with disabilities.

The plan to involve people with disabilities was conceptualized by the researchers without the input of the disabled people themselves; thus, it appeared that people with disabilities were to be used as subjects if they were needed in this process. This was evidenced by the administrative structure, which consisted of three committee levels: the advisory committee, the management committee, and the sub-groups committee. All three committees were controlled and managed by researchers. The advisory committee included only three people with disabilities out of twelve members. In theory, this committee reviewed and made decisions on the projects proposed by the management committee; however, in practice, the committee simply endorsed the proposed projects. The management committee had the most power in the administrative structure and its membership was made up of seventeen able-bodied researchers. People with disabilities were not represented at this level, which was ironic since this was the major decision-making committee. The third level was the subgroup committees, which operated under the leadership of a nominated individual who was also a researcher. These researchers were assigned to look into specific disabling conditions such as confinement to wheelchairs and visual impairment. Under these arrangements, researchers were paid to examine conditions of the disabled population, and disabled people were supposed to volunteer their knowledge, experiences, and ideas. The examination of how people with disabilities were involved in research organizations in Ontario used process indicators from previous research studies as shown in Table 8.1.

Table 8.1: Studies influencing process indicators.

STUDY	MAIN THEME	PROCESS INDICATORS
Bjaras et al. (1991)	Direct community participation	Leadership, organization, resource mobilization, management and needs assessment
Drake (1991)	Consumers' influence	Capacity to act, roles in authority, organizational network
Shalinsky (1989)	Technology development	Context, goals, status relations, motivation, communication, participation

Bjaras, G., Haglund, B.J.A., and Rifkin, S. (1991). A new approach to community participation assessment. *Health Promotion International 6*(3), 199–206.

Drake, R.F., and Owens, D.J. (1991). Consumer involvement and the voluntary sector in Wales: Breakthrough or bandwagon? *Critical Social Policy 11*(33), 76–86.

Shalinsky, W. (1989). Interdisciplinary and interorganizational concerns in the development of technology for physically disabled persons. *Disability and Society 4*(1), 65–79.

Design of the Canadian case

In this investigation, two separate questionnaires were used: one was for the research group funded by the health ministry (referred to as "providers"), and the other was for the disabled participants with whom the research group worked (referred to as "consumers"). Twenty-nine consumers working with providers were surveyed over a two-week period in June 1993. A variety of formats were used to administer the questionnaire, including telephone, TDD, on-line interviews, e-mail, diskettes, and paper and pencil forms. Responses were received from twenty providers (70 per cent response rate). This is a reasonable rate considering the brief survey period and the variety of survey formats used.

In their questionnaire, consumers were asked to rate the importance of a series of potential interview questions if research about disability was to be conducted. High-ranking questions addressed barriers and supports for consumer involvement, methods of involvement, and satisfaction. Example questions included: Are there barriers to your participation? How satisfied are you with your involvement? Consumers were also asked to define "effective involvement."

Providers were asked about how they felt regarding the involvement of consumers in all research stages. If providers responded by stating that consumers should not be involved or that they should be minimally involved, they were then asked to state reasons for their non-involvement stance and/or to identify those minimal areas of involvement. Providers were also asked about previous experiences working with people with disabilities in general and were specifically questioned about their involvement working with consumers in their subgroups. The questions teased out the nature and level of participation of the disabled in subgroups as well as the recruitment initiatives undertaken. Those consumers' responses gathered through the telephone were tape recorded and then transcribed, while those that were written on the questionnaire were preserved in their original state. All responses were studied and analyzed in order to identify common themes.

Consumers' perspectives

The responses, which can also be seen as the concerns from people with disabilities, can be summarized as follows. First, there were expressions of outrage regarding lack of accessibility facilities such as Braille and sign interpreters. Second, consumers expressed that they were often required to attend meetings for which they needed special travel arrangements and that they were expected to cover their own costs. Consumers expressed the need for easier wheelchair access to buildings and that they needed additional resources such as education and training so that they could work as equal partners with the researchers. Third, consumers expressed the need for providers to value and respect handicapped people's contributions in the same economic terms as the researchers' input. That is, people with disabilities should receive remuneration for the time they spend assisting providers in figuring out technological needs, approving the investigations of new devices, conducting the evaluation of newly designed devices, and assisting them in marketing these devices. Fourth, consumers felt that, for their contributions to be meaningful, they should be present at all major meetings, especially where important decisions are made, which would allow them to contribute suggestions and make policy-related recommendations. One consumer was so appalled by the current relationship between disabled participants and able-bodied researchers that she described it as analogous to the relationship between a dog and its food.

Providers' perspectives

Providers portrayed a more favourable relationship with handicapped people, even though these portrayals were not confirmed by the handicapped themselves. Providers stated that they involved handicapped people in all necessary research activities mandated by the research organization and that they have always provided and will continue to provide consumers with access services, including transportation and travel funding, accessible communication services such as Braille, attendant care, and reimbursement of other expenses. Nonetheless, the fact that all providers expressed the importance of involving handicapped people in research, especially in research that deals with rehabilitation technology, did not stop them from voicing reservations about the effectiveness of this kind of collaboration. Providers stated that they found it very difficult to find consumers and participants who could work together in a collaborative fashion. Additionally, they expressed reservations about the capabilities of some consumers who, even with additional resources such as education and training, could not make a meaningful contribution. Providers argued that making use of their own observations was more effective than using direct feedback from handicapped people.

Providers further stated they were not expected to spend a lot of time and funds addressing transportation and other physically related needs, which divert their attention from concentrating on "real" issues such as technology design. They further pointed out that there is danger in spending a lot of money on such social programs, and yet achieve very little in designing devices. While providers had no clear idea about the mandate surrounding the involvement of consumers in research, they foresaw problems around the sharing of expertise by consumers and providers.

ZIMBABWEAN REALITIES

The Zimbabwe study was conceptualized because of my experiences with the consequences that emanated from the Ministry of Education's resistance to employ visually handicapped teachers. The Ministry justified this resistance by arguing that visually handicapped teachers would have difficulties in marking, using visual aids, managing classes, and involving themselves in extra-curricular activities and would face resistance from students and parents. The study had three goals: first, examine the viability of the assumption that if visually handicapped teachers are hired to teach sighted students they are likely to encounter resistance from education officers, principals, teachers, students, and parents; second, uncover the nature and source of this resistance; and third, devise strategies that could be used to overcome this resistance. These strategies would facilitate the integration of visually impaired teachers into the mainstream and the government, schools, and community to achieve successful implementation of this integration.

In Zimbabwe, questions were developed and distributed to twenty-one education officers from the head office of the Ministry of Education in Mashonaland's east region. The questions were designed to uncover first, how these officers ranked the effectiveness of the visually impaired teacher in their pedagogical skill; second, to determine whether disabled teachers were viewed to possess classroom managerial abilities including methods of discipline; third, to examine if able-bodied officials viewed visually impaired teachers as an economic liability; and fourth, to tease out overall perceptions that officers held of these teachers (whether they viewed blind teachers as angry, bitter, or emotionally unstable because of the disability).

Education officers' perceptions

In examining the results from the study conducted in Zimbabwe, it is worth noting that this study had some methodological shortcomings, which were, among other things, manifestations of the political order of the time. First, the study was conducted during a period when serious debates in the Ministry were going on about the recruitment of handicapped teachers. As a result, education officers were aware of the sensitivity of the issue under investigation, which may have influenced them to offer ideas that they considered politically in tune with the public discourse at the time. Second, educational officers may have been influenced by the fact that the study was being conducted by a visually handicapped person, thus offering sympathetic views. Despite these apparent shortfalls, the study did capture a wide spectrum of attitudinal challenges confronted by handicapped teachers in their efforts to be integrated into mainstream schools.

Study participants from Zimbabwe exhibited both negative and positive attitudes towards visually handicapped teachers. Even though fewer educational officers were skeptical about the ability of visually handicapped teachers to mark, manage classrooms, and so on, the results indicate that their attitudes were overwhelmingly negative if the visually handicapped teachers' employment required extra financial support from the schools or the Ministry. They would prefer that visually handicapped teachers fend for themselves, which would include paying readers and acquiring technical devices from their own salaries.

Of the twenty-one officers interviewed, six expressed reservations about the ability of visually handicapped teachers to incorporate visual aids into their instructional methods. Registering his reservation, one officer stated,

> It looks impossible for anyone to go round this limitation. My experience with blind teachers is that they always resort to lecture methods and ask some pupils to write on the chalkboard for them. This compromises pupils' learning. There are some visual aids such as diagrams which cannot be substituted, and how can a blind teacher draw them on the board?

This quote exemplifies the many negative perceptions about people with disabilities, which were dominant in the minds of many able-bodied teachers, students, and parents. The unfortunate part of this is that, as demonstrated by the two incidents referred to at the beginning of this chapter, such attitudes influence policy decisions that are implemented without input from handicapped individuals. As an aside, it is worth noting that the concerns expressed above by the educational officer were also expressed by teachers in one school district in the United States to a blind student teacher who was being integrated into their school (Miller, 1982). In this case, the sighted teachers were concerned about how she would use phrases such as "show me" and "look at." However, unlike the Zimbabwe cases, these sighted teachers handled the situation more positively by giving the blind student teacher an opportunity to explain and demonstrate how she would execute her duties.

As a visually handicapped citizen of Zimbabwe, I too experienced similar attitudinal problems and resistance when I was hired to teach both sighted and visually handicapped students in Zimbabwe. In my situation, the resistance was from some of my colleagues, students, and parents to the point where colleagues often used derogatory and demeaning comments in my presence in an attempt to dislodge me from the teaching field. Tactics used by my colleagues included making unkind remarks about me to my students, sneaking into my classroom, and openly calling me a preacher not a teacher, since they assumed that I could not use visual aids for instructional purposes and I would be limited to the lecture method.

Contrary to the negative views expressed by the six education officers, fifteen officers offered positive views and provided alternative ways of approaching instructional challenges. These officers acknowledged the importance of visual aids in teaching, but also suggested that other methods exist that can be effectively used to achieve the same intended goals. Their ideas were best represented by the following respondent's statement:

> Visual aids are intended to assist students; however, their importance varies with the academic level of the student. At higher levels of learning, students deal more with abstract concepts. The blind teacher can still use his body as part of his visual aids. He/she can also use verbal explanations more. Some of the diagrams can be put into Braille for the teacher to explain to students.

Practical applications, such as the use of Braille, implemented by one of the blind teachers substitute visually oriented phrases while retaining the same intended and communicated meaning. For instance, instead of saying "show me," the blind student teacher cited in Miller (1982) would say "explain to me clearly what you have done." Similarly, in my teaching, I made efforts to adapt teaching techniques used by my sighted colleagues to my situation. For example, I distributed handouts and used overheads instead of writing on the board. There are now many alternative instructional strategies like the use of videos and dictating text to speech computers that can be connected to big screen projectors, making it possible for a visually handicapped teacher to type while students see what is being typed.

One of the fundamental principles of teaching is to provide students with meaningful feedback on their written assignments. Since visually handicapped teachers cannot read print, it is impossible to assess students' written assignments. This drawback is often used to bar them from the teaching field. When asked about this issue, eight education officers expressed scepticism about the ability of visually handicapped teachers to use a reader as an intervener between them and their students' written work. The following responses illustrate the general themes that recurred: the use of readers (1) slows down the blind teacher's marking speed, which often results in pupils' exercise books being returned very late; (2) forces the blind teacher to depend on the cooperation of "readers," which may also result in a late return of students' work; (3) makes it difficult for the blind teachers to really see their pupils' problems, forcing the blind teacher to trust the reader and rely on the reader's judgment. Remedial instruction also depends on the reader and his or her ability to take pedagogical issues seriously.

The above assertions depict visually handicapped teachers as helpless objects that can be easily abused and manipulated by readers. Instead of addressing issues relating to the quality of marking, respondents focused on the honesty of the readers. The unfortunate aspect of these negative perceptions is that, no matter how unreasonable they are, they are used by those in power to justify discrimination against disabled teachers.

Acts of discrimination are experienced by most, if not all, blind teachers in Zimbabwe. In my case, discrimination occurred when my school and the Ministry of Education refused to hire a reader for me and expected that I hire and pay the reader from my salary. I was also denied access to proper accommodation; moreover, the Ministry took about three months to process my initial salary. It appeared to me that these unfair working conditions were intended to ensure that I failed in the execution of my duties as a teacher, which would have provided reasons for termination of my employment.

Contrary to the negative views expressed by the eight education officers, thirteen respondents offered different perspectives on the use of readers by visually handicapped teachers. The following statements capture the positive views held by this group of respondents. One respondent stated, "Readers are only intended to facilitate communication between the teacher and the student so that the teacher will then be able to assess the written work." While another said, "A reader who is educated enough should be able to mark correctly under close direction of the blind teacher. The quality of marking gets maintained."

The difference between positive and negative responses is that the negative responses dehumanize both the visually handicapped teacher and the sighted reader. As demonstrated by the blind student teacher's practices and my own, blind teachers can successfully use readers and produce good results. In my situation, even though working conditions were not conducive, the superior quality of my marking skills was confirmed in that the feedback I gave when marking students' papers was similar to that produced by my able-bodied colleagues. Moreover, despite the fact that national and international examiners used different instruments to test my students at the end of their two years of study, my students' results were similar to those of students taught by able-bodied colleagues. Despite my teaching success, however, because of my handicap, the Ministry of Education was reluctant to designate me as an external examiner,[1] and my headmaster was unwilling to promote me to the head of my department; instead, less qualified persons were promoted. The main argument against my promotion to departmental headship was that I would need a reader when assessing other teachers' performances. Ironically, the head teacher himself had a secretary who reviewed teachers' files and wrote confidential letters to the Ministry of Education about these teachers' performances.

Another fundamental teaching principle is the ability to manage a classroom, which includes executing discipline. There is an assumption that visually handicapped teachers have difficulty maintaining discipline in their classrooms. This assumption is also used to discriminate against blind teachers because they are seen as contributing to a lack of discipline, as exemplified by the following statements made by participants of the project:

> Discipline in the classroom depends to a large extent on the tone/discipline in the school as a whole. Maintenance of discipline, therefore, will affect both the sighted and the blind teacher, although a visual handicapped *aggravates the problem*. Use of class monitors and prefects might help to *some extent* (emphasis added).

In Zimbabwe students are becoming increasingly rebellious, making school discipline a matter of disturbing concern. Some students terrorise other students in the class. Such incidents are difficult to detect since students who are bullies always threaten other students not to report them to authorities. So, discipline is an extremely difficult problem for the blind teachers.

These statements are very stereotypical and imply that classroom management is heavily dependent on the ability to see. Additionally, they suggest that students are so irrational that teachers need to adopt a military approach in dealing with them. Concerns about a blind teacher's ability to discipline students were also visible when I was interviewed by ministerial officials for a teaching position in Zimbabwe. One of the questions asked of me was, since I was visually handicapped, who would accompany me to the washroom and ensure that students did not play tricks on me and abuse me? A second question was, since I could not see, how would I know if students decided to have sex in the classroom? I found both questions condescending and reflective of how ignorant people are about blindness, to the extent that they are willing to use irrelevant and inconceivable reasons to arrive at a hiring decision.

There were, however, some educational officers who did not view classroom management as a problem for the blind teacher. One of them stated, "Class control depends on several aspects. These include the quality of teaching, rapport with students, and the teacher's personal discipline and principles. Being blind should not necessarily lead to poor discipline in class." Accordingly, another officer stated that what is required is to "keep students busy and interested ... they will not misbehave, give them worthwhile tasks, group discussions, and achievable targets." Other strategies proposed in the literature include the prefect and aide system. In fact, a study conducted by McGinnis et al. (1995) suggests:

> Schools must recognize that student learning and behaviour problems cannot be solved through continued use of reactive strategies. The occasional use of behaviour management techniques in reaction to the occurrence of behaviour problems must be replaced by consistent use of coordinated preventive classroom management system. Proactive classroom rules facilitate the operation of schools by providing structure and allowing more of a focus on academic achievement. (p. 223)

With regard to the issue of involvement in extra-curricular activities, some of the interviewees argued that, since the activities of visually handicapped teachers are limited to classrooms, this is sufficient reason to keep them out of the teaching profession. One participant stated, "The teachers' participation in extra-curricular activities is much more demanding than teaching in the classroom. Even when coaching singing and drama, the teacher has to see the students' facial expressions and body movement and correct them as they are making some mistakes. So, without sight it will be extremely difficult to coach students in any extra-curricular activity." Another respondent was even blunter, "My experience with blind teachers is that academically they argue that they can do anything. But when it comes to really doing it at the school level, they feel they are being exploited and that the sighted are unfeeling."

These quotations are insulting to visually handicapped people. This traditional attitude has deprived blind people of the opportunity to become involved in extra-curricular activities. These quotations depict visually handicapped teachers as immobile and confined to indoor activities, yet many visually handicapped teachers engage in many outdoor activities and some are prominent singers, dancers, and so on.

Other education officers supported the idea that visually handicapped teachers can participate in the extra-curricular programs. One of these officers stated, "Extra-curricular activities depend on the teacher's areas of interest. Blind people also have many areas of interest such as music, writing, playing instruments and so on. In addition, new games can now be played by both sighted and physically handicapped." Overall, there was an overwhelming support from education officers for the potential and abilities of visually handicapped teachers to execute their duties. But the support was very minimal when the implementation of programs supporting visually handicapped required that schools and the Ministry of Education provide financial support. This included the payment of readers, procurement of technical devices, and additional expenses on insurance and pension premiums. Therefore, the underlying approaches exhibited by the findings of this study are that even those who considered offering blind teachers jobs did not support them with the necessary tools, thus adopting a "we will give you the job but not the tools" stance. This is tantamount to denying visually handicapped people access to employment.

CONCLUSION: A GLIMMER OF HOPE

As both case studies have demonstrated, the discrimination and exploitation of handicapped people is institutional. The bureaucracies of the Ministry of Education and the research organization are so entrenched in their administrative structures that they are inflexible and unwilling to accommodate handicapped people. The research organization and the Ministry only agreed to work with handicapped people because government policies required them to do so. In an attempt to meet this requirement, the researchers simply went to the disability community, hand-picked a few people, and presented them to the government as participants. After using them to secure funding and to gather data, they discarded them. These handicapped people were not acknowledged in publications nor were they financially compensated for their time and ideas. They were mentioned in the research organization's annual report presented to the government. They were also displayed from time to time at workshops and gatherings conducted for the government's benefit. This strategy seems to have ensured that the research organization's funding would continue (see also Ysseldyke, J.E. et al. 1992).

The Ministry of Education in Zimbabwe has some difficulty defining an ideal or optimal "teachable standard." This standard is defined through the eyes of an able-bodied teacher. The visually handicapped teacher is expected to fit himself or herself into this standard to the point where any use of alternative methods of teaching is interpreted as incompetence and an inability to do the job. Even though these results depicted a very pessimistic view about how able-bodied professionals perceive their handicapped counterparts, there is a glimmer of hope. The fact that these able-bodied professionals agreed to discuss issues pertaining to people with disabilities provides an opportunity for honesty and candid dialogue. Such dialogue might help to erase prejudices, which are based on the lack of awareness of the needs and abilities of handicapped people. This notion was supported by a study conducted by the Canadian Association of Children with Learning Disabilities (CACLD) in Smith (1985). It surveyed the top one hundred Canadian corporations to determine their level of awareness about job applicants with learning disabilities as well as their hiring policies towards potential employees with learning disabilities. The results indicated that awareness and accommodation was very low, with nearly 50 per cent of those responding requesting information, workshops, or indicating any intention to attend one of the national symposiums on employment strategies being offered that year (Smith, 1985). Therefore, just as this study has attempted to engage researchers and education officers in this discussion, it can also raise people's consciousness about the unfair treatment of people with disabilities.

Finally, my two studies indicate that negative perceptions are not so much embedded in the words and written policies of the research organization and Zimbabwe Ministry of Education, but that they are visible in actions and in the way policies are implemented and administered. The integration into and involvement of handicapped people in a research organization should be implemented in a way that is based on mutual respect. It should acknowledge differences that exist between able-bodied people and people with disabilities and view these differences as strength in diversity and not as an excuse for repression and subjugation. People with disabilities should be provided with educational and financial support to accomplish their assigned tasks, and policies should be designed to discourage their failure and promote their success.

Since gaining political freedom from Britain in 1980, Zimbabwe has undergone formidable economic and political challenges, some of which, over the past decade, have resulted from conflicts in leadership, natural disasters such as drought, as well as chronic diseases including the outbreak of HIV/AIDS. Political freedom came through an armed struggle; a majority-rule political system was established following a civil war, all of which resulted in the creation of a large population of disabled citizens. Furthermore, as a land-locked southern African country, Zimbabwe faces economic challenges, mainly because it is agrarian-based, which causes alarming challenges for people with disability to participate in the best of times. Agrarian reforms that were accelerated in the late 1990s were met with economic sanctions from other countries. The result of the combination of economic sanctions, agrarian reform, corruption, and persistent drought has been a sharp and continuing economic decline. For example, the GDP declined by 30 per cent between 1998 and 2003, and fell another 5.2 per cent in 2004. The 2006 Human Development Report shows that the GDP is still on the decline (United Nations

Development Program, 2006). In addition it forecasted that GDP will decline by 2.3 per cent in 2007. Unemployment is estimated at 70 per cent and the adult HIV infection rate is estimated to be 20 per cent – all realities that have contributed to a sharp drop in life expectancy and increase in the disabled population.

As indicated in the preceding argument, in 1992, Zimbabwe legislated and passed the Disabled Persons Act. One of the most important objectives of this legislation is "to achieve equal opportunities for disabled persons by ensuring, so far as possible, that they obtain education and employment, participate fully in sporting, recreation and cultural activities and are afforded full access to community and social services" (*Disabled Persons Act*, 1992). By African standards, this is a very progressive legislation. This legislation makes provision for the welfare and rehabilitation of disabled persons. Under this legislation the National Disability Board was established, which is administered through the Ministry of Labour and Social Welfare. It is a consultative forum through which the government of Zimbabwe reviews its disability policies and is constituted of representatives from different disability organizations. The Zimbabwe Disability Act of 1992 further provides a framework through which the government provides funding to disability organizations and income support to individuals with disabilities. Currently disabled persons receive Z$250 (about US$1) per month for children and Z$500 (about US$2) per month for adults.

In terms of employment, since establishing the Disability Act of 1992, the government, in principle, has been encouraging all employers to consider hiring persons with disabilities and has established an affirmative action initiative. In addition, the government has tried to place disabled people in self-help projects such as piggeries, poultry farms, and market gardening. Collective community projects are also being encouraged.

Finally, it is important to end this chapter by highlighting the basis of the continuing marginalization of the disabled population in Zimbabwe, which is the integrationist approach to disability that dominates the initiatives aimed at redressing the plight of disabled people. Unlike inclusion, in integration in schools for example, the child must make adjustments to the requirements of the school while in inclusion, it is the school that must make adjustments to accommodate or include the child. This approach applies to the employment sector as well. Despite the noble intention of the law, Zimbabwean workplaces are inaccessible both physically and psychologically. The potential disabled employee has to adjust himself or herself to accommodate the needs of the workplace instead of the workplace adjusting itself to meet his or her needs.

In this light I would propose that if persons with disabilities are going to attain full citizenship a process of deinstitutionalization should take place both psychologically and physically. This approach articulates that people with disabilities should have the same civil rights, options, and control over choices in their own lives as do people without. This can be accomplished by strengthening their organizations and individual empowerment through a process of deinstitutionalization. This is an attempt to move the disability organizations and individuals with disabilities from the permanent state of dependency to the development of self sustaining programs. This is a shift away from the authoritarian medical model to a paradigm of individual empowerment and responsibility for defining and meeting one's own needs. This approach locates problems or "deficiencies" in the society, not the individual. People with disabilities are no longer perceived as broken or sick, certainly not in need of repair. Issues such as social and attitudinal barriers are the real problems both in developed and developing countries.

In contrast to Africa, the rights and needs of handicapped people in North America have been part of the public discourse since the 1960s. According to Smith (1985), "Although young people and adults with learning disabilities have been with us at least throughout this century, they were not formally identified as such or viewed as an important population until 1963 when parents and professionals banded together to form the Association for Children (and adults) with Learning Disabilities (ACLD) in Canada and America" (p. 35). However, even though there is now a high level of awareness about disability issues in North America, concepts of eugenics and euthanasia still threaten the very existence of disabled people. This was made evident when Mr. Latimer, a farmer in Saskatchewan, killed his disabled daughter with the full support of his wife, family members and neighbours. Moreover, his actions received a lot of public sympathy. This form of a publicly accepted killing builds on the principle of eugenics, which was developed in North America in the beginning of this century. According to Woodhill (1992),

The beginning of the twentieth century marked the rise of eugenics, a scientific approach to human reproduction which sought to have the "less fit" removed from the "human stock." Many studies of mentally handicapped persons and their families were carried out to "prove" the eugenics arguments, all supposedly based on "scientific methods." The results are well known – incarceration of hundreds of thousands and involuntary sterilizations in many countries including the United States and Canada. (p. 8)

All such practices altogether indicate that there is still a lot to be done in order to enhance the quality of life of disabled citizens all over the world.

REFERENCES

Beezer, B. (1991). Employment discrimination against handicapped school employees: Section 504. *West's Education Law Reporter, 65*(3), 697–712.

Brackenreed, D. (2004). Teachers' perceptions of the effects of testing accommodations. *Exceptional Education in Canada,14*(1), 5–22.

Citizenship and Immigration Canada. (2004). Speech from the Throne to Open the Third Session of the 37th Parliament of Canada, *What's New Archives – 2004.* Retrieved January 5, 2006, from http://www.pco-bcp.gc.ca/default.asp?Language=E&Page=archivemartin&Sub=speechesdiscours&Doc=speech_20040202_278_e.htm.

Colman, A. M., Fabre, R. T., & Walker, M. H. (1987). Teacher perceptions of the behavioural adjustment of primary grade level handicapped pupils within regular and special education settings. *Remedial and Special Education, 8*(5), 34–39.

Devereux, S., & Sabates-Wheeler, R. (2004). Transformative social protection. *IDS Working Paper 232.* Brighton: IDS.

Disabled Persons Act. (1992). Zimbabwe. Retrieved March 1, 2006, from http://www.dredf.org/international/zimb1.html.

Edwards, S. (2000). Canada's No. 1, United Nations says a new deemed best place to live, *National Post,* June 29, A4.

Government of Canada. (1982). *Canadian Charter of Rights and Freedoms, Schedule B, Constitution Act, 1982.* Retrieved January 5, 2006, from http://laws.justice.gc.ca/en/charter/index.html#egalite.

Hoffman v. Ohio Youth Commission. (1975). 13 FEP, case 30. Ohio.

Human Resources Development Canada. (1999). Lessons learned from evaluation of disability policy and programs. Retrieved February 1, 2006, from http://www11.hrdc-drhc.gc.ca/pls/edd/DPPTR.lhtml.

Lifton, J. R. (1986). *Nazi doctors: Medical killing and the psychology of genocide.* New York: Basic Books.

Martinez, C. (1990). A dream for me. In R. Schalock & M. Begarb (Eds.), *Quality of life perspectives and issue* (pp. 3-7). Washington, DC: American Association on Mental Retardation.

McGee, J. J., & Menolascino, F. J. (1991). *Beyond gentle teaching: A nonavasive approach to helping those in need.* New York: Human Sciences Press.

McGinnis, J. C., Frederick, P. B., & Edwards, R. (1995). Enhancing classroom management through proactive rules and procedures. *Psychology in the School, 32,* 220-24.

Miller, C. (1982). The blind student teacher: A public school perspective. *Illinois School Journal, 61*(1-4), 65-68.

Sadhu, B. (2002). Beyond program: Teachers' perceptions of conditions which impact special education. MA thesis, Mount Saint Vincent University.

Service Canada. (2001). *Canadian youth: Who are they and what do they want?* Section 9: Disability. http://www.youth.gc.ca/yoaux.jsp?&lang=en&flash=1&ta=1&auxpageid=856.

Smith, C. (1985). *Canadian perspectives on youth and adults with learning disability.* New York: World Rehabilitation Fund INC.

Smith, M. K., and Smith, K. E. (2000). "I believe in inclusion, but ..." Regular education early childhood teachers' perceptions of successful inclusion. *Journal of Research in Childhood Education, 14*(2), 161-80.

Statistics Canada. (2001). Census 2001. Retrieved June 2, 2004, from http://www12.statcan.ca/english/census01/home/index.cfm.

United Nations Development Program (2006). Human Development Report. Beyond Scarcity: Power, poverty and the global water crisis. New York: Palgrave Macmillian.

United Nations Enable. (2005). *The Secretary General message on the International Day of Disabled Persons.* Retrieved December 3, 2005, from http://www.un.org/esa/socdev/enable/iddp05sg.htm.

Waxman, B. F. (1990). *Changing stereotypes and myths about disability and ethnicity: Breaking down attitudinal barriers to employment.* (Eric Document ED 329 673).

Woodhill, G. (1992). *Critical issues in special education.* Ryerson Polytechnic Institute.

Ysseldyke, J. E., Algozzine, R. & Thurlow, M. L. (1992). Critical issues in special education. Houghton Mifflin U.S.A.

Notes

1   In Zimbabwe, in order to graduate, high school students have to write examinations in all subjects, which are evaluated by external examiners. External examiners are teachers who are not familiar with students whose answer scripts they will be evaluating and grading. Under this process teachers from one province will evaluate and grade students from another province.

8

FINANCING STUDENTS IN HIGHER EDUCATION: EXAMINING TRENDS AND FUNDING OPTIONS IN AFRICA AND CANADA

Eva Aboagye

ABSTRACT

This chapter addresses the impact of external pressures in the financing of higher education systems. The author uses both North American and African case studies to show that major challenges in the financing of post-secondary education are not limited to students and governments of developing or developed countries, but are issues that face all students and governmental bodies. The movement at the national level away from grants and towards loans means greater debt burden for students. The author demonstrates that, although there are social, economic, political, and cultural differences between the case studies, the issues of cost recovery that face students and governments are the same. The author concludes by discussing new financing directions that have been suggested and are underway in developed and developing countries.

INTRODUCTION

The world economic order is increasingly more materialistic and favours decreasing the involvement of governments in the provision of social services. This has affected social policies in many countries. In developing countries, particularly in Africa, structural adjustment, and post-structural adjustment policies have had a great impact on educational reform, especially in the area of student financing in higher education. In most parts of the world, governments are reviewing their levels of spending on higher education and examining ways of reducing subsidies to institutions and students. Currently, many of the changes taking place in the educational sector in Africa are the result of World Bank and International Monetary Fund (IMF) economic policies.

This chapter examines the effect of these external pressures on the financing of students in higher education, using data from Africa and Canada. There are reasons for choosing these two countries. Canada is currently making major changes to its student financing programs as evidenced by both provincial and federal practices. At the federal level, there is a move towards reducing student grants and increasing student loans. In addition, there is discussion about introducing an income-contingent repayment scheme. In some Canadian provinces, like Ontario, discussions on the financing of students in higher education focus on how to encourage more private involvement in the financing of students. In the African region, there are widespread attempts to review the existing systems of financing and efforts to increase private-sector involvement. Although the two areas differ economically, socially, politically, and culturally, the issues of cost recovery facing students and governments are similar. The solutions to this universal problem, however, differ because of different economic and social realities.

The general trend in the 1990s in North America and in some countries in sub-Saharan Africa was for governments to pass on part of the costs of higher education to students and their parents as well as to the private sector. This trend was usually influenced by international interests in cost recovery and the sharing of costs in the provision of social services. This chapter discusses trends that are changing the social functions of higher education institutions and addresses the questions of whether or not in a developing country these institutions are expected to be elitist or are expected to distribute benefits and privileges to the general society.

In March 1991, UNESCO organized an African Regional Expert Consultation meeting titled "Trends and Challenges of Higher Education for the Twenty-first Century." Among other discussions were debates on what delegates considered to be the functions of institutions providing higher education on the continent. The general concern of these delegates was that, in order to effectively perform their functions, African institutions would have to tackle issues of internal efficiency, including levels of financing opportunities available to the institutions and their students.

Throughout the 1990s and the decade after, governments in sub-Saharan Africa continued to look at ways to both expand access and share the costs of higher education with parents, students, and the private sector. Some of these efforts were successful while others were met with resistance. In 2003, the Association of African Universities and the World Bank jointly organized a regional training conference titled "Improving Tertiary Education in Sub-Saharan Africa: Things that Work!" The conference provided an opportunity to review progress that had been made in improving access and financing as well as the challenges that still lay ahead

In Canada, financing for students in post-secondary institutions is an important political issue. In the province of Ontario, the Liberal government of Premier David Petersen in 1985, followed by the New Democratic government under Premier Bob Rae in 1990, considered how to make the existing loan scheme more of an income-contingent loan scheme in order to make repayment more manageable for students. The advantage of an income-contingent loan scheme, as far as the governments are concerned, is to provide an avenue to increase loan levels, therefore passing on greater portions of the cost to students without the worry of creating unbearable debt burdens for them. Canadian provinces have some autonomy over higher education policies. This chapter will focus mainly on Ontario, where there have been a number of panels created to review its post-secondary system from 1995 under the leadership of Premier Mike Harris and his Progressive Conservative government to the election of Premier Dalton McGuinty and his Liberal government in 2003. These panels include "Excellence, Accessibility, Responsibility: Report of the

Advisory Panel on Future Directions of Postsecondary Education,"
in 1996, and more recently the Rae Review in 2004. The 1996 task
force was created to examine future goals of universities and colleges.
It was charged by the Minister of Education and Training to do the
following:

1. Recommend the most appropriate sharing of costs
   among students, the private sector and the government,
   and ways in which this might best be achieved,
2. Identify ways to promote and support co-operation
   between colleges and universities and between them and
   the secondary school system in order to meet the changing needs of students,
3. Provide advice on what needs to be done to meet the
   expected level of demand for post-secondary education,
   both with reference to existing public institutions and
   existing or proposed private institutions. (Ministry of
   Education and Training, 1996, p. 1)

In terms of the financing of students, although recommendations
were made for an income-contingent loan scheme, no significant
changes were made by the Conservative Government under Mike
Harris. However, there was a gradual reduction in grants and an
increase in loans combined with increases in tuition fees.

In 2003, the system of financing students that was in place in
Ontario consisted of a combination of loans, grants, and tax incentives. The federal and provincial governments partnered to provide
a student loan; the federal government also provides bursaries and
scholarships through the Millennium Scholarship Foundation; and
there are tax credits as well as a savings plan for post-secondary
education. The repayment for student loans begins six months after
students graduate and is based on a traditional, consumer loan basis
(Rae Report, 2005, pp. 18 & 21). In 2004 the Ontario government set
up a review panel led by former premier Bob Rae, which looked at
all aspects of post-secondary education in the province. Specifically
on funding, the panel was asked to make recommendations on all
aspects of post-secondary funding, including:

1. Establish an appropriate sharing of the costs of post-secondary education among the government, students, and the private sector;
2. Identify an effective student assistance program that promotes increased access to post-secondary education. (Rae Report, 2005, p. 1)

This panel submitted its review report, "Ontario: A Leader in Learning" to the Ontario government in 2005. One of the key questions concerning funding posed by the panel was: "How do we pay for higher education to ensure opportunity and excellence?" (p. 2). It made wide-ranging recommendations, including asking for more government funding for the post-secondary sector and more funding for students. Among other recommendations by the panel was a significant increase in public funding for both institutions and low income families. On grants and loans the panel called for increases of grants to low income students to cover the costs of tuition fees as well as the revision of loan eligibility to enable more middle-income families to qualify for student loans. While much discussion was generated around the possibility of an income-contingent or a graduate tax repayment plan, the panel did not make any firm recommendation on the repayment plan; rather, it urged the government to consider financing through a form of a graduate tax but noted that it would take some time to implement such a system (Rae Report, 2005, p. 22).

In a paper on Ontario Higher Education Reform, Jones (2004) examines the changes that were implemented in the post-secondary sector from the election of the Progressive Conservative government in 1995 to the Liberal government of 2005. He notes that reforms during this period were mainly characterized by privatization and had more of a market influence, which involves using cost-benefit analysis to make students more and more responsible for the cost of their education.

It is important to note that the issue of appropriate cost sharing recommended by government reviews since 1995 is the primary motivation for the passing on of costs to students and their families. Students' contributions to higher education financing are by way of loans. Loans, as a means of financing higher education, are widely used, both in the developed and developing countries, as indicated by Albrecht and Ziderman (1991). Researchers who advocate the use of loans, like Woodhall (1987), believe it is a more efficient and more equitable way of financing students than the use of grants because more students can be supported at higher rates, using the amounts that are repaid. This method is said to be more equitable than grants, which involve taking money from the general taxpayers – with average or below average incomes – to subsidize students who, some researchers believe, may come from families with above average incomes.

Researchers who are against the use of loans as a means of financing students, such as Colclough (1990), see them as less efficient and less equitable because they have a tendency to discourage the participation of students from low socio-economic backgrounds and the participation of women. Other identified problems include the cost of administering a loan scheme, concern over the debt burden, and the problem of defaulting on payments.

Albrecht and Ziderman (1991) discuss some of the main features associated with administering loan schemes, including the fact that loans can target students who enrol in fields that meet the national employment priority, as done in Colombia. It is also possible to introduce means testing based on family income or sometimes more complex socio-economic indicators as in Chile, and eligibility can be limited to students who have financial need. In Norway, Sweden, and the Netherlands, a student's financial resources are assessed independently of the resources of the student's family, and it is felt that this helps to improve access for women (Woodhall, 1987). The loan amounts can also be varied based on the difference between the cost of the educational program and the resources available to the student, as is the case in Canada, Sweden, and Brazil.

Albrecht and Ziderman also identify six different ways of arranging repayment. First is the mortgage loan, where repayment is in equal monthly instalments based on the total loan amount, which currently operates in Canada. Second is an income-contingent loan, where repayment is a fixed percentage of annual or monthly income, as is the case in Sweden. Third is a variation of the income-contingent loan repayment, where the loan is collected through the tax system. An example is the Australian higher education contribution scheme implemented in 1989 whereby students are obliged to repay approximately 20 per cent of instructional cost through an income surtax of 2 per cent, 3 per cent, or 4 per cent of their income, provided they are earning more than the mean Australian income. The fourth method of repayment is the deferral of social benefits, where repayment is made through an existing payroll tax in which benefits do not accrue until the loan has been repaid, as in Ghana. Fifth is the graduate tax or equity finance system, where students contribute through a lifetime increase in their tax contribution, which has been proposed in the United States and in the United Kingdom. In the case of United Kingdom, the government has announced plans to move ahead with a graduate tax in 2007. The sixth is an employer contribution through a tax or loan. In this case, loan repayments are shared between employers and employees, as in Ghana, where the deferred benefits include both employer and employee contributions, as also practiced in China.

AFRICAN HIGHER EDUCATION SYSTEMS

Student enrolment indicates that African higher education system is still a relatively small sector of society in comparison to other parts of the world. In most parts of the developed world, enrolment is over 2,000 per 100,000 inhabitants, with the United States reporting the highest enrolment with 5,591 students per 100,000 inhabitants and Canada following closely with 5,102 students per 100,000 inhabitants. In developing countries the numbers are lower: Peru has 3,293; Cuba 2,285; Egypt 1,698 and Malaysia 679 students per 100,000 inhabitants, (UNESCO, 1993). Furthermore, as can be seen in Table 9.1, most countries in sub-Saharan Africa have figures that are far lower than anywhere else in the world. The table divides the countries into three groups: those with less than 100 students per 100,000 inhabitants; those with 100 to 300 students per 100,000 inhabitants; and those countries with more than 300 students per 100,000 inhabitants.

Among those with more than 300 students, Nigeria doubled its enrolment from 191 per 100,000 inhabitants in 1980 to 320 in 1990; Zimbabwe doubled its students from 117 per 100,000 inhabitants in 1980 to 496 students in 1990 (UNESCO, 1993). What is interesting to note is that, during that period, Nigeria and other countries like Kenya and Ghana introduced cost-sharing measures in order to finance expansion (see Table 9.6), which caused disruptions in the higher education system.

Table 9.1: Student Enrolment in Higher Education per 100,000 Inhabitants in sub-Saharan Africa, 1990.

	COUNTRY	ENROLMENT PER 100,000 INHABITANTS
Less than 100	Angola	71
	Burkina Faso	60
	Burundi	65
	Ethiopia	68
	Malawi	63
	Mozambique	16
	Niger	60
	Rwanda	50
	United Republic of Tanzania	21
100–300	Benin	235
	Botswana	299
	Cameroon	288
	Central African Republic	119
	Ghana	126
	Guinea	122
	Kenya	140
	Lesotho	263
	Liberia	218
	Senegal	253
	Sierra Leone	114
	Sudan	245
	Togo	226
	Uganda	100
	Zaire	176
	Zambia	189
More than 300	Nigeria	320
	Zimbabwe	496

Source: UNESCO (1993).

Table 9.2: Gross Enrolment Ratios[1] in Tertiary Education for sub-Saharan Africa 2002–2003.

COUNTRY	GROSS ENROLMENT RATIO
Angola	1
Botswana	5
Burkina Faso	1
Burundi	2
Cameroon	5
Congo	4
Eritrea	2
Ethiopia	2
Ghana	3
Kenya	3
Lesotho	3
Mali	2
Mauritania	4
Namibia	7
Niger	1
Nigeria	8
Rwanda	3
Sierra Leone	2
South Africa	15
Swaziland	5
Zimbabwe	4
Brazil	21
Malaysia	29
United Kingdom	64
Canada	58

Source: UNESCO (2005).

In the Global Education Digest (UNESCO, 2005), reports on enrolment ratios for the tertiary education sector were made. Table 9.2 further illustrates that, even in 2002–2003, the disparity in higher education enrolment between the developed and the developing world continued.

When considering student financing in Africa, it is important to note the proportion of female enrolment since females make up 40 per cent of the total enrolment. The proportions range from less than 30 per cent in Benin, Burkina Faso, Central African Republic, Congo, Ethiopia, Guinea, Malawi, Mali, Mauritania, Niger, Sierra Leone, and Togo, to a few countries with almost half of their enrolment being female. In 2002–2003, some of the countries with high proportions of females in tertiary education were Lesotho, which had 61.3 per cent female enrolment, South Africa, with 53.7 per cent, and Swaziland, with 54.4 per cent (UNESCO, 2005).

In many countries higher education is seen as the means by which individuals can improve their socio-economic status; therefore, policies that govern the financing of higher education should take into account the background of students in order to ensure that access is available to all who are academically able to pursue higher education. The literature on the distribution of educational opportunities suggests that, because of the increased social mobility related to higher education, everyone who qualifies to enter university should have an opportunity to attend, regardless of income or family background. Woodhall (1992) examined studies in Sweden and the United States that show that financial assistance for students enables those who would otherwise not be able to afford tuition and maintenance costs to attend higher education institutions. She points out that in Sweden, over 40 per cent of students from low-income families said they would not have attended higher education without financial aid, compared with 12 per cent of students from higher-income families.

In 1991 the author conducted a study of university students in Ghana, and examined the backgrounds of students from all levels of the socio-economic ladder and the level of education their parents had attained, as shown in Table 9.3. This analysis showed that parents with higher levels of education held better jobs and their children were more likely to seek out a university education when compared with students whose parents had little or no formal education.

*Table 9.3: Percentage Distribution of Ghanaian Students by the Level of
Education of their Parents.*

LEVEL OF EDUCATION	FATHER	MOTHER
No education	18	29
Did not complete primary	4	10
Completed primary level	12	14
Did not complete secondary	2	4
Completed secondary level	15	11
Vocational/Technical/Teacher Training	16	22
University: Diploma	10	5
University: Graduate	12	2
University: Postgraduate	8	1
Not known	2	2
Total	99%	100%

Source: Aboagye (1996), p. 177.

The percentage distribution shown in Table 9.3 varied greatly when
students were disaggregated by gender. While only 7 per cent of females had fathers with no education, the figure for males was 21 per
cent. The difference was even much wider when fathers with only up
to primary level education were considered. Just over 40 per cent of
the male students' and 14 per cent of the female students' fathers had
up to primary level education. While 60 per cent of mothers of male
students and 30 per cent of mothers of female students had up to primary level education, 16 per cent of mothers of female students and
34 per cent of mothers of male students had no education. Just over 35
per cent of fathers of female students and 16 per cent of fathers of male
students had first and second university degrees, while 6 per cent of
mothers of female students and 2 per cent of mothers of male students
had a similar education. These proportions of parents with no education or only up to primary level education indicate that a substantial
proportion of the Ghanaian university student population are from

low socio-economic backgrounds and are the first generation in their families to attend post-secondary education. The proportions are much larger for male students in Ghanaian universities than they are for female students. For these students it is important that funding policies take into consideration the availability or lack of resources to participate in post-secondary education. To have an accessible and equitable system of post-secondary education, governments in Africa will have to examine options that do not put barriers in the way of low-income families. Even for students from higher socio-economic backgrounds, it is doubtful that they would have the financial resources needed to pursue higher education.

In addition to possessing higher educational backgrounds, parents of female students also had high-status jobs; 50 per cent of the fathers of female students belonged to professional occupations or held administrative and managerial jobs compared with 28 per cent of the fathers of male students. Conversely, 26 per cent of parents of male students were in agriculture and forestry as compared to only 9 per cent of the parents of female students. The education and occupation of parents, taken together, give an indication of the socio-economic status of the students. The female student population in Ghana, which constitutes about 24 per cent of students in higher education, can be classified as a typical middle-class group. However, since they form only a small portion of total enrolment, one cannot call all students middle class. Male students tend to come from low-income families with parents who work in agriculture, forestry, transport, and labour and who have little or no education.

In Kenya, Mwira and Hughes (1992) reported studies of family backgrounds of university students carried out in 1958, 1968, 1975, and 1983 that showed that the system of higher education became more equitable as it expanded. The backgrounds of the graduates were compared, and it was found that recent graduates more closely resembled the socio-economic distribution of the Kenyan population than was the case for the earlier graduates who were from higher-income families. They also found that female university students were more likely to come from higher socio-economic backgrounds, indicating that participation of females from low socio-economic background had not changed much since the 1960s.

Table 9.4: Enrolment in Universities in Canada, 2001–2002.

	ITEM	ENROLMENT	PERCENTAGE FEMALE
Total Enrolment	Full-time	635,639	56.5
	Part-time	251,133	60.0
Undergraduate	Full-time	527,120	57.6
	Part-time	160,392	61.2
Graduate	Full-time	84,773	49.2
	Part-time	42,115	55.1

Source: Statistics Canada (2005).

CANADA'S HIGHER EDUCATION SYSTEM

Higher education in Canada is publicly financed. While the provincial governments are the main sources of funding, the federal government also provides funding to students enrolled in universities and colleges. The university sector in 2001–02 enrolled 635,639 full-time students and 251,133 part-time students, according to Statistics Canada, as shown in Table 9.4. Canada has achieved almost equal enrolment for both males and females, although differences can still be found when enrolment is examined per faculty. The most recent statistics show more women enrolled in universities than men. Overall, the lowest female enrolment is in full-time graduate studies, making up 49 per cent of the enrolment.

Tuition fees are charged in all Canadian institutions of higher education. There are student assistance programs in all provinces, usually in the form of a combination of loans and grants. The loans, which are interest-free until six months after graduation, are means tested and are given on the assumption of some parental support. Stager (1989) conducted a study of tuition fee policies in Ontario to determine whether an increase in fees would be an efficient and equitable way of compensating for cutbacks in university funding.

Table 9.5: University Undergraduate Expenses in Ontario, 1988–89.

ITEM	AVERAGE ($) EXPENDITURE	% OF TOTAL
Tuition Fees (Arts & Science)	1,411	22.1
Other Fees (Books & Supplies)	532	8.3
Transportation	597	9.4
Food and Housing	3,843	60.2
Total	6,383	100.0

Source: Stager (1989), p. 37.

His study concludes by discussing policy with regard to tuition and student aid after thoroughly tracing trends in tuition fees, cost of instruction, family income, and student aid. He looked at private and social returns to investment in education and at the factors affecting access to education.

Stager's study provides an in-depth analysis of the changes that have occurred in tuition fees in Ontario universities and relates these changes to the total costs students have to bear. In 1988–89, fees for general arts and science and journalism in Ontario formed 27 per cent of the program cost; the fees for honours arts, commerce, and law covered 20 per cent of program cost; and the fees for more costly programs such as science, pharmacy, engineering, and architecture covered between 15 and 16 per cent of the program cost. The fees for medicine and dentistry represented less than 9 per cent of the program cost. Stager draws attention to the possibility of increasing tuition fees and also of making students in the more expensive programs pay a higher proportion of costs, mainly based on the assumption that a middle-class parent group is able and willing to pay for the cost of higher education.

In terms of other costs that students bear, Stager stated that students in Ontario are responsible for their boarding, lodging, books, educational supplies, and fees other than tuition. He noted that so far tuition fees do not represent the biggest expense that students have to cover. Table 9.5 itemizes undergraduate expenses in the 1988–89 academic year.

According to Stager, full-time undergraduate students in Ontario covered 50 per cent of the cost of their education through income that they earned during the summer and from part-time work during the academic year. Contributions from families, government grants, and other non-repayable awards were responsible for a further 25 per cent of the costs, while loans constituted the remaining 25 per cent. Of the loan component, three-quarters were from student loan plans, while the remaining were from parents and relatives.

The Ontario Student Assistance Program (OSAP) has a grant and a loan component in which eligibility is based on needs assessment and family income. Stager points out that only 19 per cent of full-time students received a grant. By his calculation, therefore, increasing fees would be an efficient method of raising more money from private sources. This is because the grant section of the program, which represents a small percentage, would cater to the low-income students. The loan section would ensure that students who could afford it would pay for their education. He noted that the concern over the indebtedness of students should not be a problem since the debt students were incurring was well within their means to repay once they became employed. It is important to note, however, that since the study used data from 1987–88, the situation might be entirely different in the 1990s and the present. In fact the employment prospects and the general economic indicators show that recent graduates are having a difficult time finding appropriate jobs which may cause defaults or difficulties in repaying loans.

We have had at least a decade of experiences with different ways of financing students; therefore, it is necessary to examine whether there has been an increase in the amount of time students spend working part-time during the school year. In countries like Ghana, Kenya, and Tanzania, which have had loan schemes in place since the early to mid-1990s, there may be opportunity to assess what impact the loan policy has had on the student population. While there exists the assumption that a mainly middle-class parent population will be willing to absorb the increases, this policy may be forcing students to spend more time on earning an income and less time on academic pursuits. In Canada, it will also be of interest to examine whether increased cost sharing may be forcing students from low-income families to apply to programs that are less expensive and therefore forcing such students to seek admission into colleges rather than universities in places like Ontario. The issue of how cost sharing is affecting low-income students is particularly important when discussing student financing in Africa because higher education tends to be the only avenue for social mobility for most students from low-income families; they, will not be able to participate in higher education without financial support.

CURRENT ISSUES IN HIGHER EDUCATION FINANCING IN AFRICA

In the current international economic order, the interests of international agencies are not always in line with egalitarianism. Most governments have to borrow from these agencies to finance their education systems, which they subsidize and for which they are having difficulties securing funds. Governments, therefore, are forced to make trade-offs in equity issues, in order to finance education. The questions to ask in this situation are: Should the meritocratic view of higher education be the prevailing influence on higher education policies? Should equity concerns override government need to reduce public spending? Given the level of population growth in developing countries and the inequities in societies everywhere, one would expect that the concern of governments would be to provide a higher education system that provides access to groups that cannot afford to attend university.

A discussion of the financing of higher education in Africa necessitated an examination of the role of international lending agencies in determining educational policies. In the early 1990s African economies went through serious changes in the education and economic sectors. Most of these changes were results of program initiatives undertaken to address the demands of the World Bank and the International Monetary Fund for structural changes under the Structural Adjustment Programs. To begin, the World Bank made recommendations for the adjustment of each level of the education sector. For instance, for the higher education level, the World Bank recommended that African countries should, in the short term, aim to improve quality, increase efficiency, and expand output in areas of strategic importance to countries. In addition, these countries were to aim to relieve the burden on public sources of financing university education and increase the participation of beneficiaries and their families. As a result of these demands, African countries such as Ghana, Kenya, and Nigeria made significant changes in the funding of education, including the gradual introduction of user fees in tuition, boarding, and lodging. In most of these countries, loan schemes were introduced as well to assist students in covering those costs. The impact was that, for the first time in most sub-Saharan African countries, there was an expectation that students would cover part of their cost of education.

Important considerations in African governments' decisions on student financing were a combination of student activism, the political clout of the middle class, and general political instability. Student activism has been evident on campuses across the continent whenever attempts are made to withdraw some of the social benefits that students enjoy. For example, in 1988, the Kenyan government was forced to abandon plans to abolish allowances because of protests from students. Similarly, protests were organized in Ghana and Nigeria, which led the governments to abandon attempts at changing student-financing policies. Dozens of students were killed in Nigeria while protesting against structural adjustment programs, and many hundreds were arrested in 1990 for protesting the conditions set for a World Bank loan to rationalize Nigerian universities (Committee for Academic Freedom in Africa, 1994, p. 59). In Ghana, although government commissions keep asking for drastic changes to the way students are financed, hardly any action has been taken because of the lack of support from the civil and public sectors and also because governments in situations of instability are unwilling to take risks. In a military takeover in 1972, for example, the introduction of student loans to replace grants was cited as justification for a coup.

STUDENT FINANCING POLICIES IN AFRICA

Most countries in Africa have free tuition at the higher education level. Maintenance costs, which include the cost of boarding and

Table 9.6: Cost-Sharing in Canada and sub-Saharan Africa.

COUNTRY	COST-SHARING POLICIES	STUDENT LOAN POLICIES AND PROGRAMS
Canada*	Tuition, accommodation, and living costs paid by students.	Federal and provincial student loans, grants, tax credits, and savings plan.
Botswana	Limited cost-sharing measures introduced in 2002–2003.	No student loan program in place as of 2003.
Burkina Faso	Introduced modest fees in 1990.	Loan with means testing.
Ethiopia	Tuition, lodging and food covered for regular but not evening and summer students.	Government considering (as of 2003) a loan program modelled after the income-contingent loan plan in Australia.
Ghana	Cost-sharing limited to small fees and user fees for lodging and food; no tuition fees.	Loan scheme linked to the Social Security Insurance implemented in 1988.
Kenya	Tuition and user fees for lodging and food introduced in 1992 but tuition fee rolled back. Parallel tuition begun in 1998 especially at University of Nairobi.	A loan program re-introduced in 1995.
Mozambique	Cost-sharing in place, including tuition fees.	No student loan scheme in place as of 2003.
Nigeria	Nominal fees for lodging and food and tuition at state not federal institutions.	In the process of re-introducing a student loan scheme.

Tanzania	Gradual cost-sharing officially begun in 1992.	Loan scheme introduced in 1993–94 as part of cost-sharing to cover part of lodging and food costs.
Uganda	Makerere University has dual-track tuition with more than 75% of students paying fees.	No student loan scheme in place as of 2003.
South Africa	Has a tradition of tuition fees.	Has means-tested income contingent loan scheme.

Source: Johnstone (2003). * Rae Report (2005), p. 18.

lodging, transportation, and other miscellaneous costs for students, are covered by scholarships, grants, and loans, or a combination of these options. The state of student financing on the continent as summarized by Johnstone in 2003 is shown in Table 9.6. In his presentation to the conference on "Improving Tertiary Education in Sub-Saharan Africa," Johnstone (2003) provided an updated summary of some of the cost-sharing policies that are in place on the continent. The table is from his presentation.

According to Saint (1992), most African countries were contemplating some form of student tuition fees. For instance, in 1991, the Kenyan government introduced tuition in universities, together with full recovery charges for student accommodation and meals and a student loan to cover those costs. Due to high default rates and other concerns, the scheme was re-organized and re-introduced in 1995. Since 1998, according to Johnstone, the University of Nairobi has been operating a dual-track or parallel program, where some students pay tuition. Since 1970, Ghana has, at various points in the discussion of the reform process, considered the introduction of tuition fees but has yet to introduce any reform to its tuition fee practices.

Zambia attempted, in the mid-1980s, to reform some of its methods used for financing students. In 1989, the government introduced cost-sharing in higher education and the students were expected to pay a small fee towards the cost of their education. In Botswana, students in the university are eligible for government scholarships, based solely on merit. In 1990, about 80 per cent of the students received scholarships, while the remaining 20 per cent were either sponsored by employers or by family or were foreign students sponsored by their governments (Marope, 1992). The scholarships cover room and board, food, books, supplies, and a subsistence allowance. Upon graduation, students have to work for the government for the number of years they received the scholarship plus an additional year. During the period of service, graduates have to contribute 5 per cent of their annual salary to the scholarship fund.

In sub-Saharan Africa, Kenya took the lead in the introduction of degree-granting private institutions. By the end of the 1980s, there were four public and eleven private universities in Kenya. The public institutions recruit the best academically qualified students and staff available, while the private institutions base their recruitment on other criteria, including ability to pay and religious commitment (Mwira and Hughes, 1992). While the central government in Kenya provides support for the university system, the public university sector receives the highest financial support from the state, a factor that has helped promote some form of equity so that those unable to pay for tuition are not excluded from the system. In 1987–88, allowances for university students accounted for 20 per cent of the allocation to higher education, and the loan scheme suffered a default rate of about 90 per cent. In 1992 Mwira and Hughes reported that both the student allowances and the student loans scheme had been earmarked for change and that plans had been made to reduce costs by admitting more day students, streamlining the operation of housing and dining facilities, and also abolishing allowances. According to William Saint (2004), Ethiopia is currently expanding its higher education system and is looking at new ways of funding it, including introducing a graduate tax, and, as Johnstone (2003) reports, a loan scheme modelled after the Australian income-contingent loan scheme is also being considered. In other countries like Uganda, Zimbabwe, Rwanda, and Kenya, universities have responded to the challenges of financing by offering parallel systems for fee-paying students, where some university spaces are set aside for students who are able to pay for their education.

In Senegal, there is a scholarship scheme, which makes higher education tuition free at the universities (Eisemon and Salmi, 1993). Scholarships are awarded based on merit from the results of the secondary school examination. For example, in 1989–90, 78 per cent of the secondary school students who were accepted into universities received a full or partial scholarship. Residences and meal facilities were subsidized, and students were required to pay only a small fee for room and board.

In my 1994 study of student financing in universities in Ghana, I examined students' sources of income. That is, the study asked questions about the sources of income that students had and of the amount of financial support they received from sources other than the government in each academic year. The results of the study indicated that 54 per cent of the students relied solely on their parents for financial support. Responses to a further question, inquiring how parents were able to make the financial commitment, revealed that only 7.8 per cent of families took loans to support their children. This was not surprising since my knowledge of Ghanaian communities is that distant and close relatives, such as aunts, uncles, and siblings, all play a major role in the financing of the education of children. Instead of borrowing from financial institutions, households ask for contribution from other members of the extended families. The families that borrow do so at a high interest in order to support their children in universities.

NEW AND ALTERNATIVE APPROACHES TO FINANCING HIGHER EDUCATION

The financing of higher education in developing countries has been made more urgent by the current economic difficulties and the inability of governments to cover all the costs in the face of social pressure to increase access. It is interesting to note that since the 1980s when African governments, academics, and multilateral and bilateral agencies started looking closely at the financing of university students in sub-Saharan Africa, the discussions have not changed much and the issues continue to be the same. Koso-Thomas (1992, p. 122) summarizes all earlier recommendations made for funding higher education in sub-Saharan Africa, Canada, and other parts of the world. They include the following:

1. Introducing tuition and other fees where there are currently none being charged and increasing them where they exist but are unrelated to real cost. This recommendation is usually made in African countries where tuition fees are virtually non-existent. The issue that is often ignored is whether African parents can afford to pay tuition fees for their children to attend higher education. There is the need therefore to critically examine the financial capacity of the average African parent to bear such a responsibility.

2. Encouraging the establishment of privately owned and financed higher education. This is increasingly more popular and could serve as a means to draw some of the excess demand for higher education from the public sector. However, most African countries do not have entrepreneurs with access to the level of capital that would be needed to run private higher education institutions. In Canada, while this proposal is viable, it is a move from a social philosophy that had been part of the country for a long time.

3. Introducing a credit system for students with repayment either in cash or in kind. Here the issue of loans as an appropriate way of funding students comes into question. Already in Canada there is discussion of whether the debt burden on students is too high.

4. Introducing a taxation system specially affecting beneficiaries of the higher education system, both graduates and graduate employers. This recommendation tends to address the equity issue in the financing of higher education students. It is important to keep in mind concerns that are expressed that this could aggravate the outward migration of educated workers, especially from developing countries where they are already underpaid.

5. Soliciting regulated and regular aid from bilateral and multilateral agencies tied exclusively to higher education objectives, particularly relevant research, and special regional courses. Governments have to be careful here that the research agenda in their countries is not unduly influenced by external forces.

6. Mobilizing new non-government resources and economic use of available resources.

7. Reducing funding on certain oversubscribed humanities course options to release funds for other more development-oriented programs.

8. Increasing the contribution from industry, particularly in the financing of research and development activities.
9. Launching special projects for the production of textbooks and development activities.
10. Joint regional funding of specialized research centres in Africa.
11. Sharing resources within and across country institutions.
12. Providing externally funded scholarship and fellowship programs tenable in higher education establishments in Africa.
13. Mobilizing resources from the more affluent African states for mutually beneficial programs located in the least-developed countries.
14. Increasing assistance from United Nations Development Program (UNDP) and other international bodies to developing countries to aid higher educational development.
15. Setting up fund-raising organs for direct appeal to local and international sympathizers for endowment and other ad hoc relief schemes.

The above recommendations are not much different from those made by Johnstone a decade later. In his summary to the conference on tertiary education in Africa, Johnstone (2003, p. 11) made some conclusions regarding tuition and student loans that brought to the fore the persistent issues in Africa. These conclusions provide a context of where Africa is, where it needs to go, the challenges involved, and the options available for confronting these challenges; therefore, they are listed below.

1. Sub-Saharan African universities and other tertiary level institutions need to supplement their limited governmental, or taxpayer, revenues with revenues from parents and students. These revenues should take the form both of user charges for governmentally or institutionally provided lodging and food and of tuition fees to cover a portion (say, one quarter) of institutional costs of instruction.
2. Given the inevitable political resistance to cost-sharing, a multi-year progression of stages should be presented, with further shifts of costs onto parents and students clearly supplemental to governmental funding, and tied

as much as possible to: a) improvements in the quality of higher education, b) expansion of opportunities and enrolments, and c) extension of participation and accessibility to hitherto under-served populations.

3. The imposition of a tuition fee should be accompanied by a program of means-tested grants, drawing on clearly identifiable and verifiable characteristics (i.e., proxies for income) such as parental occupation and education levels, prior schooling, and type of housing.

4. A student loan program should be designed to collect (according to the present value of the reasonably expected repayments discounted at the government's borrowing rate) something reasonably close to the amounts lent – less losses from defaults and other purposefully designed subsidies or repayment forgiveness features.

5. An income-contingent repayment mode should not be employed unless incomes can be reasonably verified. If income-contingent is politically necessary, it should not be the "default" repayment obligation but rather an optional means of payment that requires the borrower to demonstrate that he or she can discharge the repayments by paying a percentage of earnings from a single employer that represents the dominant earnings stream.

6. Mechanisms need to be added to the repayment process, especially if the repayment mode is a conventional, fixed-schedule mode, to accommodate borrowers whose earnings are low, either temporarily or permanently. In short, a conventional loan needs the same kind of genuine low-earnings protection that is presumed to follow by definition from an income-contingent form of repayment obligation.

Finding alternative but efficient and equitable ways of financing higher education in Africa is a problem that most African countries recognize. It is interesting to see that, while developed countries like Australia, Canada (Ontario), and the United Kingdom consider forms of income-contingent loans as a way of making their systems more equitable, Johnstone does not see it as a viable alternative for African countries. While there is a definite need to ensure that adequate collection structures are put in place in countries in sub-Saharan Africa, an income-contingent loan scheme continues to be the one option that reduces the financial burden of higher education for students and should be given serious consideration by African countries.

Under a different kind of pressure, the Ontario government's fiscal priority to reduce public expenditures in the 1990s increased the need to review the amount or level of funding that students receive from the government. The idea of encouraging the establishment of privately owned and financed institutions was one of the options that the Ontario Conservative government favoured. It is interesting to note that similar to the recommendations of Colclough (1990) for African countries, the Rae Report (2005) recommended that the Government of Ontario examine the possibility of a graduate tax as a way of financing students in Ontario. Already the Liberal government has moved towards providing more financial support for both students and post-secondary institutions.

It is important to recognize that the higher education system in Africa must expand in order to provide the skilled human resources the continent needs and to provide opportunities for social mobility within African societies. In the current economic situation, governments in Africa find it very difficult to provide ongoing financial support that the education system requires in order to operate and expand. In considering the options that have been recommended, it is important to keep in mind the social functions higher education institutions play and the importance of making them accessible to a broader cross-section of the African population. This can be done by ensuring that whatever policy is in place recognizes that the majority of African students may not have the capability of paying for their education. The level at which parents are willing to support their children financially also differs by gender and therefore has accessibility implications for low-income and female students.

A funding option that needs to be seriously considered is the introduction of payroll taxes, as suggested by Colclough (1990). Using data from Botswana, a country where overall demand for university and other tertiary-education graduates exceeds overall supply, Colclough (1990) found that the salaries of graduates tend to be higher compared with those of non-graduate workers. In such circumstances, which clearly exist in most African states, it is his view that introducing a graduate tax instead of relying on loans would be a more efficient and equitable way of financing students. He argues that a graduate tax would be more desirable because in a situation of excess demand it would help shape the structure of the demand for workers and not necessarily affect the level of employment. In addition, a graduate tax does not have equity problems that loans encounter nor does it discourage students from low-income families from pursuing higher education. Using estimates from a 10 per cent graduate tax on the 1986 graduate earnings in Botswana, he shows that graduate taxes have the capability of generating more revenue than a loan scheme.

Similarly, students in Canada are experiencing the impact of government reforms on their access to higher education. This is particularly so for students from low socio-economic backgrounds. Overall, in Canada, there is the need to examine closely the debt burden of graduates and the length of time it takes graduates to obtain a job in their fields. The average salaries of graduates in relation to their debt are important indicators of the financial situation of graduates. In addition, it is important to monitor the portion of time students spend at part-time jobs and the overall effect this has on the quality of the educational process.

CONCLUSION

This chapter has reviewed the current trends and the demands that are changing the mode of student financing in higher education systems. It has examined the conflict between the diminishing availability of funding for institutions and the need for accessibility in Canada and Africa. The chapter also discussed research on alternative means of funding students. There is a need both within African countries and in Canada for governments to take a comprehensive look at student finance in higher education in conjunction with a real commitment to equity and accessibility.

REFERENCES

Aboagye, E. (1996). *The development of student financing schemes in universities in Ghana.* PhD dissertation, University of Toronto.

Albrecht, D., & Ziderman, A. (1991). *Deferred cost recovery for higher education: The experience with student loan programs in developing countries.* Washington, DC: World Bank.

Colclough, C. (1990). Raising additional resources for education in developing countries: Are graduate payroll taxes superior to loans? *International Journal of Educational Development, 10*(2/3), 169–80.

Committee for Academic Freedom in Africa. (1994). The World Bank and education in Africa. *Race & Class, 34*(1), 51–60.

Eisemon, T. O., & Salmi, J. (1993). African universities and the state: Prospects for reform in Senegal and Uganda. *Higher Education, 25*(2), 151–68.

Johnstone, D. B. (2003). Higher education finance and accessibility: Tuition fees and student loans in sub-Saharan Africa. Paper presented to a Regional Training Conference on *Improving Tertiary Education in Sub-Saharan Africa: Things that Work! In Accra, September 2003.*

Jones, G. (2004). Ontario higher education reform 1995–2003: From modest modifications to policy reforms. *Canadian Journal for Higher Education, 34*(3), 39–54.

Kaluba, L. H. (1992). Zambia. In Burton R. Clark & Guy R. Neave (Eds.), *The encyclopedia of higher education* (Vol. 1, pp. 825–30). New York: Pergamon.

Koso-Thomas, K. (1992). Innovative ways of financing higher education. *Higher education in Africa: Trends and challenges for the 21st century.* Dakar: UNESCO Regional Office (BREDA).

Marope, M. (1992). Botswana. In Burton R. Clark & Guy R. Neave (Eds.), *The encyclopedia of higher education* (Vol. 1, pp. 12–17). New York: Pergamon.

Ministry of Education and Training. (1996). What does the Ontario education funding model need to include? Toronto.

Mwira, K., & Hughes, R. (1992). Kenya. In B. R. Clark & G. R. Neave (Eds.), *The encyclopaedia of higher education* (pp. 391–96). Oxford: Pergamon.

Rae Report. (2005). Ontario: A leader in Learning – Report and Recommendations, Toronto, Canada.

Saint, W. (1992). *Universities in Africa, strategies for stabilization and revitalization.* (Technical Paper No. 194.) Africa technical department series. Washington, DC: World Bank.

Saint, W. (2004). Higher education in Ethiopia: The vision and its challenges. *Journal of Higher Education in Africa, 2*(3), 83–115.

Stager, D.A.A. (1989). *Focus on fees: Alternative policies for universities tuition fees.* Toronto: Council of Ontario Universities.

Statistics Canada. (2005). *The Daily* (October 11, 2005). Ottawa: Statistics Canada.

UNESCO. (1993). *World education report.* Paris: UNESCO.

UNESCO. (2005). Global Education Digest – Comparing Education Statistics across the World. Montreal.

Woodhall, M. (1987). *Lending for learning: Designing a student loan program for developing countries.* London: Commonwealth Secretariat.

Woodhall, M. (1992). Financial aid: Student. In B. R. Clark & G. R. Neave (Eds.), *The encyclopaedia of higher education* (2:1358–1366). Oxford: Pergamon.

Notes

1   Gross enrolment ratio is the number of students in a given level of education expressed as a percentage of the population in the theoretical age group for the same level of education. For the tertiary level, the population used is the five-year age group following on from the secondary school exit age.

9

POSSIBILITIES IN AFRICAN SCHOOLING AND EDUCATION [1]

George J. Sefa Dei

ABSTRACT

This chapter continues to make the argument for the use of indigenous knowledge systems in current and revamped curricula, with the intent to explore possible ways to rethink the failing African educational system. The chapter further examines the implications for change and adaptation of African curricula for pedagogy and policy within African societies. The author argues that in order to imagine new curricular possibilities, policy-makers and educational development leaders must deconstruct the myth of development as progressive and indigenous as stagnant to further understand the value of indigenous knowledge systems. Finally, this chapter offers critiques and suggestions for alternative education in Africa that would serve foremost local needs and aspirations.

INTRODUCTION

Schooling and education in Africa has always been a hot topic. This is, in part, due to the realization of the powerful link between education and development. For a continent whose destiny is remarkably tied to dominant pronouncements of and about "what development is," "what development ought to be," and "why have development in the first place," it is understandable that education and development have become serious business. Literally, education is about social transformation. Education is about equipping learners with knowledge, skill, and resources that allow them to improve their own conditions and to contribute to building healthy, sustainable communities. As a community we are successful in these undertakings because we believe in the existence of quality education; as well, we understand how issues of equity, accountability, power, and knowledge are all implicated in the processes of educational delivery. Clearly, all learners bring multiple readings and knowledges to the pursuit of education and its goals of social development. Such a multiple knowledge base allows for a critical interrogation (and possible subversion) of dominant/hegemonic perspectives that have historically guided the approach to development and education in African contexts. By bringing more critical, local, and cultural resource knowledge to bear on an academic project – challenging deployment and appropriating the discourse of neo-liberal reform – we offer alternative and genuine education and development options. It is no secret that, within much of contemporary Africa (as in many parts of the West), talk of education is taken over by concerns and emphasis on standards, accountability, promotion of education excellence, search for human competencies, and human capital development (see also Kerr, 2005). The relations between quality education and education that serves the needs of a local population cannot simply be assumed. They must be theorized. Responding to this could be an additional contribution of the paper to existing knowledge. Schooling, education, and development are related in part because individually none of them are the sole sites, or avenues, for sustaining healthy communities and improving human lives.

My intent in this chapter is to share with readers ways of rethinking African schooling and education[2] and then examine the pedagogical and policy implications for African societies. The discussion has a personal political edge. As I am a continental African by birth, and I am speaking about a new praxis of African education, a politicized perspective, I am concerned about what has been happening to education on the continent over the past several decades. I may speak for many when I say that, in my schooling years, both on the continent and in North America, the education that I have received tended to least emphasize the achievements and contributions of African peoples in their own right. This has been a form of education that can only be characterized as "non-indigenized education." It is education imposed on Africa by external forces. It has been an education that has for the most part failed to deeply cultivate self-esteem and pride in peoples of African descent. It was and still is a Eurocentric education, and it continues to distort, misappropriate, and misinterpret African human condition and reality.

It is my contention that, in order to imagine new possibilities, African peoples must deconstruct the myth of *development* using local, traditional, and indigenous cultural knowledge systems. A fundamental challenge is to unravel how dominant thinking shapes what constitutes development. Today, local peoples continue to struggle for new cultural, economic, and political imaginings and imaginaries. There is a need for new visions and counter-theoretical perspectives of education and development to disentangle *development* and *education* from the grip of dominant paradigms. At the same time, in working with critical and alternative/counter ideas we think creatively about *education and development* in ways that avoid an easy slippage into the form, logic, and implicit assumptions and postulations of what exactly we are contesting. In other words, education for development is not just about an increase in physical and human capital. Education for development requires changes both in ways of thinking and in the social, political, cultural, and economic institutions of society. Local peoples have not been passive recipients of *development* knowledge. Local knowledge systems and subjective views can, and have, become important means of gaining power and resisting dominant discursive practices. It is incumbent on critical scholarship to employ an anti-colonial prism to examine some key issues of African schooling and development, specifically the role of culture, indigenous/local cultural resource knowledge, and education in the search for genuine development and educational options for the continent (see Dei, 2004). What is needed are critical discursive stances that highlight both the possibilities and limitations of locally centred development, using an anti-colonial prism to point to how local/indigenous peoples use their own creativity and resourcefulness to address broader questions of social development. The reference to anti-colonial thought is relevant in stressing local understandings of the nature and contexts of colonized relations and practices, as well as the recourse to power and subjective agency for resistance and the promotion of genuine *development* (see Dei & Asgharzadeh, 2001).

An editorial in the *CODESRIA Bulletin* (1996) identified the major challenges facing African education in the coming years. Among the challenges are "the rehabilitation and regeneration of institutions of learning and research; the renewal and sustenance of agents that produce and reproduce knowledge; the sustenance and enhancement of intellectual leadership, relevance, vitality and integrity and the capacity to transform the disciplines as they contribute to the positive and sustainable transformation of society" (p. 1). This is a tall and daunting order. There are no answers or solutions to these challenges. However, a proper identification of problems and challenges is crucial to the search for genuine solutions. Current patterns and schooling in the African context have not fully delivered on the promise of indigenous *African development*. There are fundamental problems that have to be tackled in earnest if African education is to sustain its historically immeasurable contributions to global knowledge production and human development. African education today struggles to emancipate itself from the tentacles of a colonial past and the stronghold of contemporary external dictates.

This chapter offers a critique and suggestions for alternative education in Africa that would serve foremost (but not exclusively) local needs and aspirations. Externally imposed forms of education have so far failed to critically examine how African indigenous cultural values, traditions, mythology, thought, and history constitute a sufficient body of knowledge about the African social reality and the human condition (see also Gueye, 1995). Current forms of schooling and education on the continent have not adequately addressed the complexity of the interrelationships between nature, culture, society, and the individual. Education has downplayed the acquisition of knowledge based on the interactions between the body, the mind, and the spirit.

In fact, education in Africa today can be said to be in a *crisis*. The *crisis* is rooted in a colonial legacy of often-misguided educational polices and practices (curriculum, texts, pedagogies) that failed to *speak* adequately to the variety of human experiences or to the diverse histories and ideas that have shaped and continue to shape human growth and development. Conventional processes of formal schooling (largely inherited from the colonial past) have only served to reproduce societal inequalities. Although the contemporary *crisis* in education has roots in colonialism, African governments cannot escape blame. Many African leaders, administrators, and educational policy-makers have not done much to change flawed educational policies and practices inherited from the colonialists.

Current educational policies and practices are the dictates of the international financial community. The approach to educational development by these external interests is primarily from the corporate material interests. Educational resources continue to be scarce in part because indigenous materials remain devalued and untapped for improving African education. Consequently, there is a disturbing decline in educational standards and achievements. The need to re-think new forms of schooling and educational options in an African context is more than imperative.

In the web of global knowledge production, African educators have to deal with a long history of European dominance of what constitutes valid and acceptable knowledge and how such knowledge should be produced and disseminated nationally and internationally (see Kelly & Altbach, 1978). This is particularly reflected in mainstream social science in the West as it struggles to shed itself of a negative portrayal African peoples, cultures, and histories. Within the continent itself, schooling and education policies and practices continue to marginalize and oppress local peoples and groups. Fortunately, current resistance to Eurocentric, homophobic, and patriarchal education are expressed in the call for the introduction, validation, and interrogation of *other*/subjugated/oppositional voices and ways of knowing. For current educational changes to have a meaningful impact in Africa, formal, informal, and non-formal learning and teaching systems should recover and reclaim African indigenous cultures and values as a basis for empowering local peoples. The task is not simply to reform existing curriculum and school pedagogical practices. Transformative educational change must address the internal problems of discrimination, prejudice, bias, and alienation within schools.

Transformational African education must find ways to tap the cultural resource knowledge of local peoples. Such knowledge was very much the hallmark of traditional/indigenous African education. For example, throughout history, African parents and community members have promoted learning among the youth through community- and home-based educational strategies. Colonial education, rather than tapping such local skills and knowledge, chose to devalue and/or neglect homes and community instructional strategies and practices. These strategies constitute an "untapped resource," which could be adapted by educational reformers to advance the education of African youth and all learners in today's schools. Learning from community- and home-based strategies will require creative ways to explore home- and community-based practices that promote successful learning outcomes for youth. It will require an investigation of specific community initiatives that empower youth and encourage open and collaborative learning environments. It will also demand a critical examination of the ways in which community workers can successfully assist in bringing youth learners, adult learners, and the home and community knowledge of parents into the schools.

In the context of this discussion I use the terms "traditional" and "indigenous" interchangeably. As pointed out elsewhere (Dei, 1993) the term "traditional" denotes a continuity of cultural values from past experiences that shape the present, e.g., how indigenous peoples have accommodated their new form of postcolonial experience. African scholars like Muteshi (1996) make a distinction between the "traditional" and the "indigenous" when arguing that the "indigenous" past offers a means of staking out a position as an African that is outside of the identity that has been, and continues to be, constructed in Western/Euro-American ideology. In the broader sense of this chapter, "indigenous" is defined as arising locally, primarily from long-term residents in a given community (see also Fals Borda, 1980; Warren et al., 1995).

A critical African education must come to terms with an interrogation and validation of African experiences and histories, as well as offer a profound critique of the continued exclusion and marginalization of indigenous knowledge systems from global knowledge production. Resisting global knowledge production requires new ways of thinking about schooling and education.

THE CENTRALITY OF CULTURE IN
RETHINKING AFRICAN EDUCATION

As repeatedly argued, Western knowledge has been limited by an inability of its Eurocentric theoretical frameworks to adequately adapt to the specificities of different cultures (see Asante, 1987; 1991; Ziegler, 1996). The specificities of cultures should inform social theories that purport to explain the human world. This is because academic and political questions are continually changing to reflect social conditions. There is a plurality of human experiences, and no monolithic or uniform theory can account fully for such diversity. Arguing for grand, totalizing theoretical frameworks that purport to explain away every aspect of human society can be problematic. Educational policy planning in Africa must examine multiple forms of knowledge for comprehensive educational change.

Central to developing alternative, critical ways of rethinking schooling and education in Africa is the understanding of culture. By African *culture*, I refer to the totality of life evolved by African peoples in their attempts to fashion a harmonious co-existence between themselves and the environment, a totality of life that gives order and meaning to social, political, economic, aesthetic, and religious norms (see Vieta, 1991, p. 480). African culture is both indigenous and traditional. Culture constitutes a "dynamic system of norms, values and mental representations" characteristic of a group (Gueye, 1995, p. 8). The norms and values and moral ethos allow the group members to regulate and guide their ways of living and acting.

Forms of schooling and education must adapt to the specificities of cultures. The African belief that no people can exist without a past, without a history, without a way of life, and without a culture is fundamental to rethinking education and schooling. Educational relevance is defined by how the model/style of instruction, pedagogy, and curricular change account for, and emerges from, culture. That is, education that is able to account for the real life of the people who live in the African world. In the African world all things are interconnected. Education is connected to economy, religion, society, and politics. Notwithstanding the sites and sources of disempowerment for women and ethnic, linguistic, and cultural minorities embedded in African cultures and traditions, I would argue that there is much to learn by way of making African education relevant to the needs of society through a critical interrogation of traditional cultural ethos, norms and values, and systems of thought.

Discussing the role of culture in African schooling and education brings forth some interesting questions and concerns. For example, how does the saliency of culture in African knowledge production and use assist local peoples to meet contemporary challenges of development? How does the critical examination of African culture(s) reveal a body of indigenous science knowledge relevant for African social development and Western and global knowledge? (see Ogunniyi, 1986; Bates et al., 1993). How do we resource education in the current economic circumstances of abject poverty? How is it possible to develop sustained institutional infrastructures in Africa to serve as centres of academic excellence that would promote indigenous culture and science and contribute to global science knowledge? What are the roles of the state as the sole or main provider of educational resources?

CULTURE, SCIENCE, AND EDUCATION

Culture constitutes the values, norms, and moral ethos that determine and/or influence the mentalities and behaviours of a people. There is a powerful connection between human action and culture. Gueye (1995) enthuses the idea that Africans must reflect on *science, culture,* and *development* through an integrative approach in order to produce genuine social transformation. The study of African cultures and cultural values reveal a body of indigenous scientific thought that is relevant in the promotion of social development. The search for genuine educational and social transformation in Africa demands the promotion of indigenous African science knowledge.

One problem in promoting African science knowledge is moving away from a Eurocentric definition of what constitutes *science and technology*. The erroneous assertion that Africa has no indigenous science persists (see Maddock, 1981). Historically, this assertion made it possible to superimpose or privilege Western science over indigenous African science. Science and technology cannot simply be associated with Western societies and their knowledge systems. In fact, as Jegede (1994) observes, "because science and technology are part of human culture, every society has some type of science and technology in one form or another" (p. 127). Variations among societies appear in the way science is conceived, taught, and applied to solve human problems.

There is an indigenous African science and technology which constitutes a body of knowledge to be taught in African schools (see also Thisen, 1993). An African *science* is more than a "modality of human activity investment which consists of producing objective knowledge based on the discovery of laws in the various areas of reality [which enable humans to] give a rational account [and] anticipation of events and phenomena" (Gueye, 1995, p. 8). African science extends beyond the development of "critical mind, strong commitment to truth(s), [and a] capacity to innovate and rapidly assimilate innovations" (p. 9). African science is a body of knowledge that integrates an understanding of nature, society, and culture to produce human thought and affect behaviour and action. Science is part of the belief system of a people.

Science knowledge is appropriately understood in the context of the surrounding environment. Science knowledge is relevant if it produces information about the immediate environment to explain everyday phenomena. Science education can be conceived as "a cultural and human enterprise involving the transmission of cultural heritage of a people" (Jegede, 1994, p. 123, citing Gallagher and Dawson, 1984, and Maddock, 1981). The beginning of science, as Urevbu (1984) has aptly remarked, should focus on socially relevant issues that hinge on human activity and action.

African science is built on African indigenous cultural knowledge and thought. As African educators search for innovative ways to integrate indigenous thought and practices with Western science and technology, the examination of traditional culture becomes significant (see also Yakubu, 1994). In rural African communities, one can witness the co-existence of indigenous culture and *foreign/external* cultures through the processes of globalization. African education can seek a harmonization of local cultural beliefs and values (associated with indigenous systems of thought) and so-called modern science knowledge (Jegede 1994, p. 120).

The effective promotion of a dynamic African science and technology rests on developing an institutional framework to tap into available scientific and technological knowledge and expertise for social development, for example, by developing educational infrastructures to serve as viable academic centres, which advance learning, research, and training into indigenous knowledges, practices of health and medicine, local textile printing, woodworking, and other arts and crafts. A major drawback of endogenous African development, as Thisen (1993) sees it, is the fact that "science and technology have been construed as high level of scientific research and manpower, while the application of available, on the shelf, science and technology has been ignored" (p. 6). As Thisen (1993) observes, social development depends on the transformation and exploitation of the natural surroundings. Africa must, therefore, find ways to tap and utilize its available scientific culture in the process of national development.

African educators have a challenge to bring traditional knowledge, thought, and practices into school science (see Horton, 1971). Teaching of science should place emphasis on the relation between the material and the experiential world of study, rather than on sheer facts and the "rote memorization and regurgitation" of abstract principles (Jegede, 1994, p. 126). Science education in African should "identify and use the fundamental scientific and technological principles, theories, and concepts of the indigenous practices" within local communities (Jegede, 1994, p. 126). For example, the school science curriculum should teach about indigenous knowledge governing farming practices, food-processing techniques, medicinal preparation of herbs, as well as knowledge about disease and prevention of illnesses. Schools should also teach about African spiritual cosmology as a form of indigenous science knowledge. Educational strategies should promote effective adult education that allows youth and adult learners to share indigenous knowledge in school settings. The eventual success of such practices would depend also on how the long-standing problems of science education in Africa are addressed at local, regional, and national levels, for example, dealing with the problems of poor laboratory facilities, the dearth of qualified science and technology personnel, poorly trained teachers, the poor quality of research, and the low enrolment of pupils in science classes (see Urevbu, 1984; Thisen, 1993).

RETHINKING AFRICAN EDUCATION AND THE AFRICAN INDIGENOUS SYSTEM OF THOUGHT

In speaking about African indigenous systems of thought, I want to acknowledge that there are some important questions about definitions and operationalization of boundaries as well as contestations about what constitute such knowledge forms. I would assert that different African cultural knowledge systems have a long history going back well in time and are significant for implying the intellectual agency of subjects. Unfortunately, as noted, the local resource base of African people has been the least analyzed for its contribution to genuine development. I view indigenous knowledge as constituting a part of the quest for multiple ways of knowing in the academy. When placed in a broader context as a way to rethink schooling and education in pluralistic communities of Africa and elsewhere, indigenous epistemology heavily implicates and is implicated by, Western colonialist and neo-colonialist practices of educational delivery. Thus the space and the scope of the chapter could be to engage learners, activists, policy-makers, and developers.

For example, it is common knowledge that local African proverbs, parables, tales, folklore, fables, myths, and mythologies contain words of wisdom and important information about society and its peoples and the interactions of culture and nature. These different lines of cultural knowledge have a long history and are connected to the traditions of local communities and their understandings of the social and natural worlds. Such local knowledge systems are significant for implying the intellectual agency of subjects. The current discourse of *African renaissance* is located in the need to reflect on past experiences and histories and to utilize locally contextualized, cultural knowledge to respond to contemporary problems. This does not mean recourse to a mythical or romanticized past, but rather the realization that the past, a people's history, culture, and local cultural resource base have a role to play in the search for answers to daily concerns and problems. Furthermore, the assertion of local voice is a necessary exercise in resisting domination and colonial imposition. In the African context I am using "indigenous" and "local" interchangeably to denote the complexity, dynamism, and variegated nature of knowledge systems. The use of the "local" is to gesture to how cultural norms and values (as local traditions) shape knowledge systems of communities and help offer interpretations of social existence. "Local" and "indigenous" both allude to the relevance of knowledge for particular contexts and how such knowledge can be viewed as a process of connecting place, time, and space in such a way that nothing is shown to be fixed, static, and unchanging.

There are important ethnic, class, regional, age, and gender particularities in African worldviews. The actual practices ensuing from African systems of thought and social values do vary from community to community. Furthermore, cultural values and traditions are never static or frozen in time and space. The "traditional" is not a frozen past. Tradition and the past do indeed influence the present. Life may be located in the past but is experienced in the present. Contemporary events, such as, *traffic in cultures, commoditization of cultures,* and/or the globalization of knowledge, continue to have far-reaching implications for social and educational change. The transformation of African communal moral values or systems of thought, to serve the needs of corporate capital, is a case in point. However, these developments and observations do not deny the efficacy of an African worldview as analytically and conceptually distinct from a Eurocentric, imperial, and hierarchal body of knowledge.

Elsewhere I have pointed out that, within the indigenous cultures, the African humanness as a value system speaks to the importance of relating to, rather than mastery over, nature and the social environment (Dei, 1994). The indigenous African sense of being human speaks about the wholeness of human relationships, compassion, hospitality, and generosity. It is thus problematic to ignore the cultural resource base of African peoples and its contributions to both the process and objective of social development (see also Ayittey, 1991).

A new praxis of African education could legitimize the idea that school knowledge must speak to the African human condition. Social knowledge about Africa must critique an educational system that encourages a dualistic mode of thought and seek the development of the individualist rather than the co-operative instincts of humankind. African education must resurrect the values of the co-operative individual who belongs to, and is enriched by, the group or community. This powerful ideology need to be reaffirmed in the learning processes of schools. Paraphrasing Freire (1990, pp. 57–74), African education must seek the incorporation of a tradition that stresses group work and support as opposed to an ideology of competitiveness, rugged individualism, and individual culpability.

In rethinking schooling and education in Africa, educators cannot lose sight of the common underlying themes of traditional cultures that are still very much evident in many rural African communities today. The themes of communal solidarity, collective rights and social responsibilities, mutual interdependence, respect for the elderly, and a human communion with the spiritual world could form the foundation on which to develop a new praxis of African education in the contemporary era of Euro-American capital hegemony.

Following on the pioneering works of Wiredu (1980), Mbiti (1982), Hountondji (1983), Gyekye (1987), Mudimbe (1988), Okpewho (1992), Oladipo (1992), and Tedla (1995) [among many others], I have selected twelve basic principles of African cultural knowledge as forming the basis of an African system of thought (see also Dei, 1996, pp. 96–98). These principles are interrelated and are not discussed in any order of importance:

1. All knowledge is accumulated knowledge, based on observing and experiencing the social and natural worlds. There is no marketplace for ideas, i.e., knowledge that can be bought or sold in the Eurocentric sense. This principle recognizes the link between knowledge and experience. It also takes the position that there is no sole authority on knowledge. The fact of cultural and political repositories of traditional knowledge in communities does not necessarily imply individual or group exclusive ownership of, and control over, the process of knowledge production and dissemination.

2. We are all learners of the social and natural world and social learning has to be personalized in order to develop the intuitive and analytical aspects of the human mind. In other words, every way of knowing is subjective and based in part on experiential knowledge. Such personal subjective identification with the learning processes makes it possible for the individual to be invested spiritually and emotionally in the cause of social change. It is particularly emphasized that the acquisition of knowledge is a process of interactions between the body, the mind, and the human spirit. The action of thought itself is a causal factor in social action.

3. All knowledge is socially and collectively created through the interactive processes between individuals, groups, and the natural world. This principle does not attribute knowledge acquisition simply to individual acumen, talent, or the limits of one's own senses. Knowledge comes from individuals, family, and communal interactions, as well as through the interactive processes with nature. The principle involves the collective activities of the social group, as well as natural and spiritual forces of the world (e.g., power of the ancestors and gods).

4. Humans are part of the natural world. We do not stand apart and neither are we above the natural world. This principle affirms that our basic humanness is a value system that speaks to the importance of relating to, rather than dominating, nature and the environment. This humanness stresses points of conciliation, rather than presenting the universe as a world to be studied and dominated.

5. To understand one's social reality is to have a holistic view of society. It is conceded that the social, political, and religious structures of society are connected to each other and that we cannot separate politics from economics, culture, religion, cosmology, family, and kinship.

6. History and social change are processes that do not completely lie outside the purview and power of human agency. While the act of change itself is sacred, humans nevertheless can predict and cause social change with the blessing of the powers of the natural world (e.g., ancestral spirits).

7. Both our social and natural worlds are full of uncertainties. There is no certainty in any knowledge. Every way of knowing is clouded by some uncertainty about the social and natural worlds. Humans do not need to strive to explain away everything about their world.

8. Humans do not possess the Earth. It is argued that all living beings have borrowed the Earth from the ancestors and that the living would incur the wrath of the ancestors if they destroyed nature in the process of satisfying societal and individual material needs.

9. The concept of the individual only makes sense in relation to the community of which he or she is part; the collective spirit is stronger than the individual mind. The uniqueness of the individual is recognized in terms of his or her personality, spiritual essence, talents, and *des-*

tiny. However, it is argued that such individuality must be defined and placed in the wider social and political contexts (see also Bray et al., 1986; Semali & Stambach 1995). In other words, the self is also the community. The individual is not a full person without relationship to the community (Mbiti, 1969, p. 214). The community works together as a functioning whole.

10. To every individual or group right in society is married some fundamental responsibilities. The philosophical argument is that no one gets something for nothing and that one has to give back that which is received so that others may benefit.

11. Every life form exists in paired relationships (see also Holmes, 1995, for the Hawaiian). The principle also recognizes that humans live in a continuous rather than a fixed linear time frame. Thus there are no such fine distinctions in life (as in young/old, individual/communal, mind/body, personal/political, and social/natural). To deal with these facts of life, it is contended that humans need a non-dualistic mode of thought that balances all social and natural relationships. In other words, indigenous ways of knowing are not based on fragmented categories.

12. Knowledge and survival go hand in hand. In other words, we cannot separate theory from practice. The key to human survival is the ability of society to pass knowledge down through generations by cultural transmission and through teaching by example and practice (e.g., community work and action).

These principles of the African knowledge system have relevance for educational pedagogy, curricular development, and reform of educational equity and accessibility, as well as for educational policy accountability and transparency. In particular, the idea of collective and multiple origins of knowledge means the search for new forms of schooling and education in the African context will require policymakers, educational practitioners and theorists, parents, students, and learners to all work together.

Genuine educational transformation in Africa must be informed by effective policy decisions. A politics of accountability must be eschewed as part of any political strategy for educational accessibility, inclusion, and relevance. African leaders, administrators and policy-makers, and their international allies have to re-examine the socio-economic and political implications of current economic measures that impact directly and indirectly on education.

Rethinking African education means finding appropriate ways to address all forms educational inequities in the educational system. These inequities are structured along ethnic/racial, gender, regional, language, religious, and class lines in Africa. Gender is a key area of educational inequity in Africa. Research shows that illiteracy among women in Africa is about 70 per cent on the average and more than 90 per cent in rural areas. The general school dropout rate is higher for girls; women are under-represented in the subject fields of mathematics, sciences, and technology (Njeuma 1993, p. 123; Woodhouse & Ndongko, 1993). Added to this is the feminization of poverty in Africa, which exacerbates educational chances of females. These should be pressing concerns for all.

Addressing inequities extends beyond the availability of material resources to a political and moral commitment to fight educational injustice. Issues of academic excellence and educational equity are inextricably linked.

CONCLUSION

In rethinking schooling and education in Africa, perhaps it is helpful for us to explore the place of indigenous knowledge systems in our rapidly globalizing world by discussing the relevance of such knowledge for the academy. Such a perspective views indigenous knowledge as constituting a part of the quest for multiple ways of knowing about and understanding our world. It also emphasizes the importance of teaching to link the project of indigenous knowledge systems with politics of development, global poverty alleviation, and the trend known as globalization.

While the ideas presented in this chapter may be applicable in an African context, I am mindful of the fact that the issues have broader implications for schooling and learning in other colonized and pluralistic spaces. By most accounts, such spaces are heavily implicated by Western colonialism and colonialist practices of educational delivery.

It is significant that discourses that subvert dominant thinking speak to different local and international audiences in addition to those in fields of education and academic learning. Hopefully the ensuing discussion can engage a wide audience of learners, activists, policymakers, and developers interested in questions of pedagogy, education, history, cultural studies, sociology, anthropology, and international development. We must see knowledge production in the domain of education as broadly defined.

Academic excellence is not easily attainable, nor can it be made equitable, within an environment in which national economic policies squeeze the masses at the same time as corporate and international capital interests soar. At the heart of this concern is the role of the African state in ensuring that schooling and education serve the needs and aspirations of all peoples. A rethinking of the role of the African state as the sole or main provider of education is called for. There must be alternative ways of distributing education in the current circumstances of World Bank and IMF-inspired structural adjustment policies that are reaping untold havoc on local peoples. While a discussion of the appropriate roles of the state is a crucial part of rethinking schooling and education in African contexts, the learning objective of this chapter is to urge for a reliance on local creativity and resourcefulness. Such reliance could provide some answers to the mounting problems and challenges of transcending adjustment for African education.

A relevant education is one that is anchored in cultural experience and historical cultural knowledge. African education must serve the socio-cultural, economic, and political needs of local communities. To do so, curriculum and pedagogical strategies need to be reformed. Curriculum reform will entail, among many other things, the use of local knowledge and expertise and the conduct of communicative and discursive practices that have at the centre the African experience and condition. Rethinking African education demands that educational practitioners, theorists, and policy-makers examine the instructional and learning processes in classrooms and other school settings. They must critique outdated pedagogical approaches and suggest new instructional styles to enable the youth develop critical thinking skills. Transformative pedagogies must assist youth and adult learners to empower themselves.

REFERENCES

Asante, M. F. (1987). *The Afrocentric idea*. Philadelphia: Temple University Press.

Asante, M. F. (1991). The Afrocentric idea in education. *Journal of Negro Education*, *60*(2), 170–80.

Ayittey, G. (1991). *Indigenous African institutions*. New York: Transnational Publishers.

Bates, R. H., Mudimbe, V. Y., & O'Barr, J. (Eds.) (1993). *Africa and the disciplines: The contributions of research in Africa to the social sciences and humanities*. Chicago: University of Chicago Press.

Bray, X. L., Clarke, P. B., & Stephens, D. (1986). *Education and society in Africa*. London: Edward Arnold, pp. 101–13.

CODESRIA Bulletin. (1996). The future of the social sciences in Africa. *CODESRIA Bulletin*, *1*, 1.

Dei, G.J.S. (1993). Indigenous knowledge systems: Local traditions of sustainable forestry. *Singapore Journal of Tropical Geography*, *14*(1), 28–41.

Dei, G.J.S. (1994). Afrocentricity: A cornerstone of pedagogy. *Anthropology and Education Quarterly*, *25*(1), 3–28.

Dei, G.J.S. (1996). *Anti-racism education: Theory and practice*. Halifax, NS: Fernwood Publishing.

Dei, G.J.S. (2000). African development: The relevance and implications of 'Indigenousness.' In G.J.S. Dei & B. Hall (Eds.), *Indigenous, knowledge in global contexts* (pp. 70–88). Toronto: University of Toronto Press.

Fals Borda, O. (1980). *Science and the common people*. Yugoslavia.

Freire, P. (1990). *Pedagogy of the oppressed*. New York: Continuum.

Gueye, S. P. (1995). Science, culture and development in Africa. *CODESRIA Bulletin*, *2*, 7–12.

Gyekye, K. (1987). *An essay on African philosophical thought*. London: Cambridge University Press.

Holmes, L. (1995). *Elders knowledge and the ancestry of experience in Hawaii*. Paper presented at the Learned Societies' Meeting of the Canadian Association for the Study of International Development. June 4–6. Montreal: Université du Québec.

Horton, R. (1971). On African traditional thought and Western science. In M.F.D. Young (Ed.), *Knowledge and control* (pp. 208–66). London: Collier MacMillan.

Hountondji, P. (1983). *African philosophy: Myth and reality*. Bloomington: Indiana University Press.

Jegede, O. (1994). African cultural perspectives and the teaching of science. In J. Solomon & G. Aikenhead (Eds.), *STS education: International perspectives on reform* (pp. 120–30). New York: Teachers College Press.

Kelly, G. P., & Altbach, P. G. (Eds.). (1978). *Education and colonialism*. New York: Longman.

Kerr, L. (2005). *Personal communication*. Ontario Institute for Studies in Education. Toronto: University of Toronto.

Maddock, K. (1981). Social organisation in Aboriginal Australia. *Mankind*, *13* (2), 185–87.

Mbiti, J. S. (1982). African views of the universe. In R. Olaniyan (Ed.), *African history and culture* (pp. 193–99). Lagos: Longman.

Mudimbe, V. Y. (1988). *The invention of Africa: Gnosis, philosophy and the order of knowledge.* Bloomington, IN: Indiana University Press.

Muteshi, J. (1996). *Women, law and engendering resistance: A pedagogical project.* PhD dissertation, Ontario Institute for Studies in Education, University of Toronto.

Njeuma, D. L. (1993). An overview of women's education in Africa. In J. K. Conway & S. C. Bourque (Eds.), *The politics of women's education* (pp. 123–31). Ann Arbor: University of Michigan Press.

Ogunniyi, M. B. (1986). Adapting western science to traditional African culture. *International Journal of Science Education, 10*(1), 1–9.

Okpewho, I. (1992). *African oral literature.* Bloomington: Indiana University Press.

Oladipo, O. (1992). *The idea of African philosophy: A critical study of major orientations in contemporary African philosophy.* Ibadan: Molecular Publishers.

Semali, L., & Stambach, A. (1995). *Cultural identity in African context: Indigenous education and practice in east Africa.* Paper read at the Annual Meeting of the Comparative and International Society, Boston. MA, March 29–April 1.

Shujaa, M. (1994a). Education and schooling: You can have one without the other. In Mwalimu J. Shujaa (Ed.), *Too much schooling too little education: The paradox of black life in white societies* (pp. 13–36). Trenton, NJ: African World Press.

Shujaa, M. (Ed.). (1994b). *Too much schooling too little education: The paradox of black life in white societies.* Trenton, NJ: African World Press.

Tedla, E. (1995). *Sankofa: African thought and education.* New York: Peter Lang.

Thisen, J. K. (1993). The development and utilisation of science and technology in productive sectors: Case of developing Africa. *African Development, 18*(4), 5–35.

Urevbu, A. O. (1984). School science curriculum and innovation: An African perspective. *European Journal of Science Education,* 6 (3), 217–25.

Vieta, K. T. (1991). Culture for development. *West Africa,* (April 1–7), 480.

Warren, D. M., Slikkerveer, L. J., & Brokensha, D. (Eds.). (1995). *The cultural dimension of development.* Exeter, Great Britain: Intermediate Technology Publications.

Wiredu, K. (1980). *Philosophy and African culture.* Cambridge: Cambridge University Press.

Woodhouse, H., & Ndongko, T. M. (1993). Women and science education in Cameroon: Some critical reflections. *Interchange, 24*(1/2), 131–59.

Yakubu, J. M. (1994). Integration of indigenous thought and practice with science and technology: A case study of Ghana. *International Journal of Science Education, 16*(3), 343–60.

Ziegler, D. (Ed.). (1996). *Molefi Asante and Afrocentricity: In Praise and Criticism.* Nashville, TN: James Winston.

Notes

1   This chapter was first published as "Education for development: Relevance and implications for African development." *Canadian Journal of Development Studies,* *19*(3), 1998, 509–27. The current version has some updated reference citations.

2   In the context of this discussion, I distinguish between "schooling" and "education." "Schooling" refers to the formal structures and procedures of going to school. "Education" is broadly defined to refer to the options, strategies, processes, and structures through which we (as individuals and communities/groups) come to know and understand the world and act within it. "Education" happens at/in multiple sites and contexts – schools, universities, workplaces, homes, communities, arts and media) – with a diverse body of participants involved. It could be argued that in the contemporary African context there is too much schooling with too little education taking place (see also Shujaa, 1994a, b; in another context).

INDEX

AFRICA: MISSING VOICES SERIES

Donald I. Ray and Peter Shinnie, general editors

ISSN 1703-1826

University of Calgary Press has a long history of publishing academic works on Africa. *Africa: Missing Voices* illuminates issues and topics concerning Africa that have been ignored or are missing from current global debates. This series will fill a gap in African scholarship by addressing concerns that have been long overlooked in political, social, and historical discussions about this continent.

www.ingramcontent.com/pod-product-compliance
Lightning Source LLC
Chambersburg PA
CBHW050637280326
41932CB00015B/2674